GASLIGHTING
AMERICA

GASLIGHTING
AMERICA

WHY WE LOVE IT WHEN TRUMP LIES TO US

AMANDA CARPENTER

BROADSIDE BOOKS
An Imprint of HarperCollins*Publishers*

FIRST EDITION

Illustration by captureandcompose/Shutterstock, Inc.

Library of Congress Cataloging-in-Publication Data

Names: Carpenter, Amanda B., author.
Title: Gaslighting America : why we love it when Trump lies to us / Amanda Carpenter.
Description: First edition. | New York, NY : Harper, [2018] | Includes bibliographical references and index.
Identifiers: LCCN 2017047193 (print) | LCCN 2018005410 (ebook) | ISBN 9780062748027 (ebk) | ISBN 9780062748003 (hc : alk. paper) | ISBN 9780062748010 (pb : alk. paper)
Subjects: LCSH: Trump, Donald, 1946—Language. | Deception—Political aspects—United States. | Communication in politics—United States. | United States—Politics and government—2017- | Social media—Political aspects—United States. | Press and politics—United States. | Presidents—United States—Election—2016. | Political campaigns—United States—Press coverage. | Journalism—Political aspects—United States—History—21st century.
Classification: LCC E912 (ebook) | LCC E912 .C39 2018 (print) | DDC 973.933092—dc23
LC record available at https://lccn.loc.gov/2017047193

18 19 20 21 22 LSC 10 9 8 7 6 5 4 3 2

TO THOSE WHO, AS RUDYARD KIPLING WROTE, "CAN KEEP YOUR HEAD WHEN ALL ABOUT YOU ARE LOSING THEIRS AND BLAMING IT ON YOU."

CONTENTS

GASLIGHTING
AMERICA

1

BIRTHING A PRESIDENT

Before the 2016 election, I viewed foreign lands where dictators could convince whole populations that two plus two equals five as tragic glitches in history that could never happen here. Not anymore. After living through the 2016 election, I can see quite plainly how, if the conditions are right, it can happen anywhere, anytime. I mention the phrase "two plus two" intentionally. "Two plus two equals five" was a slogan used in the Soviet Union that was later famously incorporated by George Orwell in his dystopian novel, *1984*. Joseph Stalin used the phrase to convince his people that the government would complete his ambitious Five-Year Plan in four years. But the idea is bogus on its face. Two plus two doesn't equal five, no matter what rationale is used. What Stalin didn't say when he was ginning up support for his glorious plan was that the big secret to getting it done was that Soviet workers would need to produce five years' worth of work in four years. If they did not comply, to the gulag they would go.

That's not to say that the Trump administration plans to send anyone to a work camp, although it is a long-standing joke (I hope) among Republicans who, like me, consider themselves members of the "Never Trump" crowd that we'll all be together in a jail cell one of these days.

In *1984*, Orwell's protagonist, Winston Smith, ponders the infamous equation as the novel explores whether well-meaning people, with enough pressure from Big Brother, will buckle and compromise their most fundamental beliefs. Eventually, Winston breaks. He concedes that, yes, two plus two does equal five. Why? Spoiler alert: The benefit of embracing the lie ultimately outweighs the sacrifice required to cling to the truth. Sometimes, more often than we'd like to admit, lies are easier to believe than the truth. Especially in politics.

The natures of the major characters in the 2016 presidential election, however, are much stranger than those in Orwell's fiction. At least Winston showed some remorse about succumbing to the lies. Trump and his allies did it with a smile, posing as truth-tellers while launching an all-out assault on facts and values alike. For those who wanted to board the Trump train, outward expressions of belief in Trump's grand lies were required, litmus tests of loyalty. Republicans came to believe it was necessary for their political survival and so unquestioningly repeated his mantras.

Throughout the 2016 campaign, I watched devout evangelicals champion a foulmouthed, thrice-married casino magnate who loved talking dirty with Howard Stern; profited off the young women he paraded around in various stages of undress in his beauty pageants and casino strip clubs; and bragged about grabbing women "by the pussy." Republican Party officials who spent their lives blaming Democrats for the collapse of the American Dream saluted Trump, disregarding how he had generously donated to Democratic candidates and causes. Mike Pence, the unflinchingly polite and pious evangelical congressman whom I had knocked on doors for as a college student in Muncie, Indiana, praised Trump as the "next Ronald Reagan" and happily became his vice president. Even my former boss, Ted Cruz, endorsed Trump despite once calling him a "pathological liar."

Maybe I should have expected it to happen. They are politicians after all. But I didn't. I actually believed all the talk from the Tea Party Republican types about sticking to their principles and doing all they could to regain the voters' trust. Somehow, the GOP found a way to win in 2016 without keeping those earnest promises. Does that make it right? A lot of people will tell you yes, winning cures all. I'm not one of them. Winning is great, but if it doesn't bring real, positive change, it's not worthwhile and most likely won't last long, either. That's proven true already. Trump's victory hasn't united the party; it's corrupted it.

It's not like we didn't see this coming. Since day one of Trump's candidacy, the New York real estate mogul has acted as if the Republican Party was something he intended to co-opt rather than join. He hardly expressed any loyalty at all to Republican principles, yet he demanded unwavering allegiance from members of the party.

Tell me, is this what Republicans waited for years in the political wilderness for? To babysit Trump's Twitter account and compete in a never-ending tournament of mental gymnastics to defend Trump from one self-manufactured crisis to the next? I know we have a higher calling than that. There is far more important work before us—the kind of work that if Republicans don't do, will never get done.

If the Republicans don't stop the out-of-control government programs, endless spending, and continued assaults on constitutional freedoms, who will? Not the Democrats. All they have to offer is more government control over the most personal parts of our lives—namely, our money, our health care, and our education. Things like the tax code, Obamacare, Medicare, and Medicaid aren't abstractions. They are government programs that hit home, literally. But, more important, to our conscience, if the Republican Party folds up for good, will anyone ever advocate for the most dearly vulnerable among us, the unborn, in public office again? I fear not.

Going forward, all GOP candidates, from those running in the biggest, most expensive races to the ones in the smallest Podunk places, will have a choice to make. Will they endorse and mimic the sleazy but effective precedent Trump set in his stunning 2016 win, or will they risk sticking their necks out to demand something better for America? If you think that's an easy choice, let me dissuade you, much as it saddens me to do so.

Trump is president. That means he is "the establishment." He has all of the GOP's political power. *All of it.* And I see very few people in the party willing to challenge him for it.

As a top staffer to two party members who famously took on the so-called establishment—Senators Jim DeMint and Ted Cruz—I know what it takes for someone to do so and the consequences that come from it. Before Trump came along, DeMint was the rare senator who dared to oppose incumbents and backed candidates willing to challenge the status quo in Washington. This made then–Senate minority leader Mitch McConnell, who preferred to run more "electable" candidates such as Arlen Specter and Charlie Crist, fume.

DeMint was practically outcast in Washington when he told McConnell in 2010: "I'd rather have 30 Marco Rubios than 60 Arlen Specters." It was a pointed comment and I was proud to assist him when he said it. At the time, McConnell was backing the incumbent senator Arlen Specter in the Pennsylvania GOP primary; DeMint was backing the outsider Pat Toomey. In the Florida primary, McConnell was backing the well-known and well-funded Charlie Crist; DeMint was backing the upstart candidate Marco Rubio. McConnell's allies tried to depict DeMint's comment as some kind of surrender to permanent minority status. Their PR machine went into overdrive against DeMint, but he withstood it well. We knew what Specter and Crist would do in the Senate. More of the same. Nothing. We felt our party would be more effective with a principled minority than we would be as a party that sat on its duff until some lucky fate gave the GOP the White House, the House, the Supreme Court, and a supermajority in the Senate.

We did find out who was more "electable," too. Rubio and Toomey became GOP United States senators. Upon seeing their chances for political success wane in the GOP, Specter and Crist became Democrats. Their actions proved that DeMint had been right all along. Those turncoats hadn't been real Republicans; they had ditched the party the minute it no longer served their ambitions. Still, DeMint was treated by the establishment class like he, not the Republicans who left the party, was a traitor.

In the wake of Trump's election, many people started worrying about political "tribalism." Meaning, the membership and intense affinity some people have toward a particular group, or "tribe," to which they belong, such as a political party. In extreme cases, membership and loyalty become more important than the function of the group; it becomes the purpose. Some people apply these descriptions to Trump supporters, but the GOP had gone tribal long before Trump came along. Leaders who expected Republicans to blindly support candidates, such as Specter and Crist, who simply put an "R" after their names and waved the red flag rather than a blue flag, without giving a thought as to whether they would reliably represent the party's principles falls into that definition pretty well.

I resisted those impulses at the time and will continue to do so. I will not choose a politician over my values. For this, I've been accused of being a "purist" but it's about something much bigger than that. I believe those kinds of choices make the difference between a life lived in freedom and a life lived in dictatorship. It's the difference between being an American who enjoys liberty and justice for all and those forced to live under cultish political regimes. In the United States of America, our public servants need only take one oath, a pledge to support and defend the Constitution. Not some loyalty oath to a fellow politician, candidate, or party. I'll be damned if someone thinks he or she has to submit to some mumbling suit, let alone be hazed by a bullying president, to serve. It makes me nauseous to watch the Republicans who think they do.

Chris Christie comes to mind. I remember cheering him on as I watched the YouTube clips of the New Jersey governor's early town halls, where he would get into heated exchanges with union officials and school educators who demanded higher taxes and handouts. He stood his ground and gave them the straight truth about what he intended to do with his budget and how he would make things better for everyone in New Jersey. Fast forward to 2016, when Christie made an appearance to endorse Trump where he looked so blank-faced and feeble that it was compared to a hostage video. (And that's being grossly unfair to actual hostages.) Among the last few times Christie was seen on the national stage he was spotted binging on M&M's in an airport and looking dazed and confused on the beach in the middle of his state's budget crisis. I can rattle off the names of other Republicans, elected and aides alike, who similarly became zombies for Trump: Jeff Sessions, Ben Carson, Reince Priebus, and Sean Spicer, to name a few. Everyone Trump brings into his inner circle has a way of eventually turning into a stooge.

"Never Trump" conservatives commiserated that watching Republicans fall under Trump's spell through the 2016 election was like a political horror show: *Invasion of the Republican Body Snatchers*. *National Review*'s Jonah Goldberg wrote that he felt "drained as I try to resist what feels like a kind of crowd-sourced brainwashing spread across the land like a wet rolling fog."

I kept replaying the disturbing scenes of people caving to Trump over and over in my mind. I had to find a way to stop the vicious negative feedback loop; I spent serious time reflecting on the race, trying to figure out what had happened. And now that I know, I want you to know, too.

The most surprising thing? How Trump's political playbook has been hiding in plain sight all this time. He keeps everyone, not just Republicans, spellbound in a rote and methodical way. Donald J. Trump is president, but he's also a professional gaslighter. Only when enough people identify how his gaslighting works and why it's so successful will anyone have a chance to stop it.

His gaslighting method utilizes the tactics he honed to keep his name in the tabloid press as a New York City business mogul in the 1980s and 1990s. Made-up sources, heresy, and bluffs were the go-to tools of his trade. Before *The Apprentice* and Twitter, Trump would reportedly phone reporters masquerading as a publicist with fake names such as "John Miller" or "John Barron" to brag about famous women who wanted to sleep with him. The reporters often knew it was Trump and they played along anyway. It all made for juicy stories that were good for Trump and good for attracting readers. Trump quickly learned how to hold the public's attention with his tall tales. And with enough trial and error he stumbled onto a terribly effective method of controlling and manipulating the press.

He learned that people actually love it when he lies. He loves it because he gets stories about his prowess—whether it be sexual, business, or political—in the press. The media loves it because it keeps people reading the papers, watching their shows, and clicking their links. And his enemies love it because they keep thinking that this time will really, finally, truly be the time Trump does himself in with his jaw-dropping yarns. We're all suckers.

You can't help but get drawn in; we're sold on superlatives. Everything he does is amazing, phenomenal, or—one of his most used descriptors that happens to be most accurate—"unbelievable." Even if we know in our hearts it's "unbelievable," we can't help but entertain the possibility that it might be true. It's only human. Wouldn't life be difficult to get through if we fact-checked every piece of information we received before deciding to believe it? To get through the day, we are inclined to accept these lies, at least momentarily. Questioning everything is exhausting. Eventually, we let some misinformation slip in. We are even more biased toward the information if it happens to be something we would like to be true, like the promise of a great American success story.

If Trump says that he's built the most incredible, beautiful buildings in Manhattan, isn't there a part of you as a red-blooded American who gets excited and wants to believe? Or, at the very least, wants to see those buildings and find out for yourself? Go ahead and take a trip to Fifth Avenue. The onlookers who have been coalescing for years on the street outside Trump Tower, taking photos, craning their necks to see the top of the building and poking their heads inside to get a glimpse of the pink marbled walls and golden escalator, tell you all you need to know.

You may hate his lies, but Trump sells them with unshakable confidence. He forces us to pay attention. Trump even keeps those who don't believe, as he has said, "in suspense." We are a captive audience, living in constant anticipation of his next move. We're glued to the tube, computer, and smartphone. I speak for myself on these points. I'm always keeping tabs on Twitter and checking my email. I have a

TV monitor in my kitchen so that I can watch it while I cook and fold laundry. Whenever I'm traveling by train or car, I have an audio feed of all the TV news and talk radio piped through my car radio and iPhone. No one makes me do it. I *want* to. I feel like I must. Yes, it's part of my job, but when everything seems to change from minute to minute, how can I turn away? It's the most compelling show on earth and I can't stop watching. I'm transfixed.

Like it or not, we're all living in Trump's world now. This is a book about what happens when a politician knows he can't win by competing in everyone else's reality, so he creates his own. When we watch Trump start spinning his next ridiculous narrative, we often misunderstand what he's doing. We get his motives wrong and misinterpret the results. We want to think his crazy lies are his greatest weakness when they are, in fact, the source of his strength. He has no shame in telling them and won't be embarrassed about it, either. His intense commitment to his outlandish ideas is a form of virtue signaling to his base. It says, "I'll do anything to win and beat the people you don't like." This is the attitude that's convinced a sizable population of this country that he's a winner, and if they invest in him, they'll win, too. And they have! Against all odds, they made him President of the United States! This mentality will never bring him down because it is what's raised him up all his life.

We need to recalibrate our thinking when it comes to understanding Trump. The conventional wisdom currently says that when Trump tweets something laughably incorrect, the fact-checkers will reveal the truth, the public will turn against him, and his political allies will desert him. That has not borne out. That's *our* false narrative.

What we have to admit is that President Trump will continue to say whatever he wants. The whole country will continue rushing to debate it, and his allies will continue to fall in line. So what is it about this trick that keeps working, that we can't pull ourselves away from? Here is where things get interesting. What I want you to notice is how all the major influence groups—the media, the political parties, the voters—are incentivized to go along with the gaslighting for their own self-interested reasons.

Reflect for a moment on the 2016 election.

The media loved all the content he gave them and the eyeballs he brought to their various platforms. Most of Trump's GOP primary rivals were content to watch him savage their mutual opponents, thinking it would benefit them in the end. The Democrats egged Trump on, thinking his buffoonery would drive voters into the arms of Hillary Clinton. The more outlandish Trump became, the more in demand his surrogates found themselves and were handed media and political opportunities that were never before within their reach. Even the victims of his gaslighting had reasons to let it go unchallenged, as any kind of response only legitimized his illegitimate accusations. Trump's gaslighting method is practically foolproof. Everyone gets caught up in it; he always gets what he wants in the end.

Trump's birtherism gambit is a textbook example of the technique he uses again and again. Let me walk you through the steps.

The very first thing he does is stake a claim over political terrain other candidates consider risky but has a lot of potential. This is Step One. Remember, Trump is a real estate man at heart. He knows how to find an empty building that might look unsavory but can be developed into something valuable. In this case, it was birtherism.

When Trump started dipping his toe into the conspiracy waters in 2011, the birther fervor, which had broken loose during President Barack Obama's first presidential election in 2008, had mostly died down. Sure, it was something Republicans still cracked jokes about, but no one was seriously willing to indulge in it for more than a laugh. Most considered birtherism a nonproductive waste of time, if not totally racist. Conservatives, by and large, thought it was only something promoted by liberals to make Republicans look like stupid tin-foil-hatters.

I remember being booked for an MSNBC TV debate segment about it in 2008 and having to painstakingly explain that even the Senate's most conservative senator, Jim DeMint, whom I later worked for on

Capitol Hill, called the issue a bunch of "nonsense" in an interview with the *Huffington Post*.

Around that time, I also attended a Tea Party event hosted by the group FreedomWorks that was being infiltrated by members of the radical LaRouchePAC who said Obama wasn't a citizen and tried to sneak signs depicting Obama as Hitler into the event. I worked with FreedomWorks organizers to identify people carrying birther signs so they could be asked to leave the event. On another occasion, I was nearby former GOP majority leader Dick Armey, who was doing a TV interview on the National Mall, when I saw someone carrying an embarrassing sign with the obvious intent of holding it behind Armey to make him and the Tea Party look bad on television. I jumped in front of the man and held up a large American flag to block the view. These were the types of things my friends and I were doing in our own little ways to try to hold the line.

Fast-forward a few years later. Along comes Donald Trump, calling himself a Republican and on a mission to become the biggest birther in America. But Trump didn't go full birther at first. No, no. He had to create some interest. He started slow, by raising questions about what *other* people were saying and thinking. This is Step Two of his gaslighting method. This is how Trump slyly both advances and denies the very claim he has staked out in Step One. See how this works.

"Everybody that even gives a hint of being a birther . . . even a little bit of a hint, like, gee, you know, maybe just maybe this much of a chance, they label them as an idiot," he told ABC's *Good Morning America* on March 17, 2011. Trump wasn't exactly coming out and saying he was a birther, but he was using his platform to express sympathy toward the large number of birthers who could be watching. He was advancing the narrative without committing himself to it. Gear up the presses! "Is Donald Trump a Birther?" asked *Inside Edition*. His gaslighting was catching. He got everyone to start asking questions about birtherism. He didn't have to answer them to make his point. You see, when Trump is gaslighting, he rarely tells an outright lie. When pressed, he avoids specifics but keeps everyone chattering away with speculation on the topic.

The press egged him on, as did the Democrats who thought birtherism would help them by drawing sympathy to President Obama. Obama's re-election campaign even sold T-shirts and mugs mocking the movement.

Trump made himself available for all kinds of high-profile interviews on the subject, denying all the while that he was a real "birther." He just had a lot of questions about it, you see. "Why doesn't he show his birth certificate? There's something on his birth certificate he doesn't like," he told the women of *The View* on March 23, 2011. On March 28, 2011, he told Fox News, "I'm starting to wonder myself whether or not he was born in this country."

Do you see how this advance-and-denial step works? He was only "wondering" about Obama's citizenship. When this step is carried out correctly, it generates lots of attention. It induces intrigue, laying the groundwork for a much grander narrative.

Then he did something that you will learn to recognize as Step Three of his method; he created suspense to keep the media's interest in him and the subject. Trump promised evidence would come out "soon" to support his inquiries. He told *Morning Joe* on April 7, 2011, "His [Obama's] grandmother in Kenya said, 'Oh, no, he was born in Kenya and I was there and I witnessed his birth.' She's on tape. I think that tape's going to be produced fairly soon. Somebody is coming out with a book in two weeks, it will be very interesting."

The tape never came out. Obama, however, did finally produce his birth certificate on April 27, 2011, after Trump stoked questions in the press over it for six weeks straight. In doing so, Obama lectured the press for having their priorities wrong. He pointed out that he was in the middle of a big budget debate with Republicans but "the dominant news story wasn't about these huge, monumental choices that we're gonna have to make as a nation, it was about my birth certificate."

Without saying exactly who was responsible, Obama vented about the "carnival barkers" and "sideshow" that had been created. The people who pushed "just make stuff up and pretend that facts are not facts," Obama said. "I have been puzzled at the degree to which this thing just kept on going." Later on, many members of the media realized the role they played in giving oxygen to Trump's gaslighting. The *New York Times* posted a story to this effect, "In Trying to Debunk a Theory, the News Media Extended Its Life."

A rational person would have thought the story would end there. But Trump had no interest in rationality. The issue was too politically fruitful to let go of so easily. Besides, Trump had found other GOP politicians who were willing to play along. In October 2011 Texas governor and then–2012 presidential hopeful Rick Perry had dinner with Trump. No one knows for certain what they talked about, but pretty soon after that Perry was on the birther bandwagon, happily taking cheap shots at President Obama. Perry told CNBC, "It's fun to poke at him a little bit and say, 'Hey, how about—let's see your grades and your birth certificate . . . it's a good issue to keep alive."

It sure was. For Trump. More than a year after Trump started gaslighting Obama, he was still going, fully engaged in Step Three. In August 2012, he upped the suspense and interest in his storyline by tweeting: "An 'extremely credible source' has called my office and told me @BarackObama's birth certificate is a fraud."

In 2013, ABC's Jonathan Karl asked Trump if he had taken birtherism too far. Trump said, "I don't think I went overboard. Actually, I think it made me very popular, if you want to know the truth, OK? So, I do think I know what I'm doing."

That's exactly why he kept stoking the fire. In 2014, Trump was still pushing it. He tweeted: "Attention all hackers: You are hacking everything else to please hack Obama's college records (destroyed?) and check 'place of birth.'" (Note: this wouldn't be the only time Trump called on foreign hackers to help him cast aspersions upon a political opponent, either.)

What did all this do for Trump? A poll conducted by Fairleigh Dickinson University in May 2016 found that 77 percent of those who supported Trump believed President Obama was "definitely" or "probably" hiding important information about his early life. Birtherism, without question, put Trump on the political map; Republican voters liked how he needled Obama. And so Trump kept dabbling in birtherism well into his presidential campaign, building as much suspense as he could for his final thoughts on the matter.

In September 2016, Trump summoned the national press corps to his newly opened Trump Hotel in Washington, D.C., with the tantalizing promise that he would make a "major statement" regarding the circumstances of Obama's birth.

Reporters had long grown tired of the birther shtick and resented being marched into the hotel, calling the charade an "infomercial" for his property. But Trump had a way of guilting them into it. Medal of Honor recipients would be attending, reporters were told. Before Trump's remarks, there would be a serious discussion about national security. Trump was giving the media a dare. Would reporters turn down a major event with decorated veterans? If they skipped it, Trump would accuse them of not respecting the troops and not giving proper attention to military issues. So the press dutifully assembled and waited patiently as the veterans gave their speeches and Trump praised his new luxurious digs.

At the end of the event, Trump made his long-awaited statement regarding President Obama's birth certificate. Here he would unveil Step Four and Step Five of his gaslighting method. The discrediting of his real opponent and the declaration of victory.

"Hillary Clinton and her campaign of 2008 started the birther controversy," he said. "I finished it. I finished it. I finished it, you know what I mean. President Obama was born in the United States period. Now we all want to get back to making America strong and great again." That was it. Trump tossed the conspiracy off as an unfortunate incident propagated not by him, but by his opponent, Hillary Clinton. That's Step Four, the discrediting. "Finished it," he said. He won. Trump told the world that the single most defining issue of his political career-to-be was someone else's mishap that he fixed. That's Step Five, the victory.

Reporters who covered the issue for five long years were exasperated. CNN's Jake Tapper lamented, "[I]t is hard to imagine this as anything other than a political Rick Roll"—a reference to a common Internet prank, where people are tricked into clicking on a link that goes to a music video of Rick Astley's 1987 hit "Never Gonna Give You Up." Little did anyone know at the time that Trump's entire presidential campaign could be likened to a giant Internet prank that would ultimately make him president. We weren't being rickrolled. We were being gaslit.

"Gaslighting" is a psychological term for what happens when a master manipulator like Trump lies so brazenly that people end up questioning reality as they know it. I cannot tell you the number of times I heard reporters and political observers ask one another questions like "Can you believe what Trump said?" or "Is this really happening?" over the course of the 2016 campaign. It was all so unreal. We simply couldn't believe what we were seeing and hearing with our own eyes and ears.

Oftentimes, Trump says something so long and so confidently—and with so much outside support—that you can't help but wonder if he isn't right. That's gaslighting.

The term comes from a 1938 play, later made into the film *Gaslight*, in which a man attempts to convince his wife she is delusional in order to distract her from the murder he committed. Gaslighting is far more malicious than a little white lie; it's a lie told in such a way that it makes the person being lied to feel crazy, and, in dramatic cases, start acting like it.

New York Times columnist Maureen Dowd launched the term into the political realm in the 1990s when she used it to describe how Democrats intentionally provoked Newt Gingrich to make him fly off the handle and appear "hysterical" in the press. But the term didn't go mainstream until 2016 when so many people began grasping for ways to explain the maddening effect Trump was having on them.

I experienced the phenomenon personally from my perch as a CNN commentator who followed every minute of the 2016 primary and general election campaigns, going head-to-head against Trump's most fervent surrogates in a high-stakes media atmosphere for hours on end. But I wasn't alone. Trump was gaslighting America. He still is.

Of course, we are all familiar with politicians who lie, break promises, or obfuscate the truth. President George H. W. Bush's "Read my lips" promise not to raise taxes went bust. President George W. Bush's weapons of mass destruction in Iraq were never found. President Barack Obama's "If you like it, you can keep it" vow about Americans being able to keep the doctors and health insurance plans they liked never held up. Each of these presidents made statements they knew might not prove to be true.

Gaslighting is far more aggressive than any of these misguided lies. It's an elaborate scheme undertaken with the goal of gaining control over people. Trump is an expert gaslighter and what I want you to understand is that there is a very specific method to his madness.

I showed you how Trump worked through the steps when he was gaslighting people about Obama's birth certificate. Those very same steps are almost always present in his political attacks. Here they are:

- **STAKE A CLAIM**: Trump finds a political issue or action that competitors are unwilling to adopt and that will ensure a media frenzy. Such as: "President Obama is not a U.S. citizen."
- **ADVANCE AND DENY**: Trump casts the issue into the public realm without taking direct responsibility. He does this by raising questions about or discussing what *other* people are saying, reporting, or thinking. Tabloids, YouTube videos, tweets from unknown origins, and unverifiable Internet news stories are often used as sources.
- **CREATE SUSPENSE**: He says evidence is forthcoming that will soon get to the truth of the matter. Trump can remain in this mode for weeks, months, or even years.
- **DISCREDIT THE OPPONENT**: If critics gain traction, Trump attacks their motives and personal character.
- **WIN**: Trump declares victory, no matter the circumstances. This step usually takes a long time to reveal itself, and Trump will often engage it when he is ready to drop the matter.

There it is, Trump's gaslighting method, which he has used time and again. This is how he achieves the true goal of every megamanipulator: attaining complete control over his environment and the people in it. It's enough to drive sane people mad if they don't understand how it works and why he uses it. But now that you have this book, you won't be one of them.

What are the benefits of gaslighting? For starters, when Trump does this, no one has time to talk about his tax returns, his business failings, or even why he told Howard Stern it was okay to call his daughter, Ivanka, "a piece of ass." He keeps people buzzing with gossip, innuendo, and conspiracies about his opponents. It's the political equivalent of twerking like Miley Cyrus. Nobody really likes it, but everyone is going to watch and have something to say about it. Trump's gaslighting method is not honorable (you wouldn't tell your daughter to do it!), but it is extremely effective for someone willing to do anything to be the center of attention.

I'll show you what gaslighting looks like from all angles, starting with how the Republican base was a prime target for it. Then I'll show you how Trump gaslit his Republican rivals to secure the nomination and how I was personally gaslit on live television. You'll see how Trump and his surrogates gaslit the media, too. Lastly, I'll show how previous presidents have tried it, but how Trump has perfected the method.

By the end of this book you'll understand Trump's gaslighting method well. Take it from me, I've been all the way down the rabbit hole of this curious and curiouser world of politics. And just like Alice in Wonderland, I met both fantastic and frightening characters along the way and fought the Jabberwock firsthand. Now I'm out of the tunnel and ready to tell you the unbelievable tale of how a man got elected president by telling people as many as six impossible things before breakfast.

WINNING UGLY

Trump has always positioned himself as a showman on the make, but that doesn't explain why so many people in 2016 were so eager to buy what he was selling. Much more enormous forces than his own larger-than-life personality were coalescing on his behalf.

Going into the 2016 election Republican voters had only one thing in mind. You might think it was to "win." Wrong. The GOP tried that in 2008 and 2012. This time the goal was something else altogether: beat liberalism. Winning and beating liberalism sound similar, yet they each create a totally different appetite for the kind of Republican candidate voters would choose to represent them. Let me explain.

For two straight election cycles, the GOP tried to win by nominating the most "electable" candidates possible. Cue the courageous Vietnam POW John McCain, who went on to serve his country as the maverick United States senator from Arizona. Cue the former Massachusetts governor Mitt Romney, the perfectly groomed family man and business turnaround artist who saved the 2002 Winter Olympics. Both men of incredible personal achievement whose lives were rich with patriotic biopic material. Both of them committed Republicans but willing to moderate on big-ticket items like immigration and health care in order to, theoretically, pick up independent voters.

Needless to say, that didn't happen. Obama found a way to gut both McCain and Romney on the issues where they should have been the stronger candidate. Obama, the inexperienced Illinois senator, prevailed against McCain in 2008 by promising to quickly end the Iraq War—a "dumb war" in his words—which the military veteran McCain supported and vowed to win. Obama didn't have a plan to end the war, mind you. Or a plan to close the detention facility in Guantanamo Bay like he promised, either. No matter. He still won.

The 2012 re-election was tougher for Obama. Romney, the Republicans' "jobs" candidate, thought he could win by promising to revive the economy, which suffered throughout Obama's first term despite the trillion dollars the president had spent on stimulus. To woo voters to his side, Romney pointed to his record and offered detailed PowerPoint presentations about his plans. Phooey to that, the Democrats said. They didn't even bother running on Obama's record, let alone seriously counter Romney's ideas. Rather, the Obama campaign caricatured Romney as a rich and ruthless out-of-touch bully. One progressive group ran an ad holding Romney personally responsible for the death of a cancer patient at one of the companies he'd restructured. The media dug up people from Romney's prep school who said he'd pinned a schoolmate to the ground and clipped his hair because Romney, supposedly, the strict rules enforcer, thought it was too long. A story about how Romney had strapped their family dog to the roof of a car during a road trip surfaced to further demonstrate his cruelty. Without any proof, then–Democratic Senate majority leader Harry Reid took to the Senate floor to accuse Romney of not paying any taxes for ten years. (He never apologized for floating the unfounded rumor, either.)

Did it work? Yep. Obama won handily. The editorialists at the *Wall Street Journal* conceded the effectiveness of the ugly campaign, bemoaning in a post-2012 editorial that Obama

> *said little during the campaign about his first term and even less about his plans for a second. Instead his strategy was to portray Mitt Romney as a plutocrat and intolerant threat. . . . This was all a caricature even by the standards of modern politics. But it worked with brutal efficiency—the definition of winning ugly. . . .*

Game, set, match. The Democrats had found their groove and had no reason to alter their methods for the 2016 election. It didn't matter who the GOP nominated. So long as the candidate was male, he would be deemed some kind of sexist, patriarchal *Mad Men* throwback who couldn't wait to drag America back to the pre-1960s when white men dominated the upper echelons of power. (And if Republicans had happened to nominate a woman, I have no doubt they would have found a way to tag her with the same sneering labels, too.)

What could Republicans do to stop it? The lesson was clear. Republicans would have to get ugly back. The man who spearheaded the devastating swift boat ads used to defeat Democratic presidential candidate John Kerry in 2004 said that the GOP had to dust off their knives. Advertising consultant Rick Reed wrote:

> *Every winning presidential campaigner in recent memory— George H. W. Bush, Bill Clinton, George W. Bush, and Barack Obama—was unafraid to launch blistering, sharp-edged ads that took aim at their opponents, while simultaneously crafting positive biographical narratives about themselves that tied into their policy philosophies. Mitt Romney, an exceedingly fine man, did neither. Before we get too "sophisticated" in our analysis of what went wrong in 2012, perhaps it is as simple as we played nice and the other guys didn't.*

The psychology is on Reed's side. Many voters want candidates who will get down and dirty, even if it means telling lies, to win. As Dan Ariely, a behavioral economist at Duke University and author of *The Honest Truth About Dishonesty*, said, "[I]t turns out that people want their politicians to lie to them. People view politics as a means to an end, and if they care about the ends, they're willing for the means to be a little bit more crooked."

Over the next four years the Democrats made it awfully easy for Republicans to stop being nice. Repeatedly labeling nearly half the country as bigoted, homophobic sexists for failing to march in lock-step behind a progressive agenda will do that.

While there were heaps of petty insults leveled between Republicans and Democrats during the Obama years, there were typically two ways a Republican was guaranteed to be smeared as a racist while Obama was in office: by opposing Obamacare and/or open borders. Republicans had genuine policy objections on these issues, and yet the Democrats and their allies in the media made it seem like Republicans were just being hostile to the first black president and minorities more than anything else.

Democratic senator Jay Rockefeller said, in a Senate hearing no less, that "people who made up their mind that they don't want it [Obamacare] to work because they don't like the president . . . Maybe he's of the wrong color, something of that sort. I've seen a lot of that and I know a lot of that to be true."

Conservatives who advocated border control and a stricter immigration system were constantly accused of harboring bigoted ideas, even when expressing dismay over the death of a vibrant young woman such as Kate Steinle who was shot by an illegal alien. One *Huffington Post* headline said the killing gave conservatives a "license to hate." The argument from progressives, in short, was that tragic murders happen all the time. Violent crime is everywhere; don't single out one minority community. But conservative media pounded the fact that Steinle's killer had seven felony convictions and had been deported five times before he came back to the United States and ended her life. Still, most Democrats refused to even have a discussion about keeping these people out of the country unless Republicans, mind-bogglingly, agreed to provide a path to citizenship to all illegal aliens first.

The examples of Republicans being demeaned for raising legitimate questions and concerns could fill volumes of books. Plenty of other conservative writers spend their lives documenting this, but that's not the point of this book. For the sake of brevity, accept the point that the incessant accusations of racism pushed conservatives to the brink. And once one party decides the other party's thoughts are beyond the bounds of polite conversation, that doesn't mean the conversation is over. All that means is that polite conversation ends. The conversation goes somewhere else; it spirals. One rant about President Obama's amnesty plans by then–Fox News personality Glenn Beck summed the frustration up perfectly. Beck told viewers, "Maybe I'm alone, but I think it would be faster if he just shot me in the head, you know what I mean? How much faster can he disenfranchise us?" He proceeded to impersonate Obama and pretended to pour gasoline on guest Bill Schulz. (Beck, thankfully, was only using water.) For added effect, he brandished some matches as if he were going to burn Schulz alive. Transitioning back to his own persona, Beck said, "President Obama, why don't you just set us on fire? For the love of Pete, what are you doing? Do you not hear—do you not hear the cries of people who are saying, stop? We would like some sanity in our country for a second!"

Liberals laughed at Beck for his loony posturing. They kept suggesting Republican views on immigration and Obamacare were racist and bigoted. Drawing on monologues like this, the *Washington Post*'s Dana Milbank published a book about Beck titled *Tears of a Clown*. Their mocking didn't have the intended effect, though. Conservatives became more entrenched and determined to keep turning up the volume, not only so they would be heard but until they eventually drowned their liberal naysayers out completely.

Some liberals eventually came to the realization that they had been too unfair to conservatives. By then it was too late. One pre-2016 election comment from HBO's Bill Maher was telling. "I know liberals made a big mistake, because we attacked your boy Bush like he was the end of the world, and he wasn't," he said. "And Mitt Romney, we attacked that way. I gave Obama a million dollars because I was so afraid of Mitt Romney. Mitt Romney wouldn't have changed my life that much, or yours, or John McCain. They were honorable men who we disagreed with, and we should have kept it that way. So, we cried wolf, and that was wrong. But this is real. This is going to be way different." Oh yes, it was.

3

#WAR

By the time Trump became a candidate, conservatives had gotten very good at making themselves heard through Tea Party protests, Fox News, radio, and most important, the new universe of conservative media online. Republican voters no longer had to depend on any lecturing liberals for their news and commentary. During the Obama years right-wing websites, such as *The Blaze, The Federalist, RedState, Townhall, Daily Caller,* and *The Gateway Pundit* flourished by publishing stories that catered to a right-of-center audience.

Among the most successful was *Breitbart News,* founded by the excitable, intriguing libertarian Andrew Breitbart from sunny California. I met him in 2004 when I was a college student and he was working for the *Drudge Report.* He came to address a group of us who were interested in media at the Leadership Institute in Arlington, Virginia. He spoke to us about how to choose interesting story angles and devise enticing headlines for conservative readers. (No one had heard of the term "clickbait" at that time.) I remember him relaying his now well-known mantra, "Politics is downstream from culture," and explaining the importance of bringing our conservative perspective to the media. Someone offered to get him coffee from Starbucks. His order was a huge cup of joe with two shots of espresso in it—even then he was running at 200 percent. In the middle of his speech, he took a quick break to update the website. We were all dazzled. The *Drudge Report*! Updated before our very eyes!

A few years later Breitbart struck out on his own, founding *Breitbart News* with the hashtag motto #WAR, telling anyone who would listen, "We didn't declare war on the Left, they declared war on us." He and his like-minded friends were sick of complaining about the liberal media; they were going to be the media and do everything they were tired of the liberal media doing to conservatives. *But better.* They would target political adversaries, which included liberals working in government, nonprofits, think tanks, campaigns, and the media alike. The Breitbart generation of conservative writers didn't aspire to be Bill Buckley leading high-minded debates; they aspired to be political versions of Chris Hansen who ran sting operations in *Dateline NBC*'s "To Catch a Predator." During my time at the Leadership Institute, I also had the occasion to meet James O'Keefe, the conservative provocateur who would later make headlines on *Breitbart News* by styling himself and a colleague, in their words, as a "pimp and a prostitute" to seek advice on how to start a brothel at the nonprofit voter registration organization ACORN. When I met him he was only pranking campus officials. In one memorable stunt, he convinced university workers that he, as an Irish American, was deeply offended that the cafeteria was serving Lucky Charms cereal. He secretly filmed the meeting, showing how they fell for it and agreed to take his complaint to their higher-ups. At the end of the film, he showed himself gorging on the cereal. The whole point was to demonstrate how stupid he thought political correctness was on campus. It was hilarious. Conservatives were learning how to turn the tables on the liberals and, damn, were they having fun.

By giving a platform for these kinds of hijinks, Breitbart was running much more than a conservative website; he was shaping a new no-holds-barred conservative attitude toward politics. And you were either with him or against him.

Shortly before his untimely and sudden death, Breitbart lectured members of the Conservative Political Action Conference audience in

2012 who were disappointed with Romney's conservative bona fides that "Anyone that is willing to stand next to me to fight the progressive left, I will be in that bunker. And, if you're not in that bunker because you're not satisfied with that candidate, more than shame on you, you are on the other side." Those in Romney's bunker lost that year, as we all know, but the spirit of Breitbart's words continued to gain strength after he passed away and Republicans looked toward 2016. Support the nominee or join the other team. This. Was. War. Breitbart and his like-minded members of the right-of-center media world had no interest in being objective editors, writers, and reporters. They were activists wielding keyboards, tape recorders, and cameras for the cause. In the wake of Breitbart's death, Steve Bannon, Trump's future campaign chief, took over *Breitbart News*—a critical development.

Please understand, however, that this wasn't a battle that always fell along clearly defined lines of red versus blue, like it typically does during a presidential election. This band of conservatives were fighting against a bipartisan ruling class they believed was putting America on a perilous, likely terminal, path to ruin. They were determined to seek victory, meaning blunt conservatism, anywhere possible. Even when the chances of success were slim.

The government shutdown over Obamacare is a good example. When I offered the idea to brand Ted Cruz's historic twenty-three-hour filibuster against Obamacare with the hashtag #MakeDCListen, I wanted to send the message that this wasn't about Cruz standing up and giving a big speech. It was about forcing Washington to listen to what conservatives had to say. We wanted everyone to hear how the Obamacare exchanges were going to crash, how premiums and deductibles would keep going up, and how people wouldn't be able to keep the insurance plans and doctors they liked, no matter how many times Obama promised otherwise. Cruz, in the truest sense, had to grind Washington to a halt to make the Democrats take these concerns seriously. As much as we hoped the shutdown would force a showdown on Obamacare with the president, the Republican leadership undercut Cruz throughout the entire process. But the network of conservative media, especially on Twitter, had his back. Without them, it would have been difficult to demonstrate much support for the shutdown. The avalanche of hashtags and favorable comments online made it impossible for Cruz's opponents to dismiss him. Anti-establishment Republicans weren't winning in Washington but they were gaining momentum.

This was one of the first tangible signs that conservatives were beginning to wield social media and other online media platforms in powerful ways. Outside Washington, more battle lines were being drawn over the raging culture debates that broke out all over the country during Obama's two terms in office. Many of these emotional issues never saw the light of day in places such as the U.S. Senate. Yet millions of Americans were grappling with social issues that were quickly redefining the culture at a whiplash pace—a factor more powerful than any single government shutdown.

Even though President Obama was unwilling to endorse gay marriage as a 2008 candidate, by the time his second term rolled around Christians were told that they must, through court order, not only accept it but celebrate it, too. Without much debate, judges began quietly instructing Christians that they must bake wedding cakes, provide floral arrangements, and photograph gay weddings one court case at a time. Although Obama was permitted time to, in his words, "evolve," any such grace period was closed off to everyone else after his evolution was complete. Business owners who supported pro–traditional marriage causes in their personal lives found themselves under attack. The Christian-owned Chick-fil-A was subjected to boycotts over reports that the foundation operated by its founder, S. Truett Cathy, had donated to organizations that opposed gay marriage. Mozilla cofounder, Brendan Eich, was forced to step down from his own company over a $1,000 donation he made toward Proposition 8, a California ballot initiative to ban gay marriage. To many Christians, these were not run-of-the-mill news events. They represented direct threats to their religious freedom, and accordingly, they increasingly turned to media sources who viewed it as such.

Gay marriage wasn't the only issue liberals demanded rapid acceptance of during the Obama years that generated lots of attention in right-wing media. In 2008 transgenderism was barely known, but by 2016 Democrats were calling to provide government-mandated benefits for it. The idea that sex-change therapies and surgery should be freely available came into vogue, on demand for middle schoolers and members of the United States military alike. Conservatives, for the most part, questioned the wisdom of allowing minors to transform their God-given bodies with drugs and surgery or taxpayer funding of such procedures for convicted soldiers like Chelsea Manning. They wanted a safe place to hash this out. Conservative media provided that.

Then there is abortion, the gruesome matter that sends people running into opposing party bunkers faster than anything else. I hesitate to even discuss it; it's so sickening, so upsetting, but that's all the more reason not to shy away. Here we go. A few years ago, a legitimate house of horrors was discovered in West Philadelphia, run by Philadelphia abortionist Dr. Kermit Gosnell. He was murdering infants born alive by sticking scissors into the back of babies' necks and snipping their spinal cords. At the clinic, the Philadelphia district attorney's office found urine-splattered walls, cat feces, and corroded suction tubing, which was also the only tubing available for resuscitation purposes.

In May 2013, Gosnell was convicted on three counts of first-degree murder. In light of the trial, a number of conservative senators wanted to pass a resolution to call on the Senate to seek information about "abusive, unsanitary, and illegal" abortion practices. Pro-choice Democrats blocked it. California Senator Barbara Boxer said that if Republicans wanted to investigate Gosnell, they'd have to go after all the "unsanitary" health-care practices, as if the cold-blooded murder of a newborn child is somehow akin to improper handwashing techniques.

I cannot overstate how unsettling these revelations were to conservatives. Even so, they barely warranted a shrug from most members of the media. One *Washington Post* reporter described the Gosnell murders as a "local crime story" that didn't warrant national attention. After facing the fury of conservatives online, she later admitted she was wrong. But it didn't make a difference. If you were a conservative who cared about abortion, you most likely found yourself turning to places such as *Breitbart News* and *LifeNews.com* to find out what was happening.

The modern Democratic Party and the mainstream media had, almost overnight, turned radical on abortion and it was as if no one outside the conservative bubble cared.

President Bill Clinton's old approach that abortion be "safe, legal, and rare" would have him drummed out of the party today. The pro-choice left advocates abortion on demand, anytime, anywhere, and many members of the mainstream media seem to agree. Texas Democrat Wendy Davis is lionized by the left and in women's magazines for standing up for the "rights" of women to terminate their pregnancies at *twenty weeks*. Let me remind you, that's the same week a baby is so well developed that a doctor will usually schedule an appointment to reveal the gender of the child. In 2015, the hashtag #shoutyourabortion went viral as progressive activists helped to "normalize" the life-ending procedure. Liberal activists framed abortion as a source of pride and female empowerment, a callous attitude that is now frequently expressed by women. Consider the following. *Goonies* actress Martha Plimpton appeared at a Planned Parenthood event in Seattle where she told the audience, "I've got a lot of family here, some of whom are here in the audience tonight. I also had my first abortion here at the Seattle Planned Parenthood! Yay!" She continued, "Notice I said 'first' . . . and I don't want Seattle—I don't want you guys to feel insecure, it was my best one. Heads and tails above the rest. If I could Yelp review it, I totally would." The old Clinton mantra practically seems quaint.

Lastly, in addition to identifying compelling policy and social stories to pursue for conservative readers, right-leaning websites had plenty of scandal to write about during the Obama years. For example, the mainstream media mostly covered the passage and enactment of

Obamacare as a process and political story; conservative media dug into it as a snow job full of kickbacks, scams, and broken promises.

Most conservatives could tick off a laundry list of affronts by name. While most of these events barely registered a blip on mainstream media, they were long-running stories in conservative media, and part of the shared conservative folklore of the Obama years. Just to name a few, there was Solyndra, the stimulus boondoggle where the government gave a $535 million loan to a solar panel start-up that went bankrupt; Fast and Furious, the federal gunwalking operation where the Bureau of Alcohol, Tobacco, Firearms, and Explosives illegally sold weapons to suspected gun smugglers, two of which were later found in the Arizona desert where Border Patrol agent Brian Terry was killed; the devastatingly long wait lists at the Veterans Affairs hospitals; the Associated Press spying scandal, where AP reporters, as well as Fox News reporter James Rosen, were improperly surveilled by the Department of Justice. To be sure, all of these stories popped up in places like the *New York Times* and NBC, but they were analyzed and discussed in great detail, with real dedication for many months, by the conservative media. Your standard GOP activist could talk at great length about any one of these controversies, while most of it would be nothing more than a foggy memory to anyone not paying attention to right-leaning media networks.

But there is always one defining message delivered by the conservative media that never changes and is broadcast each and every day, regardless of the outrage du jour: The liberals running the government and the media can't be trusted. They constantly remind their audiences how conservatives will never get a fair shake from them. The Media Research Center, a conservative organization devoted to tracking liberal bias in the media, has sold a bumper sticker for many years you're likely to see anytime you take a long drive on any red-state highway. It reads: DON'T BELIEVE THE LIBERAL MEDIA. The folks who put these bumper stickers on their vehicles have tuned out of the mainstream media. They listen to TV and radio hosts—think Rush Limbaugh, Sean Hannity, and Laura Ingraham—who blow up the Democrats in government and the big-time anchors on the mainstream networks for hours on end. It's a total win-win for the righty talkers, too. They get to score big ratings by trashing their competition and, bonus: They don't have to spend money on their own shoe-leather reporting. All they have to do is click on the news or flip through the papers, find something to disagree with, and hammer away. It's fast, cheap, and easy programming that also deters the audience from taking their eyeballs and ears anywhere else.

This combination of content is extremely effective in persuading listeners to distrust nonconservative outlets. Perhaps *too effective*. Former conservative talk-radio host Charlie Sykes wrote in his 2017 book *How the Right Lost Its Mind* that "[W]e succeeded in convincing our audiences to ignore and discount any information whatsoever from the mainstream media. The cumulative effect of the attacks was to delegitimize those outlets and essentially destroy much of the Right's immunity to false information."

So much so that, over time, a sizable number of conservatives came to give credence to anyone who branded himself or herself as one of them. Like, say, Alex Jones, the popular Texas-based talker and well-known conspiracy theorist who gained legitimacy among many conservative readers by being linked by the heavily trafficked *Drudge Report* with increasing regularity during Obama's second term. Looking back, I see how one particularly alarming conspiracy theory that emerged in early 2015 should have served as a warning of what kinds of voices could influence the presidential election.

At the time, I was working as communications director for Texas senator Ted Cruz. Multistate military training exercises, known as Jade Helm, were beginning and people were panicked about the heavy military presence congregating in certain areas. Jones had been telling people to fear the worst—the military was preparing for a war against the American people. "They are training to attack and beat and arrest and shoot and kill patriots," he said in one spring broadcast. After a fleet of refrigerated Blue Bell ice-cream trucks was spotted rolling down Texas highways, it was theorized that they were going to be used as morgues for the military to store all of the dead bodies. Normally such ideas would be readily dismissed. Not this time. Texas residents made so many inquiries that Texas governor Greg Abbott had to ask the Texas State Guard to monitor the operation.

Although that did alleviate some concerns, no one could tamp down on the theory. The *Texas Tribune* commissioned a poll to survey Texans' feelings about the exercises and found 44 percent of Texans believed the government would use the military to impose martial law. Daron Shaw, the codirector of the poll and a professor of government at the University of Texas at Austin, said, "It cuts into everybody's suspicion. Nobody trusts the federal government. About a third of Democrats are concerned about the government going nuts. Among Republicans, it's between 55 percent and two-thirds."

You don't have to be a polling expert, or even do math that well, to figure out something was going on. People were scared and willing to believe Internet rumors. Moreover, those kinds of numbers represented a majority of Republicans and enough Democrats to win an election. *A winning coalition*, you might say. One someone could take to #WAR.

4

TERRORIZED

I was sitting at my desk in Senator Jim DeMint's press shop on the eleventh anniversary of 9/11. The day was already fraught with anxiety and sadness, remembering how terrorists had killed thousands as they plunged planes into the World Trade Center and the Pentagon. While working in the Senate, I thought a lot about Flight 93, which had been headed for the U.S. Capitol. The names of its passengers and crew members are etched on a beautiful bronze plaque outside the Capitol Rotunda. They saved the U.S. Capitol by storming the cockpit and forfeiting their lives to stop the terrorists from destroying the building in which we had the honor of working.

When I looked online that day, it appeared a mob had stormed the U.S. embassy in Cairo. They had ripped down an American flag and in its place hoisted the dark black flag of the Islamic State. My heart sank as I wondered what was to come. I worried if we were witnessing the beginning of something reminiscent of the Iranian hostage crisis. Later that same day, an attack was launched on the American consulate in Benghazi. The Obama administration passed it off as a "spontaneous protest," but that wasn't believable. Not on the anniversary of 9/11.

Everyone was looking to the State Department for answers, but Secretary of State Hillary Clinton was quiet. She released a statement that evening that vaguely referred to an anti-Muslim video. "Some have sought to justify this vicious behavior as a response to inflammatory material posted on the Internet. . . . There is never any justification for violent acts of this kind," she said.

Clinton was much more honest behind closed doors. Unbeknownst to the public at the time, she was running a secret email system for herself outside of government networks. Her system, which was used to conduct official business and handle classified information, was only discovered when Congress launched an investigation into the Obama administration's handling of Benghazi years later. Even after her secret server was discovered, Clinton was loath to turn over the emails to investigators and stonewalled Congress for months before handing them over in parceled allotments. To this day, no one has seen all of them; about 33,000 remain "missing," because her lawyers claimed they were all "personal." Congressional investigators were able, however, to learn something significant from the parcel of emails she did turn over: what she really thought about the Benghazi attack in real time. While she was appearing to go along with the line that a YouTube video had sparked the attack, she made a different assessment in an email that evening to her daughter, Chelsea. Clinton said:

> *Two of our officers were killed in Benghazi by an Al Qaeda-like group: The Ambassador, whom I handpicked and a young communications officer on temporary duty w[ith] a wife and two young children. Very hard day and I fear more of the same tomorrow.*

The next afternoon she called the Egyptian prime minister Hisham Qandil and was even more plainspoken. According to State Department notes of the September 12, 2012, call released to congressional investigators, Clinton said, "We know the attack in Libya had nothing to do with the film. It was a planned attack—not a protest." Meanwhile, she maintained her silence in public, letting other Obama administration officials deliver a different message. In her place, National Security Advisor Susan Rice assumed briefing duties, agreeing to do the "full Ginsburg"—a reference Clinton would likely want to avoid. It refers to how lawyer William Ginsburg famously did all five Sunday morning shows in 1998 when representing his client Monica Lewinsky as she took her affair with former president Bill Clinton public. Hillary Clinton stayed mute as Rice continued to peddle the lie that the attack in Benghazi was a "spontaneous reaction" to the events in Cairo that were prompted by an anti-Muslim YouTube video. Longtime Clinton chroniclers Jonathan Allen and Amie Parnes described Clinton's decision to hang back thusly in their 2014 book *HRC*: "She didn't need the platform, it was a politically risky proposition in the middle of a crisis." The truth eventually came out. And when it did, it reinforced the worst characterizations of Clinton. That she was a cold, calculating ladder climber. That Americans could be murdered in a terrorist attack and she would still prioritize her political ambitions above all else.

Clinton and others in the Obama administration weren't being honest because they were dead-set against saying anything that would give Americans the idea that terrorism had increased on their watch. In his farewell address, President Obama sought credit for keeping America safe. "[N]o foreign terrorist organization had successfully planned and executed an attack on our homeland," he said. In a lawyerly way, Obama was right. But Americans had watched the body count of terrorist victims rise during his time in office, and many didn't appreciate how the president was playing semantic games to create the illusion that everything was fine. We knew better. We saw it with our own eyes.

American journalist James Foley was beheaded by ISIS in August 2014, the gruesome video of his murder was blasted by the terror group as grisly propaganda for all to see. More beheadings followed: Israeli American journalist Steven Soltoff, Indianapolis man Peter Kassig, and British aid workers David Haines and Alan Henning, among them. In 2015, another ISIS propaganda video showed militants marching twenty-one Coptic Christians to a beach in Libya, where they were beheaded.

The terror had come home, too. During Obama's second term, America stood witness to radical Islam-inspired shootings in Little Rock, Fort Hood, Brooklyn, Garland, Chattanooga, San Bernardino, and Orlando. Bombings in Boston and New York. Another beheading was carried out in the small town of Moore, Oklahoma. But because these attackers weren't card-carrying members of al-Qaeda, or wearing some standard-issue ISIS uniform, we were supposed to believe we weren't under attack.

Obama could keep saying that all he wanted, but he couldn't make it feel true to everyone. The security atmosphere had gotten too hot. We could feel it.

I sure did. The entire time I worked on Capitol Hill, death threats, lockdowns, and anthrax scares were a regular part of life. We were always being threatened by something or other. One day in October 2013, in the middle of a government shutdown, things got even scarier.

At that time, I was working as a senior staffer for Senator Ted Cruz, and we were in the middle of the government shutdown he had led over Obamacare. I was typing at my computer and was jolted from my work when I heard what sounded like a large jackhammer outside our first-floor window overlooking Constitution Avenue. The noise was so unusual and jarring that a few of my colleagues got up from their desks to go to the window and see what the fuss was about. In an instant, a fleet of police cars and motorcycles, more than I've ever seen at once, came screaming through the intersection. Our chief of staff, Chip Roy, flew into the office. "Everyone in here now!" he said, gesturing toward an interior room where someone had shut off the lights. I felt a gust of wind from other doors being slammed shut and locked. Someone said shootings were under way.

Scenes of the Washington Navy Yard shooting where a dozen people had been killed only a few weeks earlier flashed in my mind. Was someone trying to send us a message because of the shutdown? Did someone want to teach us a lesson about our pro–Second Amendment stance? Was this terror? Thinking I may need to run, I took off my heels and slipped into a pair of flats that were under my desk. "This is what women did on 9/11 when the Capitol and White House were evacuated," I thought. Quickly, I entered the room where people were crouched on the floor. I saw a tiny closet, where people usually made coffee, and ran in.

Our press assistant followed. I told our legislative director, a slim and petite mother of two, to get in. She said she couldn't fit. Without saying a word, I picked her up and shoved her inside. We shut the door, sat, held hands, and began praying for Capitol police to quickly bring this matter to an end. I checked social media on my phone. A shooting had taken place. Other Capitol Hill offices were instructed to shelter in place, which meant the threat was imminent. No escape. No more details were available.

Then someone violently started banging on one of the outer office doors that faces the public hallway. "Open up!" a voice yelled. We all remained silent. The doorknob started shaking hard. "Open up!" the person yelled with more force, pounding the door again. Still we all stayed silent. "Capitol police!" Then—and I must tell you I've never been prouder of the men I've worked with in the Cruz office—came a loud retort. "NO!" a resounding chorus of male voices boomed back. I wasn't the only one who believed that whoever was on the other side of the door wasn't a friend.

"Show us your identification!" someone yelled from our side of the wall.

After some back-and-forth they made an agreement. All of our offices connected through a series of interior doors down a long hallway. The person knocking would meet Roy near the front office, far away from where we were hiding, and produce identification. I buried my head in my hands. My God, was Roy offering himself up to take the first bullet for our staff? Everything was surreal. After a few minutes, which felt like much longer, we got word. It was the Capitol police. The shots were fired to protect us, not *at* us.

Turns out, a woman had crashed into a White House security checkpoint, struck a Secret Service officer, and led a high-speed chase down Pennsylvania Avenue toward the Capitol right outside our offices. There, Capitol police fired multiple shots and she was finally forced off the road and killed. She had an eighteen-month-old child in the backseat of the car, who thankfully was unharmed. Her motives remain a mystery to this day.

I did, however, discover something about myself I hadn't previously realized. I was terrorized. Not by the events of that day per se, but by everything leading up to that day that made me believe someone awful was knocking on our door. Maybe I got too many suspicious package alerts on my government-issued BlackBerry. Maybe I got too many harassing comments on Twitter. Maybe I watched too many episodes of *Homeland*. Maybe I consumed too much media that focused on the rise of ISIS and their horrifying methods. Maybe this, maybe that, maybe everything. I can't tell you exactly why. All I can tell you is that I was. In this environment, the absolute worst seemed absolutely possible.

I wasn't alone in my thinking. Terror loomed large in the decision-making process for many Republicans when it came to the 2016 election. One of the most persuasive essays of the cycle supporting Trump's candidacy explicitly made the case for him on do-or-die grounds inspired by terror. Writing for the *Claremont Review of Books*, Michael Anton, using the pseudonym Publius Decius Mus, bluntly stated: "2016 is the Flight 93 election: charge the cockpit or you die. You may die anyway. You—or the leader of your party—may make it into the cockpit and not know how to fly or land the plane. There are no guarantees. Except one: if you don't try, death is certain."

If that deadly analogy wasn't clear enough, he had another one ready. "A Hillary Clinton presidency is Russian Roulette with a semi-auto. With Trump, at least you can spin the cylinder and take your chances."

The piece rocketed through conservative media. Rush Limbaugh spent an extensive amount of time on his program reading it, exalting the piece for how well it shamed the so-called Never Trumpers. "It is shot between the eyes of conservative intellectuals who say that Trump is beneath them," Limbaugh said. Trump campaign strategist Steve Bannon later said the essay presented a "seminal moment when Trumpism really started to get an intellectual basis."

Psychologically, Anton's essay fired up all the right synapses. One postelection study presented at the American Psychological Association annual dinner conducted by cognitive neuroscientists at George Mason University found stimulation of morbid anxieties helped Trump win. The study found:

> [W]hen individuals were made to think about death, their support for Donald Trump increased, regardless of their party affiliation and whether or not they had an overall negative attitude towards Trump. These findings imply that the recent terror attacks in San Bernardino and Orlando, which undoubtedly aroused existential anxiety, may have played an essential role in Trump's mindboggling ascent from Reality TV to the most powerful office in the world.

INSIDE JOB

I n the beginning of the Republican presidential primary Donald Trump had one job: destroy Jeb Bush. Here is where the real gaslighting begins.

It cannot be overstated how much the idea of another Bush-versus-Clinton general election made conservative activists groan. To them, Bush was the epitome of the Republican-in-name-only (RINO) types who had lost the last two elections to Obama. Bush did have a commendable record as Florida governor, but he was no trusted conservative warrior. He'd been mostly absent during the Obama years, avoiding all the ruckus, basking somewhere in the Florida sunshine. When he did pipe up, the only things he seemed interested in discussing were policies the Tea Party railed against, namely some version of amnesty for illegal aliens and adoption of Common Core standards. Conservative activists had a word for his type: "squish." Besides, the memories of the previous Bush presidencies hadn't grown fonder over time. Those presidencies recalled broken tax pledge promises, busted budgets, and the beginning of the never-ending wars in the Middle East. A third Bush presidency was too much to ask.

Adding to the displeasure among GOP voters was how the media was obviously ginning up a food fight among the uncomfortably large field of Republican candidates. The long march of debates and forums seemed much more geared toward benefiting the media outlets hosting them than the candidates or voters. The whole situation was begging for someone with a brash voice to cut through the clutter. Yet the mild and moderate Bush was considered to be the presumptive front-runner.

Something else made Bush an attractive target for Trump. Although many Republican voters felt this frustration, Republican candidates weren't willing to verbalize it . Sure, candidates such as Ted Cruz recognized Bush was "establishment," but there was an imaginary line the candidates wouldn't cross. It wasn't gentlemanlike courtesy; there was too much risk in alienating the deep-pocketed donors who had donated generously to the past two winning Bush presidential campaigns. Like vultures, most of the other candidates were hoping to pick off Bush's biggest funders, as well as his choice staff members, as soon as his campaign croaked.

Trump, however, was a line crosser and most of the other candidates were happy to see him waltz right over it. In a crowded primary with seventeen GOP candidates, every one of them was looking for ways to clear the field. Thus, the conditions for Trump's gaslighting of Bush were set.

Broadly, here is how it worked. When Trump engaged Step One, making unfair claims about Bush, many of the others stepped aside and let him do it. They believed Trump would bulldoze Bush away, while driving his own unfavorables so high in the process that it would put someone more appealing, such as Cruz or Rubio, on a glide path to the nomination. It's politics 101: If your rival is self-destructing or someone is helping him or her do it, get out of the way. In those hazy days of the GOP primary, everyone seemed to think Trump would be a political suicide bomber, taking out the main target and vaporizing his own candidacy in the process. But Trump was crafty. He, as you will see, always avoided taking direct responsibility for his smears, which activated Step Two, the advance-and-deny phase. Again, the other Republicans running had no reason to intervene. They let Trump dance around the facts, thinking voters would see how much more "presidential" they were in contrast. Everyone went along with

Step Three—the suspense. Either bad information would come out about Bush, or Trump would be proven a liar. Pure benefit for people like Cruz and Rubio, who wanted to see them both damaged. Or so they erroneously thought. It always proved to be a giant ruse to benefit Trump and Trump alone. By the end of it, all of the other GOP candidates would be defeated, discredited, and worst of all, blamed by many in the press for not doing enough to hold Trump accountable for the bad behavior he exhibited all along the way.

A key takeaway of Trump's gaslighting of Bush is how well it forced him into an unescapable psychological box. No, it wasn't how Trump called Bush "low energy" although that did hurt Bush quite a bit. Trump's real feat was how he forced everyone to remember that Jeb Bush was a "Bush" and would never be anyone else.

The Bush campaign deliberately left the last name "Bush" off their signage because they knew how reluctant the country would be to back him if he came off as a dynasty candidate. Therein lies the sick genius of Trump's gaslighting method. When Trump gaslit Bush, he did it to gain total control over Bush's campaign narrative. Remember, gaslighting is all about control. Trump wasn't going to let Jeb Bush run on his record as a Florida governor. He would make him run on his brother's presidential record, which was deeply scarred by the politics of war.

But first, Trump did a gaslighting test run to see how Bush would fare against his method. To do it, Trump went after Bush's wife, a plan of attack long considered no-man's-land. That's the first step of his method: staking a claim no one else would take. Trump suggested Bush's soft position on immigration was due to his Mexican-born wife. It was a cheap shot, but the people who disliked Bush were willing to look the other way. During a September 2016 debate at the Ronald Reagan Presidential Library, Bush was asked to respond. Bush turned to Trump and began lecturing him. "To subject my wife into the middle of a raucous political conversation was completely inappropriate," Bush said. "And I hope you apologize for that, Donald."

Nope. Time for Step Two—advance and deny! Trump owned up to talking about Bush's wife but called the hubbub "a total mischaracterization." Then Bush made his request again. "Why don't you apologize to her right now?" Little did Bush realize he was dealing with someone who would never comply with such a request. "No, I won't do that because I've said nothing wrong," Trump said. Jaws dropped. The whole exchange was astonishing. Bush made a hard play to stand up for his wife, which should have been a slam dunk but somehow got stuffed. It was embarrassing to watch. Trump didn't even need to employ Step Three. He skipped right ahead. Step Four—the discrediting of Bush—was accomplished.

Trump took a victory lap on *Morning Joe* the next day. "I thought he was going to push me harder to apologize to his wife," Trump said, further reinforcing how pathetic he thought Bush was. There it was—Step Five, the step that we don't always see right away. Trump was telling him how easily he won the argument. It was Trump's way of declaring victory.

Trump got everything he wanted from the exchange. He tested Bush and found that Bush was someone he could gaslight and that he could reap the benefits for doing it, too. This was only a warm-up. Soon enough he would grab the third rail of Bush family politics and gaslight Jeb right out of the race.

Trump was about to move into the most fringe-infested area of American politics, which strangely enough unites the far-left and far-right ends of the political spectrum. In this case, the conspiracy theory that 9/11 was an inside job and that George W. Bush—Jeb's brother—was somehow responsible for it. Just like birtherism, this was a subject plenty of people on the right and the left obsessed over. The territory was rich, should someone have the nerve to take ownership of it. Trump did.

Trump started his taunts in the fall of 2015. During an interview with Bloomberg TV, the subject of President George Bush and 9/11 came up. "He was President," Trump said. "Blame him, or don't blame him, but he was President. The World Trade Center came down during his reign."

To be sure, questions about the country's decision to engage in long wars in the Middle East were fair. Blaming Bush for the terrorist attacks was not. Trump was twerking in the gray area in between, riling up all of the conspiracy theorists who had long believed the collapse of the World Trade Center was an "inside job" conducted by the U.S. government. He was being just vague enough to energize the truthers who blamed Bush for not doing enough to stop the attack.

Bush, naturally, defended his brother. He used the smooth, poll-tested line that President George Bush "kept us safe." At the same time, he was incredulous. "Does anybody actually blame my brother for the attacks on 9/11?" he asked in an interview with CNN. "If they do, they're totally marginalized in our society." Bush wanted the topic made out-of-bounds. How dare anyone raise questions about it! What he didn't know was that he was playing right into Trump's hands.

Time for the second step of Trump's gaslighting method. Advance and deny. The ol' Shaggy defense: *It wasn't me,* Trump told *Fox News Sunday*:

> *"Jeb said, 'We were safe with my brother. We were safe.' Well, the World Trade Center just went down. Now, am I trying to blame him? I'm not blaming anybody, but the World Trade Center came down, so when he said we were safe, we were not safe. We lost 3,000 people. It was one of the greatest—probably the greatest catastrophe ever in this country."*

In one fell swoop, Trump advanced the blame narrative while expressly denying it at the same time. This rhetorical device is *critical* to understanding Trump's gaslighting method. (Don't worry, there will be many more examples.) Trump kept at it, seeding the idea that President Bush was responsible for 9/11. Then, during a February 13 debate, one week before the South Carolina primary, Trump called the Iraq war a "big fat mistake," forcing Bush to choose a side. Trump said:

> *"I want to tell you. They lied. They said there were weapons of mass destruction and there were none. And they knew there were none. There were no weapons of mass destruction."*

Bush, just like Trump wanted, leaped to defend his family honor, saying:

"I'm sick and tired of him going after my family. My dad is the greatest man alive in my mind. And while Donald Trump was building a reality TV show, my brother was building a security apparatus to keep us safe. I'm proud of what he did. And he has the gall to go after my brother."

Trump shot back, "The World Trade Center came down during your brother's reign. Remember that!"

Bush complained that Trump "has had the gall to go after my mother," referring to how Trump had tweeted earlier that Bush "had to bring in his mommy" to a previous campaign stop. Bush told the debate audience she is "the strongest woman I know." Trump cracked, "She should be running."

Bush was walking right into the box Trump wanted to trap him in. The method was working. Trump forced Bush to draw attention to his greatest weaknesses: the fact that he was a Bush and the Bush family record in Iraq. Gleefully, Trump turned up the heat, drawing in the Clintons, too. A pox on both dynastic houses! A perfect permutation.

"The World Trade Center came down because Bill Clinton [didn't] kill Osama bin Laden when he had the chance to kill him," Trump steamrolled. "And George Bush—by the way, George Bush had the chance, also, and he didn't listen to the advice of his C.I.A." The Bush-friendly crowd booed Trump resoundingly, but Trump kept right on at it. He wasn't giving an inch. He fought on. "How did he keep us safe . . . excuse me, I lost hundreds of friends!"

Conservative talk-radio powerhouse Mark Levin said Trump's remarks were a "disgrace" and sounded like "a radical kook."

Trump didn't care one bit. He wasn't intimidated; his method was succeeding. In fact, Trump's gaslighting only works if people get outraged. Making people choose sides and argue about his topic of choice is exactly the point!

Trump kept on pushing Step Two—advancing and denying the idea that the Bush family should be held responsible for 9/11. He went on *The Mike Gallagher Show* to keep driving the point home.

"I am just giving the facts. The World Trade Center you understand, Mike, I mean the World Trade Center came down during his reign. And I said what about that? Did it come down during his reign?

"So, you can't say your brother kept us safe because after the World Trade Center—the World Trade Center came down during his reign. And, frankly, there was a lot of information that the CIA and the NSA, you know, you had a lot of different agencies that were poorly coordinated because they could have found out about this.

"You know, there's a lot of theories. They did not get along and they did not share information properly and they could have done something better. Who knows? Who really knows? But you can't say the World Trade Center was not like an event—I mean, he was president and the World Trade Center came down.

"You have Jeb, who doesn't even like using his last name—you have Jeb—and for good reason, I understand that. But you have Jeb saying his brother kept us safe."

Bush was already flailing before Trump started his gaslighting, failing to come in as one of the top three candidates in the first two contests in Iowa and New Hampshire. Now, Trump was on his way to finishing him off well before the winner-take-all Florida primary in Bush's home state. During a February 17 rally in Bluffton, South Carolina—three days before South Carolina Republicans would go to the polls—Trump upped the ante. Time for Step Three, the suspense and promise of something more intriguing to come!

Trump said:

"We went after Iraq, they did not knock down the World Trade Center. It wasn't the Iraqis that knocked down the World Trade

Center, we went after Iraq, we decimated the country. Iran's taking over, okay. But, it wasn't the Iraqis, you will find out who really knocked down the World Trade Center. Because they have papers in there that are very secret. You may find it's the Saudis, okay? But you will find out."

We "will find out"? Talk about tantalizing. Trump was taking what was thought to be a settled matter and throwing all kinds of questions into play. He didn't even pretend to have any facts on his side. Those would come *later*.

Although Trump didn't commit himself to anything tangible, he was giving a siren call to the conspiracists. They knew he was referring to the twenty-eight "missing pages" of the 9/11 Commission report that the Bush administration had ordered classified. Many of those who believed 9/11 was an "inside job" thought these documents would "prove" that the U.S. government was complicit in the 9/11 attacks. And like every good conspiracy theory, there were some legitimate people who wanted to see the pages as well. Some family members of 9/11 victims advocated for their release, desiring the complete record. The Obama administration later released the documents in July 2016. And Trump was on to something. The pages did show that 9/11 hijackers had had relationships with Saudi officials. Nothing that substantially changed the findings of the report, though. During the 2016 primary, however, the contents of the pages were somewhat of an open question. No one knew what those pages said.

To help push back against Trump, Jeb Bush's brother George and mother campaigned with him through his final swing in South Carolina. Surely Trump was grinning. It was the perfect snapshot of a royal political family in a nonestablishment year.

Bush had been totally sucked into the fire Trump had lit. "The more outlandish things he says about my brother . . . knowing about 9/11—you can't make this stuff up," Bush said at a stop in Summerville. "This is Michael Moore talk!" Right—it was just the kind of bipartisan nuttery Trump excelled in trafficking. (Note: Michael

Moore was one of the few pundits who predicted Trump would win the presidency.)

Trump's goal had been met. All the work Bush's staff had done to depict their candidate as a man of his own destiny, not the favored son and brother of previous presidents, was undone. Trump won the South Carolina primary by 10 points. Step Five complete. Trump won. Rubio came in second, Cruz third, and Bush a distant fourth, claiming only 7.8 percent of the vote. Bush dropped out of the race that night. I was on set for CNN the moment he withdrew and watched his speech in the camera monitor. The moment he went to the podium, I extended a palms-up hand to Trump supporter Jeffrey Lord, who was sitting beside me. Wordlessly, he high-fived me. We both felt the same. "That's it," I thought. "We beat the establishment. We can only go up from here." How terribly wrong I was. In a postelection piece for the *Daily Beast,* former Bush adviser Tim Miller reflected:

> *In politics, the road to defeat is forever paved with good intentions. Ask my fellow presidential campaign staff losers about our efforts and I suspect you will hear us comfort ourselves with the notion that "at least we stayed true to our values." That we campaigned with the "best intentions."*
>
> *The idea was met with mockery by Trump supporters and advisors. Instead the value that drove the Trump phenomenon was a promise to win above all things. To defeat all enemies, be they Democrats, ISIS, illegal immigrants, or anyone investigating the campaign's ties to Russia. "At least he fights" was the refrain from his fans anytime someone would try to convince them that he was not pure, not conservative, not trustworthy. Scoreboard taunts largely replaced ideological arguments. Belittling took over debating. It's hard to argue with the results.*

Trump's formula took out the giant of the GOP primary. Although I was pleased at the time to see Bush drop out of the race, Trump's attacks on the rest of the field began to worry me. On the air, I frequently expressed my hope that the GOP race would come down to a choice between Cruz and Rubio. Trump was dangerous. Nothing about him was conservative, civil, or remotely reliable in my mind. He was crude and lied all the time, seemingly for fun. Conservatives had to hold the line for the good of the party, I believed—and still do. Many other commentators were so closely tied to their candidates for their livelihoods, but as a CNN contributor, I feel a weighty responsibility to give viewers my honest assessment. Even when it comes to my former boss. The night Cruz won the Iowa primary, for example, I knocked him on CNN's air for using tired old talking points and not using the opportunity to speak to a national audience that was getting their first look at the first-in-nation caucus winner. Although I had worked for a presidential candidate, I was on my own at CNN and the idea of blindly supporting any candidate with my commentary was unimaginable. But then an attempt was made to disqualify me from the discussion altogether and derail my career.

It all started in March 2016. No doubt I drew attention to myself from the Trump campaign mid-month when I publicly called for a blacklist of Republican politicians who endorsed Trump, which attracted lots of attention. The influential conservative website *RedState* favorably excerpted what I wrote:

> *It's time to make a list. A list of those so-called conservatives and Republicans endorsing Donald Trump, the megalomaniac who regularly threatens his opponents and the press, raves about making members of our military adopt ISIS-like tactics, has funded Gang of Eight Democrats, promises to forcibly relocate American companies to his liking, and has demonstrated again and again he intends to govern as a tyrannical King rather than a President. Call it a boycott, call it a blackball, call it blacklist, call it whatever you want. I'm done with these folks and other conservatives should be, too. Anyone who will defend a man condoning random acts of violence at his rallies has lost their morals; they will defend*

anything at all. So, I'd like to remember who supported Trump so I never give any kind of credence to their judgment. "Never Trump" means never those who support him as well.

That's when I really made myself a target. Of course, the piece outraged Trump-friendly websites, especially *Breitbart News. Gateway Pundit*'s Jim Hoft, whom I had met during my DeMint days, blasted the list, telling his readers it was written by "Amanda Carpenter who is usually kind and intelligent but now suffers from a severe case of Trump Derangement Syndrome."

Former vice presidential candidate Sarah Palin was among the Trump supporters I called out. Criticizing her wasn't something I enjoyed doing. I hardly felt affection for any politicians, but during the 2008 election I was downright thrilled the McCain campaign had selected her as his vice presidential pick. On many occasions, I happily defended her in print and on TV from the multitudes of attacks she received. When she abruptly resigned as Alaskan governor, I was disappointed but sympathetic. As a *Washington Times* reporter, I wrote about the massive legal bills she faced due to the barrage of ethics complaints lodged against her. It was so unfair. The complaints cost nothing to file and cost her severely. She must have noticed because she thanked a person named "Amanda" in her book. One of her associates took care to point it out to me. Make of that what you will.

We met once briefly. While I was working for Cruz, she made a special trip to thank his staffers for our work. It was a last-minute event on the weekend, but my husband and I quickly hustled our kids into the car to attend. I really wanted to meet her in person. During our short exchange, she complimented my children, and we had a photo taken. Her aides later followed up with me, asking if I would be interested in doing some speechwriting for her, which I grudgingly declined. I just didn't have the bandwidth. My hands were full working as a senior staff member for Cruz and tending to my babies, whom she oddly went out of her way to mention when she blasted me months later for criticizing her jumping aboard the Trump train.

I had publicly said, "What has Donald Trump done for Sarah Palin?," asking what Trump had done to promote any of the values Palin's supporters had been advocating for the past several years. Trump had supported the bailouts and Obama's stimulus bill, and even talked favorably about universal health care. So what exactly was Palin getting out of this endorsement, in terms of policy or otherwise? A very fair question that she didn't want to answer.

In a Facebook post she wrote:

Rallying a group of young conservative DC staffers when I travelled across the country to support their bosses' efforts to defund Obamacare. Since I'm supporting a Republican candidate promising to do away with Obamacare, some of these same staffers are now hell-bent on blacklisting me, and have even gone so far as accusing me of "trashing the constitution" and lying—accusing me of being paid for my endorsements! They know better but spew the lies anyway. Some of these young folks started out bright and talented, but they're corrupted by power in Washington. Still, I'll hold out hope for them and echo the words of Mr. Buckley once again: "I won't insult your intelligence by suggesting that you really believe what you just said." (Oh—and to one of those staffers-turned-talking-head, Amanda, who now helps lead this charge against me . . . I meant what I said when you brought your kids all the way to meet me that day not long ago—they really are cute.)

She was trying to shame me. Like a parent lecturing me about how disappointed they were in their child. The moment she dragged my kids into the discussion was the instant I regretted ever thinking of her as any kind of a role model. But this was par for the course for hardball politics. Besides, something far worse happened soon after that made me forget all about it.

My own personal gaslighting session was about to begin.

BURNED

never imagined I would be considered an enemy by anyone working on the Republican side, but those were the very people who would gaslight me during the 2016 election for everyone in America to see.

Some background is necessary so you can see how blindsided I was.

I got my start as a Midwest conservative activist, spearheading a rabble-rousing political blog in college that tracked how tuition dollars were being misspent. From there, I packed my bags for Washington. I had landed an internship at the Leadership Institute, an organization that works as a feeder tank of sorts for conservative think tanks, media outlets, and campaigns. After that I got a job right away with *Human Events*, a now-defunct print publication that prided itself as being Ronald Reagan's favorite newspaper. I roamed the halls of Capitol Hill with a tape recorder as a credentialed congressional correspondent. Very early on in my career, Regnery Publishing asked me to pen a book: *The Vast Right Wing Conspiracy's Dossier on Hillary Clinton.* From there I moved into the digital world at Townhall.com and then into a newsroom at the *Washington Times.* Throughout my different moves, I frequently appeared on cable TV, even gaining a coveted weekly segment on *The O'Reilly Factor.*

In 2009, I got a call from South Carolina Republican senator Jim DeMint's office asking if I'd like to be his speechwriter. Even though my media career was going gangbusters, many of the top-flight media personalities I admired had political experience. They had the kind of credibility very few people in my cadre of talking heads had. Here was my chance to hone my writing skills, observe the legislative process from the inside, and see how to navigate the political scene. Until receiving that call, however, I always thought doing so would require working for some mealy-mouthed, do-nothing politician. A dreadful thought. I realized how special this offer was; DeMint was taking real risks challenging the party. I went from reluctantly considering the idea to counting down the hours until my start date, afraid DeMint would change his mind. I excitedly handed in my Capitol Hill press pass and exchanged it for a shiny, new Senate ID.

During my tenure on Capitol Hill, I found myself in the center of the GOP's internal civil war as DeMint took on the Republican establishment, backing hard-charging conservative candidates in primary contests who later became the stars of the party, such as Rand Paul, Ted Cruz, and Marco Rubio. In December 2012, when DeMint accepted a job to become president of the Heritage Foundation, I didn't anticipate staying in the Senate. Returning to the media had always been my plan, but some Texans who knew about my work for DeMint had something else in mind.

"Are you interested in working for Ted Cruz?" I was asked. Although I was aware of Cruz's sterling credentials and flattered to be recruited, the notion didn't thrill me at first. "Freshman members are usually pretty boring," I said. "Can you assure me this guy will actually want to do something?" They said I wouldn't be disappointed. Give it a couple of months, I was told. Again, I was being offered a once-in-a-lifetime opportunity that I wasn't wise enough to immediately appreciate.

So I moved my things a few floors from DeMint's well-appointed office in the stately Russell Building into a cramped Dirksen basement where a team of spirited and friendly Texans were on a mission. In short order, Cruz started rocking Washington, challenging the old white hairs in the party and Democrats alike.

My colleagues and I were taking on the establishment and loving every minute of it, happy warriors. During my time there, *Roll Call* published a front-page story calling me "Cruz's Twitter Torrent" that highlighted my willingness to criticize the GOP leadership and crowned me Capitol Hill's most followed staffer. Then in the spring of 2015 a new chapter began. Cruz became the first GOP candidate to announce his bid for the GOP nomination in March 2015, executing a flawless rollout.

When I first joined the Cruz office in 2013, I knew there was a possibility he would run and viewed it as my job to ensure that the path would be available to him if he so chose. That meant going to work every day as if it were a make-or-break kind of day. No mistakes. Some days were tough; we worked in a pressure-cooker atmosphere where lots of people were gunning for Cruz. We all got tougher in those years and I can say the mission was accomplished. He successfully launched. But continuing the job would have meant moving to Texas, where the campaign was headquartered, impractical for me, my husband, and our two small children, who, at the time, were both under three years old. Sure, I could have stayed in the Senate office, but I couldn't stand the thought of manning a quiet, boring desk in D.C. while all the action was happening on the campaign trail. That wasn't for me. As his official headquarters geared up, I prepared to say good-bye to my dear Texas friends. This was the time for me to take the plunge and try to return to my media career. Not long after I departed, much to my delight, CNN asked me to become a political contributor. I cheerfully said yes, but having no idea of the roller coaster of a ride I was about to embark upon.

I continued to think my time working for Senator Cruz was one of the most standout aspects of my résumé. What I didn't realize was that in the rough-and-tumble 2016 presidential campaign, it would make me a huge target.

The first step of my gaslighting had long been in the works. An indecent claim had been made, but no one was willing to take ownership of it. A rumor had been flying around among political operatives and reporters that Cruz had some kind of affair he was hiding. Someone just needed to stake a claim on it to thrust it into the public domain. Until that point, it was the typical kind of crap seedy campaign hacks tried to pass off to reporters, hoping one would be willing to at least write a speculative story to get people talking about it. From time to time, a reporter would ask someone in the Cruz universe about it. We weren't stupid, though. I knew, as did many other former and present Cruz staffers, that if someone went on the record refuting the story, reporters would use the denial to publish it. "Cruz staffer denies rumors of affair" would be the headline. The better response was to tell them something like "Listen, off the record, if you have some kind of evidence I'll look at it. Show me the picture, the video, the emails, or whatever you've got." They never had anything. So, no story.

Then in spring 2016, long after I had left my position with Cruz in July 2015, and I was comfortable in my new role at CNN, the inquiries started increasing. A pair of writers who flitted around conservative circles issued pointed interview requests to me, saying it was urgent that I talk to them about an important matter regarding Cruz. A story was to be published soon, I was told. They said I needed to respond without ever telling me what I was supposed to respond to. The messages were aggressive in a way that annoyed me. "Who do they think they are talking to me like that, I'm not a Cruz staffer anymore," I thought. "Get lost." Then, one afternoon as I was pulling out of my church's driveway after dropping off a load of clothes to donate, I got a phone call from someone with the Cruz campaign. On the other end of the line was a friend I had worked with in the Senate since my DeMint days. He wasn't calling to catch up on old times. The campaign had gotten word that the *National Enquirer*—owned by one of Trump's oldest and proudest fans—would soon publish a nasty story about an affair I was going to be named in. I pulled my car over as I struggled to absorb what I was being told.

"You're kidding, right?" My voice cracked. He was not. He apologized that I was being put in this position and I knew how much he meant it. I imagined how they must have tried to stop the story, which had no facts at all to back it up. The gaslighting was now imminent. The *National Enquirer* was going to claim that I had had an affair with Ted Cruz. Step One was coming right at me.

I knew that I needed to end the conversation quickly. I was on my own now; no one at the campaign could help me even if they wanted to. If anyone had reason to believe we were coordinating a response, it would only look like we were trying to cover something up. It occurred to me that there was a chance that someone could be trying to record my reaction. My paranoid instincts were kicking in as I considered all the ways someone might try to frame me. I raced home to tell my husband, a conversation that seems comical upon reflection. "Honey, please don't be upset. The *National Enquirer* is going to report that I cheated on you with my boss." My husband knew it was all absurd but we still didn't know how to explain it to people, like his parents. Honestly, we couldn't decide whether to laugh it off or cry. (We split the difference. He laughed. I cried.) All we could do was brace ourselves, having no idea how this would unfold. While we waited, my manager instructed me to take the precaution of consulting with a good lawyer to see what could be done to protect myself. I did that and steeled myself for the days ahead.

A few days later, the *National Enquirer* story went online. The Internet went berserk, especially on Twitter under the hashtag #Cruz-SexScandal. When I read the digital story, however, I initially felt a massive rush of relief. I was not named. No women were. But, it was clear to me that Trump associates were taking ownership of the story—Step One—because Roger Stone, the onetime Nixon aide who prided himself on dirty tricks and who was advising Trump at the time, was quoted.

"These stories have been swirling around Cruz for some time," Stone told the publication. "I believe where there is smoke, there is fire. I have to believe this will hurt him with his evangelical Christian supporters." Pure conjecture. I felt like the story was a giant whiff and the whole thing would blow over soon. Or so I naively believed. That's because I didn't see the print cover of the *National Enquirer* until later.

Five barely blurred-out faces of women accompanied the allegations of a sex scandal on the front page of the publication, seen by millions and millions of people while they waited in the checkout aisles at their local supermarkets. One of them was of me. "IT'S OVER FOR PERVY TED" the headline blared. "CRUZ'S 5 SECRET MISTRESSES!" *Salon* posted a story describing the clamor: "Internet Scrambles to Identify Women in *National Enquirer's* 'Bombshell' Report Alleging Ted Cruz Had Five Affairs." Outlets like *Salon* acknowledged how unlikely the story was but ran with it anyway—even referencing Alex Jones as someone who was promoting the smear.

This is an important part of how a smear spreads: Outlets that would never cover a story like this on their own would still cover the coverage. The right fake narrative seduces outlets across the spectrum. Here is what *Salon* said:

> In its latest issue Friday, *The National Enquirer is alleging Ted Cruz has had at least five extramarital affairs. The rumors started as just that—rumors. But as more of the puzzle is pieced together, the rumors are gaining traction. (Remember, the Enquirer broke John Edwards' campaign-ending affair in 2007.) Probably less reputable than the Enquirer, Alex Jones earlier this month warned of a "looming" Cruz sex scandal during an interview with consultant and former Donald Trump staffer, Roger Stone.*

In other words, we have no reason to believe this is true, but we are going to write about it anyway. The only "puzzle" being pieced together was that Trump operatives thought these rumors would damage Cruz with his evangelical voters. Thanks, *Salon*!

It didn't take long for people to figure out I was one of the women pictured, linking the photo the *National Enquirer* used to a photo *Roll Call* had taken of me to use in a profile about my work for Cruz. Although the story itself hadn't named me, the *National Enquirer* made me a cover girl for their smear. It couldn't possibly have been a coincidence. Of all the millions of photos of women on the Internet, my photo was selected by their staff and used in a manner in which the public could easily identify me. And the public did. Internet users quickly tagged me as a supposed mistress. All because the *National Enquirer* used my image for their made-up story. I was floored by how underhanded it was. The gaslighting was under way. Step Two, where the Trump campaign both advanced the story and denied responsibility for it, was next.

The *National Enquirer* also used the images of four other women, one of whom was Katrina Pierson, who had once volunteered for Cruz's Senate campaign and since became a spokeswoman for the Trump campaign. She rushed to confirm her photo in the story, fanning tons of media attention to the story. Even the most junior media professional would know that this would only make the tabloid story more enticing. She tweeted: "Of course the National Enquirer story is 100% false!!! I only speak for myself, however." Not me, she was saying, while pointing the finger firmly at me and the other women shown on the cover. There it was. Step Two in pure and perfect form: advance and deny.

Her comments egged on the mob to get me and the other women to respond. This was the trigger for Step Three—the suspense! What would we say? Why weren't we talking? Who would confront us? Everyone was watching.

As a cable-TV commentator and former aide to high-profile senators, I was quite used to the normal barrage of negative social media commentary that comes to those who work in politics and media. Once during the government shutdown, a Democratic operative in California wished death upon my children. The endless barrage of slime the *National Enquirer* uncorked was on another level. I couldn't even begin to keep up with the stream of accusations, falsehoods, and filth coming my way.

As I watched it all pile up, I was helpless. There wasn't a single thing I could do as people rifled through my professional and personal histories online, either. Every silly Instagram photo I had taken was scrutinized, especially those where I had vainly shown off dresses I enjoyed wearing or tried out different hair and makeup looks. (You try being made up for TV by the country's most talented hair and makeup artists and resist the urge to capture the moment!) The real photos I could deal with, though. After all, I put them out there. It was the fake ones that people Photoshopped to supposedly "confirm" the affair that were infuriating.

But I knew I had conducted my career honorably. There was nothing they could hang on me. Although I worked around the clock, I was always one of the first people to leave the Cruz office each day and rarely staffed off-campus events. I had two very young children at home and commuted a long distance on the train to and from work. I even declined attending all-staff retreats held in Texas, refusing travel that would put any more distance between me and my babies than the miles between my home and the United States Capitol. Though at the time I had felt a bit guilty about ducking so many after-hours activities, it became a blessing in disguise. Everyone who knew me knew I was all about work, family, and not much else. The whole idea of an affair was ludicrous and everyone who knew me knew it.

A brief side note: Every once in a while, there is a big debate on Capitol Hill over the kinds of unspoken rules used by conservative offices that dictate that male and female staffers are never to be alone together. This doesn't mean men and women can't talk privately. What it does mean is that if there is a one-on-one meeting, the door stays open. It's not complicated. Vice President Mike Pence once disclosed that he doesn't eat dinner alone with any female except his wife. Many liberal types expressed shock over his statement, but to me it wasn't remarkable. I knew many conservative men who followed similar guidelines, especially those who traveled frequently and were oftentimes away from their families. It was widely viewed as a matter of respect for the wives who were at home hundreds of miles away. When the Internet mob went looking for anything to link me illicitly to any of my male bosses, I thanked God for those rules. There would never be a picture of me having a one-on-one dinner with some male superior that could be taken out of context. No grainy footage of me in an elevator with a senator or climbing out of some chauffeured car with just the two of us late at night or early in the morning. Nothing. Those rules may have very well saved my career.

I had nothing to hide, but that didn't change the fact that my livelihood was being threatened. I confirmed to my supervisors at CNN that there was nothing to the story and the network agreed that I should continue doing the segments I had been doing since they hired me. While the story was burning up the Internet, no serious news outlet was going with it, so we agreed to proceed as normal.

On March 25, I went to CNN's D.C. bureau for a live segment on Kate Bolduan's 11 a.m. show about the latest happenings in the GOP primary. I was to debate Trump supporter Adriana Cohen, a columnist for the *Boston Herald*. Any debate with a Trump supporter carried a risk of going sideways, but I felt reasonably confident she would stick to the moderator's topics. Again, how naive.

While the Internet trolls were going crazy over #CruzSexScandal, Trump had publicly insulted Heidi Cruz's looks, retweeting a photo that compared an unflattering image of Heidi (a beautiful woman) with a posed shot of his wife, Melania, from her professional modeling days. Bolduan asked Cohen if Trump should "move on" from attacking Heidi. That's when Cohen hijacked the segment and took the smear mainstream. The transcript gives me chills to this day.

COHEN: Oh, absolutely. We should move on. Where we should move to is the National Enquirer story that has reported that Ted Cruz has allegedly had affairs with five mistresses, including— you've been named, Amanda.

BOLDUAN: I'm sorry. I don't think that's moving on at all, Adriana.

COHEN: No, well I'd like to know, if we're going to call Donald Trump's character into question, I would like Ted Cruz to issue a statement whether or not the National Enquirer story is true, whether he has had affairs with many women, including, uh, you were named, Amanda. Will you denounce this story or will you confirm it?

As Cohen dripped those words out of her mouth, I saw my media career flash before my eyes. Was this really happening? This was Step Four. Happening in real time. I was being discredited in a way that everyone could feast on my humiliation; I was being gaslit on live television! The denial I would give would only feed the flames.

Going into the bureau that morning, I planned for the possibility that a reporter would buttonhole me about the rumors. Someone could stake me out on the street outside CNN or possibly in the greenroom. Never did I think someone would do this to me on camera. Not in the middle of a live segment.

Would this exchange be the first thing that would come up when people Googled my name now? After all I had worked to accomplish? Would I ever be able to work in politics again? The sheer cruelty of it all was staggering. When Bolduan turned the conversation to me I knew I would only get one shot to answer, and if I misspoke one word, everything would get much worse, fast. Thankfully, I said everything I wanted to say in a single sound bite. The segment continued.

BOLDUAN: Let me just—let me just step in, really quick. Amanda, I will give you a second. Let me just be very clear. It will come as no surprise to our viewers. CNN has no reporting on what you're talking about from the National Enquirer. Amanda, go ahead.

CARPENTER: What's out there is tabloid trash. If someone wants to comment on it, they can talk to my lawyer. It is categorically false. You should be ashamed for spreading this kind of smut. I will not be intimidated. I will continue to make my thoughts known about Donald Trump and I am not backing down.

What was only an Internet and tabloid rumor was now national news in the most-watched presidential primary in history. Even the most seasoned political journalists were aghast and unhappy they now had to cover the hit job. The *Washington Post*'s Callum Borchers summed up the sucker punch Cohen threw at me. He wrote:

Cohen, a media professional, surely knew what she was doing. And she succeeded. A story without any solid reporting behind it, which many news outlets had managed to dismiss for two days, was suddenly out there on a major cable news station. Cohen created a spectacle that she knew others in the press, who had exercised restraint, would have to cover. This is how Trumpism works. The disheartening reality for journalists is that the Republican presidential front-runner and his allies are getting frighteningly good at forcing them down roads they have tried to avoid.

I'm not eager to give Adriana Cohen any more of the attention she clearly craves, but we have to recognize why she would do such a thing. I'll discuss Trump's army of surrogates later in the book, and Cohen is a textbook case. She went from being a cable-TV striver to a hero in the Trump crowd in a matter of seconds. Associating herself with the slimy narrative posed no risk to her reputation because she had barely any recognition to begin with. It's no accident that the talking heads who rushed to Trump's side during the primary are people you hadn't heard of before. He attracted the types who had nothing to lose by associating with him. For those desperate to make it in the media, the risk of attaching themselves to an intensely negative story was worth it if it provided a sliver of a chance at stardom. For her efforts, Cohen got herself written up in major publications that never would have even glanced her way otherwise. She proved her loyalty to Trump's candidacy.

After the segment finally ended, I unhooked my microphone and walked quickly into an empty office. I shut the door and slid down behind it. I texted my manager two words: "It happened." I was surprised to see my hands trembling a little. Before I could speak with her, my phone started ringing. Bolduan's producer was calling to apologize, something I said wasn't necessary. There was no way anyone could have known that Cohen would do something so dirty. Bolduan called me herself soon after. Many others at CNN were as stunned as

I was and rushed to express how upset they were about the segment, which was extremely comforting to me as I tried to figure out how to proceed.

Outside of CNN, all kinds of reporters started blowing up my phone for comment. Now that the story was out in the open, everyone wanted a piece. "Ignore, ignore, ignore," I thought as the requests streamed into my phone.

One fortunate coincidence. My manager, who is based in New York City, was on a field trip with her daughter at the National Air and Space Museum that day. Various media websites put up the clip of the explosive segment immediately; she watched it while standing in line with her daughter. She wanted to see me, but I didn't want to ruin her daughter's trip. She insisted. (She later told me she believed I was in a state of shock and she needed to make sure I was all right.) So I agreed to meet her at the museum, and standing outside the gift shop as tourists shuffled by to purchase freeze-dried ice cream and space-themed tchotchkes, we strategized. We agreed that I should lie low while the campaigns duked it out. I would go home, turn off my phone, turn off my computer, and hunker down.

As we spoke, the Cruz campaign blasted out a statement calling the story "garbage" and blaming Trump for enlisting his "political henchmen to do his bidding." Trump sounded off as well, writing a doozy of a statement in response. He said:

> *I have no idea whether or not the cover story about Ted Cruz in this week's issue of the National Enquirer is true or not, but I had absolutely nothing to do with it, did not know about it, and have not, as yet, read it. I have nothing to do with the National Enquirer and unlike Lyin' Ted Cruz I do not surround myself with political hacks and henchman and then pretend total innocence. Ted Cruz's problem with the National Enquirer is his and his alone, and while they were right about O.J. Simpson, John Edwards, and many others, I certainly hope they are not right about Lyin' Ted Cruz. I look forward to spending the week in Wisconsin,*

winning the Republican nomination and ultimately the Presidency in order to Make America Great Again.

The *Washington Post*'s Chris Cillizza described the statement as "perfectly Trumpian." It was precisely because it contained so many elements of Trump's trademark gaslighting. In that statement, Trump drew attention to the story, denied responsibility, created suspense, and discredited Cruz all at once. Trump's gaslighting Steps One, Two, Three, and Four were fully operational.

That evening I visited a friend who works outside the world of politics. She had no idea about the events that transpired earlier in the day. We drank wine while the kids played and barely spoke of it. I briefly tried explaining what had happened, but the whole thing sounded so far-fetched and bizarre coming out of my mouth. Try to picture this conversation. Her: "How was your day?" Me: "Oh, well, someone from the *Boston Herald* asked me about an affair I never had on live television and then two presidential campaigns fought about it." It sounded delusional. I'm not sure she even believed me until her mother-in-law, an avid political observer, approached me in church on Easter Sunday to ask what on earth was going on.

Trump was later asked on ABC News about the story. Anchor Jonathan Karl asked, "But let me ask you, this story, this that we see in the *National Enquirer*, this kind of rumormongering, should this kind of thing just be off limits? Do you condemn this story?"

He wouldn't. Trump replied:

"I don't care. I mean really I don't care. The National Enquirer did a story. It was their story. It wasn't my story. It was about Ted Cruz. I have no idea whether it was right or not. They actually have a very good record of being right. But I have absolutely no idea. Frankly, I said, I hope it's not right."

Advance and deny. There it was again. Trump's tried-and-true way of deflecting responsibility while encouraging others to pursue it.

Meanwhile, the online harassment was brutal. A friend of mine who does online analytics told me that there were more than 46,000 tweets directed at me in the seventy-two hours after my CNN appearance—a stunning number.

When I did finally log back on a few days later, I was crushed. People had Photoshopped images of me and my children in hurtful ways. Fake social media accounts were being created in my husband's name lamenting his cheating wife. Friends of his from high school and college whom he hadn't heard from in years were messaging him, saying things like "I'm here for you if you need to talk," as if our marriage was crumbling. Internet trolls lied, saying they had contacted members of my family who had confirmed the affair. The incoming fire wasn't targeted at just me anymore; they were going after my family one by one. I swung between wanting to bury my head in a pillow and sob and fantasizing of personally tracking down every one of these jerks and taking a sledgehammer to their computers.

Then I broke. I was at my computer when the social media director for Trump's presidential campaign, Dan Scavino, tweeted out a ridiculous video full of photos of me claiming to "prove" the affair I never had with Cruz. I was getting a personal dose of Step Four, the discrediting, dished out to millions of people by a presidential campaign.

I couldn't believe it. Rage consumed me. No longer could I sit silently by as people made my husband and dear, sweet, beautiful babies into Internet jokes. The idea that my son or daughter would Google his or her name one day and be subjected to these images infuriated me. I had been pushed past the point of no return.

Barely thinking, tweets flew from my mind, through my fingertips, and out to the world. I posted a plea for my friends to screenshot what Trump's social media manager was doing to me. "Donald Trump CANNOT say he isn't smearing women when his own social media director is doing it," I wrote. Scavino posted a reply on Twitter: "#ICYMI: Ms. Carpenter wants friends to abolish me from Twitter for replying to a Twitter users video clip? #Priceless."

He was, predictably, twisting my words. I clarified, telling him that.

"I want you to be accountable for harassing me. That's what I want. This is harassment by a presidential campaign."

In my anger, I told the trolls to "get back to huffing chem trails" and, in the process, called all kinds of negative attention to myself. My husband told me to stop, that I was "going crazy," but I didn't see it. My manager called. That's what brought me back to reality and forced me to realize what a mistake I'd made. I had promised to endure the storm quietly and I broke it. Not just to her, but to CNN. I made the story juicier instead of letting it die. I gave what all my detractors wanted. A spectacle. My gaslighting was complete.

Now it was a question of whether my career was even salvageable. I didn't see it, but I had managed to stay on the high road until I fired off those tweets. My decision to discuss the matter more online meant I needed to answer more questions on television as well. An interview with Jake Tapper was arranged where I would be asked about the allegations on the record. I stood in my walk-in closet thinking, "How do I pick out a dress to wear to deny an affair I never had? Which dress might I like to burn afterward?" The whole thing was so embarrassing and what hurt the most is that I had brought this part of the predicament on myself. Although I was fully confident of my innocence, I knew the court of public opinion wasn't always fair. If I screwed up one question or showed any kind of hesitation, it could be the last interview I ever recorded.

At that moment, Brooke Bacak, the colleague I had stuffed into the closet the day I thought our office was under attack, emailed to see how I was doing. I wrote back that I couldn't talk at the moment, because my career was teetering. All I told her was that I had to be perfect in my next interview. While I was still standing in my walk-in closet, she messaged me a pair of psalms. I sat down quietly and reflected on them both before rising again. Then, trying my best to put my faith in God and reminding myself that He is in control, but dreading every second of what was to come, I packed up my things and took the longest drive of my life to CNN's D.C. bureau, wiping tears off my steering wheel all along the way.

The interview went smoothly, mostly because it felt like an out-of-body experience, I think. While the cameras rolled, I told Tapper I had always been 100 percent faithful to my husband and had no higher priority than being a good wife and mother. I explained the professional conundrum the allegations had put me in. "I don't want to run away from this," I said. "I want to address it. But, at the same time, the hardest thing is defending myself, but not making it worse."

We talked about why I was targeted. I didn't think it was any great mystery. I was an effective commentator who often espoused anti-Trump views on a network Trump watched obsessively. His campaign couldn't dismiss me as some liberal hater. My conservative credentials were solid and I had a significant following on Twitter, his preferred mode of communication. It made sense that Trump folks would want me sidelined. Trump once complained about his surrogates being put on debate panels with "killers." It wasn't all that far-fetched that he probably thought I was one of them.

"I'm stuck in this box," I told Tapper, "where I am forced to try to defend every smear that comes after me, my husband, my children online or suffer in silence. And so, I just want to encourage everyone to look at the broader context of this campaign. There's a toxic culture being produced this season. We all need to recognize what's happening, look at the facts, and go into this with our eyes wide open and be unafraid to confront it."

After my interview ended, Tapper interviewed Trump campaign spokeswoman Sarah Huckabee Sanders. I listened to her on XM radio as I drove back home, wary to hear myself become the subject of yet another cable-TV segment.

Sanders suggested that "for the sake of" my family I should sue the *National Enquirer*. I glared at the radio as I heard her say that. As if I had thousands of dollars to spare on a legal battle that, win or lose, would almost certainly hinder my media career. Besides, I was already being billed for pricey legal consultations; I barely earned any money that month after paying the fees for a few advisory conversations. All I wanted was for this episode to be over, wiped from the public memory. The last thing I wanted was an expensive legal fight that would take the focus off my job.

Sanders said she had no knowledge about what the campaign's social media director had done. Not one to let someone wriggle out of a question so easily, Tapper brought her up to speed. He said:

> *"The story is apparently, according to Amanda, a smear job, no truth to it. Your campaign, I'm telling you, as a factual matter, is pushing it. Your social media director tweeted out a crazy video suggesting that Amanda Carpenter, who's married with two children, and this married senator who also has two children, that something untoward was going on. There is no actual evidence that it happened. I mean, at some point, aren't you just ashamed? This is the Trump campaign sending it out."*

After repeated pushing, Sanders chalked the whole dustup to the nasty business of politics at large and slammed the Cruz campaign as "one of the dirtiest and nastiest campaigns out there." It was a flabbergasting performance, but one that would well qualify her for her future role as Trump's White House press secretary.

Thankfully, the press moved on to other stories quickly enough. Still, I was forever changed by what happened in March 2016. When I reflect on the situation, my eyes well in gratitude for all who supported me, especially those at CNN. It was awkward for everyone and I am deeply thankful for the support the network provided that allowed me to rise through it.

At the time, I knew my situation reminded me of something. It took me a while to realize what it was. It was Trump's birtherism. All of the damaging elements of Trump's gaslighting method were present in my story. How the scandal was defined, how Trump denied involvement, how he created suspense, how Trump discredited his opponents. But, most important, how everyone, especially those who stood to lose the most, were left with no good options while they endured the barrage.

The more I thought about my situation, the more I realized how foolproof Trump's method was. There's no way of stopping it. In my case, Trump's allies selected politically toxic territory that no other person would touch but that was certain to get tongues wagging.

Think about it. Is there anything more enticing, especially in the political world, than the possibility of a sex scandal? No. People can't help but gossip about it once they catch wind of such a rumor. So Step One, check. Next, those spreading the rumor were ever so careful to push the story in a way to avoid any direct responsibility. I wasn't specifically named, but my photo was used. Trump's spokeswoman denied it happened, but said she was only speaking for herself. Step Two, check. The suspense that came with setting the Internet off to identify the five women was a thrilling development that drew everyone, willing and unwilling, into following the story. Step Three, check. When I was publicly confronted about it, I had to respond. "No comment" is not an option on live camera. Thus, I couldn't help but be tied to the disgusting smear. Step Four, the discrediting, check. What could I have done differently? Other than be more careful about what I tweeted, not much. I had no options, other than to run and hide, which many people in the Trump camp would have liked me to do. Step Five would come later. Remember, this wasn't being done to me per se, but to hurt Ted Cruz.

That's how I discovered there was a method to Trump's gaslighting madness. Over time, I realized he kept employing the same strategies again and again. He had a pattern. An effective one, too. Make no mistake: Trump would keep gaslighting America because it worked.

THE PLEDGE

Now that you know how Trump gaslit Obama, Bush, and me, I'll tell you how he gaslit the entire Republican Party.

To the random observer, Trump is a political savant with a supernatural ability to pass off the most inconceivable stories. No, no. Trump is good at one thing and one thing only. Gaslighting. Once you learn how to identify the steps of Trump's gaslighting method, you'll see it present itself in almost everything he does. He's a one-trick political pony.

Let's back up a little. Think of the characteristics that Trump supporters say they love about him. They praise the president because Trump "says it like it is." He fights. He doesn't back down. He isn't politically correct. He exudes strength. These aren't a bunch of distinct qualities that Trump possesses; these character qualities are necessary for his gaslighting.

Look at each one of these features independently. When Trump "says it like it is," it's usually because he's picked up on some non-politically correct subtext lots of people are thinking about but no one else of his status would be willing to say—all part of Step One, choosing the fringy, but politically rich narrative. His gaslighting is typically an offensive move to take control over an opponent; that's the point. That's what leads his supporters to say, "Ooo! He fights!" While Trump is selling his story, he always turns the heat up with a good dose of suspense, which makes it look like he never backs down. Through it all, Trump is totally committed to his story, like a method actor. That's because there can be no halfway measures of gaslighting; it's an all-or-nothing proposition. If he doesn't appear to fully believe what he's saying, he could never convince anyone else. Thus, Trump never, ever breaks character or gives his audience reason to doubt their confidence in him. It all has the net effect of making him look and sound strong. Voilà! The things Trump fans love about him are the specific traits he best exhibits when he's gaslighting.

Therein lies the real secret to Trump's success. It's not the "art of the deal," as he titled his bestselling memoir that made him famous. It's in the *sell*. And Trump's cunning ability to sell anything is what propelled him to gaslight America all the way to the White House. All he does is keep applying the same method to different circumstances. By the time you reach the end of this book, you'll be able to predict Trump's—that supposed political madman—next move with ease.

So, let's go back to 2015. The beginning of his campaign. Conventional wisdom was that you win the primaries by explaining your biography and qualifications, securing a solid base that can be expanded upon in a general election, and turning out the vote. Opposition research was something that had to be done, but only used in a pinch, lest you risk turning off your opponent's voters in the general election when you'd want their votes.

Trump threw all that out the window. That's not how gaslighting works. And, before he started torching individual candidates, he torched the party itself.

From the start, Trump openly flirted with launching a third-party bid—something no other candidate would think about threatening. This was the first step he took to gaslight the Republican Party—the claiming of uncharted political territory. Who else would try to appeal to the GOP by saying he might very well up and leave it? It seemed nonsensical, but in retrospect, oh how savvy it was. He understood that trust in political institutions—organizations such as the Republican National Committee—was in the gutter for GOP base voters. And the more he fulminated against the party, ironically, the more Republican voters liked him. A strange dynamic was at play. According to a Gallup poll conducted from January through December 2015, conservatives represented the largest ideological group in America. Yet that same year, the number of voters who identified as Republicans was near record lows. Meaning, there were plenty of conservatives willing to vote for a GOP ticket, but a historically small number had any affinity for the party. These were the right conditions for a rebel candidate to thumb his nose at the GOP kingmakers and be rewarded for doing so. Which is exactly what Trump did.

Naturally, the GOP party leaders freaked. They worried that if Trump went third party, he would likely siphon off voters and cripple the GOP's chances of beating Clinton in the general election. The RNC had no choice but to go along with Trump and whatever gaslighting he did. The party wouldn't object because the party leaders were willing to put up with anything to keep him inside the tent.

Fox News anchor Bret Baier sought to peg Trump on the question of party loyalty during the network's August 2015 debate. Baier asked the candidates to raise their hands if they were "unwilling tonight to pledge your support to the eventual nominee of the Republican party and pledge not to run an independent campaign against that person." Only Trump raised his hand, making it clear that he stood alone on this question. Step One, done. He was always differentiating himself, going to the outer limits of the debate where no one else would go, you see.

"Experts say an independent run would almost certainly hand the race over to Democrats and likely another Clinton," Baier said. "You can't say tonight that you can make that pledge?" Trump would not.

Step Two was next. Trump advanced the idea that he might go ahead and go third party, but denied that he really wanted to leave the GOP. Trump said, "I cannot say." He wouldn't consider the fact that he would lose. He went on:

> *"[I]f I do win, and I'm leading by quite a bit, that's what I want to do. I can totally make that pledge. If I'm the nominee, I will pledge*

not to run as an independent. But—and I am discussing it with everybody, but I'm, you know, talking about a lot of leverage. We want to win, and we will win. But I want to win as the Republican. I want to be the Republican nominee."

Trump was playing games. Why wouldn't he just say he would support the nominee if it wasn't him? Would he really bolt? But, his confusing answer had a distinct function. It kicked off Step Three—the suspense!

The word "leverage" made people wonder, too. What was it that Trump wanted? What was he going to do? What would the Republican National Committee do? The possibilities for political analysts to chew over and debate were endless!

This is where the RNC walked right into the fire Trump was setting. Desperate to quell such talk, RNC chairman Reince Priebus came up with an idea. He would make each candidate sign a "loyalty pledge" affirming that if he or she did not win the nomination he or she would "endorse the 2016 Republican presidential nominee regardless of who it is." The pledge also required candidates to promise not to run as an independent or write-in candidate, or seek or accept the nomination from another party.

Even though Priebus didn't have any way of enforcing it other than threatening to deprive the candidates of party resources for future campaigns, most of them were eager to show how confident they were that he or she would win. And so everyone but Trump quickly signed. It was easy for them to do because no one thought Trump would win. For example, after signing the pledge Rand Paul told CNN he would "support whoever the nominee is," but said that he believed "Donald Trump would be a disaster for the country."

Trump wasn't going to give away his signature without getting something in return. He was going to make the party bigwigs grovel for it, getting all kinds of extra attention that made the other candidates green with envy.

Priebus buttered Trump up, telling everyone the New York businessman was a "net positive" for the party. The chairman told reporters Trump "brings a lot of interest" to the field and bragged about the fact that the "Trump show" helped lead 30 million people to watch the first GOP debate. Then he made a special trip to New York's Trump Tower to extract the signature. Trump finally signed it, telling reporters, "The best way for Republicans to win is if I win the nomination and go directly against whoever they happen to put up. And for that reason I have signed the pledge."

"We were absolutely furious," a Jeb Bush staffer told *Politico*. "[Trump] is openly chiding us for communicating a conservative message in Spanish and they get on a train and go up to New York to give him a press conference and a pat on the back for joining the party. It was a total affront to us—because [the RNC] was no longer calling balls and strikes, they were actually helping him." Similarly, a John Kasich staffer huffed, "Every time Trump would do something dumb, Reince would be up in New York shining his shoes."

Priebus considered the pledge a success, calling it a symbol of "party unity." Never mind that the pledge was needed precisely because of the divisions Trump was sowing in the party. Priebus believed he had averted a crisis by handcuffing Trump to the GOP. In reality, he had handcuffed the GOP to Trump. Advantage, Trump.

Anytime commitments from the RNC seemed to waver, Trump would throw it in the faces of the party leadership, proceeding to Step Four of his method. He would discredit party officials, accusing them of "rigging" the election against him. Party rules required the presidential nominee to earn 1,238 delegate votes outright. Trump was the clear front-runner, but some states had preset rules that did not automatically award the majority of delegates to the candidate who won the state's primary contest, which sent Trump into fits of rage against the RNC. In one barrage of anger Trump accused the party of running a "dirty rotten disgusting system." Sure enough, the RNC would come scurrying back to Trump after every rant to affirm their commitment to him.

Trump did get some unexpected help taking over the GOP. From the Democrats, surprisingly enough. The Democrats believed Jeb Bush was the most formidable candidate in the GOP field. They wanted him to lose the GOP primary so, theoretically, it would be easier for Clinton to win the general election. Accordingly, they developed a strategy to build Bush's rivals up in hopes they would tear him down. Emails obtained through a hacking carried out by Russian operatives and publicized by WikiLeaks (more on this later) showed that in the early stages of Clinton's campaign, her top aides had prepared a memo for the Democratic National Committee that discussed exactly how it should be done. It said:

> *The variety of candidates is a positive here, and many of the lesser known can serve as a cudgel to move the more established candidates further to the right. In this scenario, we don't want to marginalize the more extreme candidates, but make them more "Pied Piper" candidates who actually represent the mainstream of the Republican Party. . . . We need to be elevating the Pied Piper candidates so that they are leaders of the pack and tell the press to [take] them seriously.*

Another hacked email showed Clinton aides planned a summer 2015 conference call to, in part, discuss "how do we prevent Bush from bettering himself" and "how do we maximize Trump and others?"

It wasn't like the desire for the Republicans to nominate a disastrous candidate to improve Clinton's chances of winning were any big secret, though. Many prominent liberal writers openly said as much. Jonathan Chait, of *New York* magazine, assured his fellow liberals that they could "earnestly and patriotically support a Trump Republican nomination" for this reason.

It was as if no Democrat stopped to consider the fact that if Trump cut down the whole GOP primary field of governors and senators, his techniques just might be good enough to win the general election, too. Especially against a candidate Republicans had been waging political warfare against since the 1990s.

The main thing that threw them off is how eager Trump was to fight. (One of his biggest selling points to GOP voters.) They were sure it would backfire eventually. Normally a candidate will delegate the rhetorical knife-fighting to his aides and surrogates. Not Trump. He liked to do combat himself.

Epistemologist Jeremy Sherman noticed how Trump was doing this in 2011, when he first began toying with birtherism. Sherman called the tactic "nounism," explaining that Trump had a history of using "psychology as taxonomy, identifying what sub-species of winner and loser people are." Trump used nounism to great effect when gaslighting individual opponents, such as Jeb Bush, Marco Rubio, and Ted Cruz. Labeling people in unfair, unscrupulous ways is, in part, how he staked a claim over them, the first step of this method.

One would think that Trump would damage his own credibility by talking about others in such derogatory terms. The research, sadly, is on Trump's side. A 2013 study conducted by the College of Journalism and Mass Communication at the University of Georgia found that the risk of levying a negative attack is well worth the reward, as any negative blowback on the person launching the attack tends to dissipate while the attack takes effect. "For voters who react with disdain toward the candidate (whether or not a defensive message follows), a sleeper effect is likely to occur," the study said. "That is, the overtime impact of the negative attack increases.

"We conclude, albeit unhappily, that negative messages are risky only in the short term; that any initial damage done to the attacker, either through an effective defense mounted by the target or by initial low credibility ratings from voters who do not like attackers will not last," the researchers said.

After Trump secured his blessings from the RNC and pushed Bush out of the field, the nation looked to the winner-take-all GOP primary in Florida on March 15. At that point, Trump had Marco Rubio in his sights. He dubbed the fresh-faced Hispanic Florida senator "Little Marco," drawing negative attention to Rubio's inexperience and youthfulness. Not one to let the attack go unanswered, Rubio matched Trump tit-for-tat. Very soon their feud took on the tone of a schoolyard fight. The only things missing were the "Yo Mama" jokes. Rubio called Trump "the man with the worst spray tan in America" and said that since he likes to sue people "he should sue whoever did that to his face."

"He's always calling me Little Marco," Rubio said at a stop in early March. "And I'll admit he's taller than me. He's like 6'2, which is why I don't understand why his hands are the size of someone who is 5'2. And you know what they say about men with small hands? You can't trust them." Of course, everyone knows that's *not* what they say about men with small hands, a physical aspect Trump has reportedly been self-conscious about ever since *Vanity Fair* editor Graydon Carter called him a "short-fingered vulgarian."

Trump wasn't about to let Rubio get away with the dig. During a live debate in Miami—with millions of people watching—Trump dramatically held up his hands. "Look at those hands, are they small hands?" he said. Alluding to Rubio's comments, Trump said, "And he referred to my hands—'if they're small, something else must be small.' I guarantee you there's no problem. I guarantee." One of the big, national headlines recapping the exchange was: "Donald Trump Defends Size of His Penis." Trump didn't need to go any further with his gaslighting method. Rubio self-immolated on Step One. Trump called Rubio little and then, crudely, created a discussion about how much of a bigger man he was. Rubio ended up looking like a struggling stand-up comedian, rather than a stately U.S. senator. It was a distressing development. But the numbers don't lie. Trump beat Rubio in the winner-take-all state of Florida by 18 points and Rubio ended his campaign that evening. Trump boasted later that Rubio "played Don Rickles, and then I played Don Rickles times five." Give him credit, Trump was very upfront about this approach. If his opponents went low, he'd go lower.

Trump's next opponent to defeat was Cruz. Cruz's strength during the GOP primary was that he was the tried-and-true conservative who had been battle-tested not only as a winning Supreme Court litigator but as a U.S. senator, too. The campaign ordered T-shirts and signs that touted him as a "courageous conservative," which, to tell you the truth,

I found cringe-worthy. I felt so strongly that while I was still working for Cruz I told him that I couldn't go along with the messaging and that it wouldn't work. "Why?" he asked me. I said no one would want to wear a T-shirt that said that. I never would; it was self-congratulatory, and limited to self-identifying conservatives. Still, the team went forward with it. My heart sank when I saw Trump's red Make America Great Again hats. Yes, Trump had shamelessly ripped off Ronald Reagan's winning 1980 campaign slogan, but no one really cared. It was still relevant. Upbeat, optimistic, inclusive. A slogan anyone could buy into and easily support. Other Cruz signs featured the word "trusted" in all capital letters with the last three in red. It was meant to convey that voters could "trust Ted." Another messaging loser, in my eyes, as it implied that the candidate had impeccable judgment about everything. Yes, Cruz is extremely intelligent, but everyone is wrong at some point or another. Stuff like that begs opponents to disprove the branding. More concerning was the fact that they didn't make the messaging about an idea bigger than Cruz; they made it about Cruz.

Trump countered that succinctly with "Lyin' Ted." Step One. "Lyin'" was a broad claim Trump used to silo a number of attacks on Cruz, including, strangely enough, another round of birtherism. One of the first things Trump accused Cruz of lying about was his birth story. Birtherism had worked well enough against Obama, Trump must have thought. Why not Cruz?

Cruz's birth story wasn't as simple as most but it wasn't that complicated, either. His father was born in Cuba and his mother in Delaware. Their son, Ted, was born in Canada while they were both there working in the oil and gas business. Cruz was always a U.S. citizen because his mother was always a U.S. citizen. But that didn't mean Trump wouldn't muddy the waters. In January, Trump pretended as though he was helping Cruz clear up the issue, going on CNN and telling America that Cruz had a "big problem."

"How do you run against the Democrat, whoever it may be, and you have this hanging over your head if they bring a lawsuit?" he said in an interview with CNN's Wolf Blitzer. This was Step Two. Trump was advancing the idea that Cruz wasn't eligible to become president but denying he would be the one who would make the charge. He claimed other reporters were forcing him to talk about the subject. "This was not my suggestion," he told Blitzer. "I didn't bring this up. A reporter asked me this question. . . . I'm doing this for the good of Ted . . . I like him. He likes me." "For the good of Ted" Trump tweeted to his millions of Twitter followers that Cruz must "preempt the Dems on citizen issue. Go to court now & seek Declaratory Judgement—you will win!" All superb examples of advancing and denying the story.

Liberal writers celebrated, enjoying how the birtherism was being turned against Republicans after their Democratic president Barack Obama had endured it for so long. "Donald Trump Is a Ted Cruz Birther and It's Fantastic!" said one headline from the *New Republic*. "Will Trump, the most famous of the Barack Obama birthers, hurt Cruz's candidacy with his innuendo?" writer Ryu Spaeth asked. "Will he start demanding Cruz's Consular Report of Birth Abroad, as he did President Obama's birth certificate? Could this crazy primary campaign get even crazier? We are hoping the answer to all these questions is yes."

This is why Trump's gaslighting of Ted Cruz worked. Not only did Cruz have to grapple with properly rebutting an unfair smear while not giving it oxygen to spread, but there were lots of people who delighted in watching Cruz squirm. Who was going to defend him? Not the Washington establishment types he'd spent his short-lived career in Washington castigating. Not the Republican candidates who wanted Trump to take Cruz out and make it easier for themselves to win. Not the Democrats who had already suffered through Trump's birtherism schemes. They went into fits of giggles as they watched Ted Cruz try his hand at dealing with it.

(Side note: For a short time Trump even tried concocting a double birther fantasy against both Cruz *and* Rubio, whose parents immigrated to the United States when he was a child. In late February, Trump retweeted a tweet that said "Mr. Trump . . . BOTH Cruz AND Rubio are ineligible to be POTUS! It's a SLAM DUNK CASE!! Check it!" He was later questioned by ABC's George Stephanopoulos, who asked, "You're really not sure that Marco Rubio is eligible to run for president? You're really not sure?" Trump remained firm in the second step of his method. "I don't know," Trump replied. "I've never looked at it, George. Honestly, I've never looked at it. Somebody said he's not, and I retweeted it." Twitter was very helpful to Trump in this way. He could retweet practically anything and claim complete ignorance.)

Later that spring, as the race came down to Trump and Cruz, Trump proceeded to Step Three of his method—the suspense. He said that Cruz must take down all negative ads against him or he would "bring a lawsuit against him relative to the fact that he was born in Canada and therefore cannot be President." Cruz told him to bring it on. "I would encourage you—if you want to file a lawsuit challenging this ad, claiming it is defamation, file the lawsuit," he said.

Cruz was calling Trump's bluff, but Trump kept up the act of suspense to buy himself time before starting a new round of gaslighting. Trump wasn't going to beat Cruz with only one round of gaslighting. More was on the way. "If I want to bring a lawsuit it would be legitimate," Trump said in a statement responding to Cruz's challenge. "Likewise, if I want to bring the lawsuit regarding Senator Cruz being a natural born Canadian I will do so. Time will tell, Teddy." Trump never brought the lawsuit on either charge but used all the controversy to move on to Step Four to discredit Cruz.

This is why Trump can look so erratic at times. He doesn't care about winning his arguments on the merits. He uses the media to cause confusion and chaos and get people on his turf. He will pick up and drop different fables with ease until he forces his opponents into a defensive posture.

To engage the discrediting process, Trump's campaign made an ad, promoted on his Twitter account, titled "Lyin' Ted" that accused the Texan of being "just another all talk, no action politician." He was going to make everyone say "Lyin' Ted."

Other Republicans helped Trump, picking up the messaging. An ad from a super PAC backing John Kasich said, "Many just call him Lyin' Ted . . . if Ted Cruz's mouth is moving, he's lying."

Around that time, the *National Enquirer* story alleging Cruz's infidelities took off, beginning the gaslighting episode that ensnared me as detailed in a previous chapter. Then, as if things couldn't get any weirder, Trump embraced another Cruz conspiracy theory put forth by the *National Enquirer*.

Near the end of April, as the primary in the ruby-red state of Indiana was becoming do-or-die for Cruz, the *National Enquirer* came out with a bewildering cover, claiming that Cruz's father played a role in the assassination of President John F. Kennedy. Pure conspiracy bait. Theories regarding the circumstances of JFK's death had driven all kinds of mania over the years. Even though the Warren Commission unequivocally stated that Lee Harvey Oswald murdered JFK, numerous theories continued to circulate that somehow the CIA, the Cuban government, or even the KGB was responsible for the killing. In fact, more people were willing to entertain these theories than to accept the findings of the Warren Commission report. A 2003 Gallup poll found that three-quarters of Americans believe more than one man was responsible for the assassination. An overwhelming majority. A fruitful political market. And so the *National Enquirer* gave those 75 percent of Americans another angle to consider—the possibility that Ted Cruz's father had something to do with it.

The front-page story said: "TED CRUZ FATHER LINKED TO JFK ASSASSINATION" with an image of a blood-spattered First Lady Jacqueline Kennedy cradling her dying husband alongside a giant photo of Ted Cruz. To make their preposterous allegation, the tabloid relied on a grainy photo of Kennedy assassin Lee Harvey Oswald standing next to a man that, the *National Enquirer* said, "top DC insiders have confirmed" was Cruz's father.

This was the print equivalent of Trump's favorite hedge, "Some people are saying [insert the blank]." This story was nothing more than "Some people are saying this is a photo of Ted Cruz's father." The story didn't get that much attention until the day voters went to the polls in

Indiana, May 3. Trump went out of his way to play up the story in an interview with *Fox & Friends* the morning of the Indiana primary.

The hosts didn't bring it up, but Trump was determined to make it a topic of conversation that morning. He said:

> *"His father was with Lee Harvey Oswald prior to Oswald's being— you know, shot. I mean, the whole thing is ridiculous. What is this, right prior to his being shot, and nobody even brings it up. They don't even talk about that. That was reported, and nobody talks about it. I mean, what was he doing—what was he doing with Lee Harvey Oswald shortly before the death? Before the shooting? It's horrible."*

There, Trump was fully advancing the conspiracy while denying responsibility. Step Two! "That was reported," Trump said without saying by whom. He pretended like he was only asking questions— "What was he doing?" Well, nothing, because it never, ever happened.

That was enough to push Cruz over the edge. Trump had gaslit Cruz about not only his eligibility to become president and his faithfulness to his wife, but also his father's supposed criminality. Three rounds of gaslighting! At this point Cruz probably knew he was not likely to win the Indiana primary and felt free to speak his mind about Trump, knowing he wouldn't need to court his voters later. Cruz unleashed. "I'm going to tell you what I really think of Donald Trump," he said. "This man is a pathological liar. He doesn't know the difference between truth and lies. He lies practically every word that comes out of his mouth."

Trump responded thusly: "Today's ridiculous outburst only proves what I've been saying for a long time, that Ted Cruz does not have the temperament to be President of the United States." The gaslighting extraordinaire had struck again. Trump wasn't unhinged, you see. Cruz was. Trump's victory was imminent.

I was on the air for CNN early in the evening of the Indiana primary and even before the polls closed, it didn't look good for the Texas senator. The campaign had pulled out all the stops, even announcing Carly Fiorina as his choice to be vice president should he get the nomination, but nothing seemed to be breaking Cruz's way. The most attention-getting moment of the short-lived Cruz-Fiorina ticket came when Fiorina fell off a stage while introducing Cruz at an event.

Still, no one expected it all to end that night. Not like that. I was cleared from the set before the race was called. I was almost home when a reporter texted me a message saying she'd gotten word that Cruz would be dropping out that night, could I confirm?

I ignored the message but urgently called a friend at the campaign. No one picked up. I called another number. No answer. And another. Nothing. The phones went straight to voice mail. Anyone who works in politics knows what that means. It's a death knell. All the phones were off because they were in a cone of silence to receive the bad news. A few minutes later a senior staffer texted me a message back. One word. "Yes." I saw the word flash onto my phone while I was driving. Automatically, I pulled the steering wheel right toward the highway exit ramp that was just ahead to make a U-turn to head back to the studio. CNN would be calling me back at any minute.

The race was a blowout; Trump won by 20 points.

I watched Cruz's concession speech on set. While most members of the media knew what was coming, the crowd of Cruz supporters who gathered to hear him speak didn't. Watching their reaction was the most painful part. They gasped in shock when Cruz told them, "From the beginning I've said I would continue on as long as there was a viable path to victory. Tonight, I'm sorry to say it appears the path has been closed." Some of them shouted "No!" at Cruz. His staffers told me later that disappointing their supporters was the hardest part about dropping out.

While Trump should have been graciously celebrating his all-but-certain nomination, he wouldn't get out of the gutter. The morning after Cruz suspended his campaign, Trump was on ABC's *Good Morning America* still pushing the JFK conspiracy. "All I was doing was referring to a picture that was reported in a magazine," he said. "I think they didn't deny it. I don't think anybody denied it." Still advancing, still denying. He couldn't stop the gaslighting.

Cruz had, in fact, said it all was "nuts," "not a reasonable position," and "just kooky." Still, Trump kept doddering on. "It was picked up by many other people and magazines and periodicals and newspapers, and all I did was refer to it," he said. "I'm just referring to an article that appeared. It has nothing to do with me." Sure, nothing to do with Trump at all.

SURROGATE SECRETS

Throughout his career Trump has cultivated an army of allies to obscure the fact that he is a chronic liar.

Tony Schwartz, the ghostwriter behind Trump's 1987 hit book *The Art of the Deal,* was better at it than most. He came up with the phrase "truthful hyperbole" to make Trump's wayward ways sound harmless and charming. Schwartz, who has come to regret the work he did for Trump, said, "[I]t's a way of saying, 'It's a lie, but who cares?'" He said that Trump loved it. Similarly, many of Trump's surrogates in the 2016 campaign adopted the same attitude. Sure he tells lies, but who cares?

Most of his media surrogates were Tea Party misfits and other striving activists who would never survive the vetting of any professional GOP campaign. They didn't have anything to lose in supporting Trump and neither did Trump in accepting their support.

He didn't even have to pay most of them; they volunteered, eager for the attention. These people ran to the networks, dotting televisions across the nation to speak on his behalf, but because they were nonofficial surrogates Trump didn't bear any direct responsibility when they screwed up. It was an extremely nontraditional surrogate operation for a presidential candidate. For Trump, however, it was just fine.

Trump's gaslighting gave them lots of media opportunities. The media needed Trump supporters willing to go on TV and stand by his narratives to provide balance to their segments. When Trump advanced and denied the claims and built suspense, he extended the story. Thus, Trump extended their marketability. And the more Trump's gaslighting methods succeeded in dismantling the competition, the more valuable they became. The supply of people willing to publicly attach their reputations to Trump was low and the demand was high. "If I accepted all the requests I would be on TV seven days a week, three to four times a day," Omarosa Manigault told *Time*.

Trump was their golden ticket. He put stars in their eyes. "When Donald says, 'I think you're great, I really want you to work for me,' I don't think any sane person would say no to that," said Katrina Pierson, who worked her way from freelance Trump surrogate to official Trump campaign spokeswoman. "It's definitely boosted my profile, obviously, for good or bad," Pierson told *GQ*. Scottie Nell Hughes recalled how she felt when Trump invited her to board his private plane. "It's like the song from Journey," she said. "Just a small-town girl . . . amazing."

They were so thankful, they almost groveled at his feet in gratitude. They spoke their own reverent Trumpian language, peppering their speech with superlatives such as "incredible," "phenomenal," and "unbelievable" to praise their man in the highest terms possible. Most were careful to refer to him as "Mr. Trump" at all times.

The deification of Trump appeared to be compulsory—even for members of the family. In her convention speech to introduce her father, Ivanka Trump said: "No one has more faith in the American people than my father. He will be your greatest, your truest, and most loyal champion." Even Trump's physician got the memo. "If elected, Mr. Trump, I can state unequivocally, will be the healthiest individual ever elected to the presidency," Dr. Harold Bornstein said in a signed statement given to the press. His former campaign manager Corey Lewandowski once described Trump as the "Ernest Hemingway of Twitter."

The over-the-top expressions of admiration from those within Trump's circle didn't decrease when he became president, either.

White House cabinet secretaries felt compelled to prostrate themselves before the president. During the introductions in Trump's first cabinet meeting, White House chief of staff Reince Priebus told Trump that it was a "blessing to serve your agenda" and then everyone sitting at the table took turns expressing their thanks to the president. A sampling of the remarks included:

- **VICE PRESIDENT MIKE PENCE:** "It is the greatest privilege of my life to serve as the vice president to a president who is keeping his word to the American people."
- **ATTORNEY GENERAL JEFF SESSIONS:** "It's an honor to serve you."
- **SECRETARY OF LABOR ALEXANDER ACOSTA:** "I'm deeply honored and I want to thank you for keeping your commitment to the American workers."
- **OFFICE OF BUDGET AND MANAGEMENT DIRECTOR MICK MULVANEY:** "At your direction, we were able to also focus on the forgotten men and women who are paying taxes, so I appreciate your support on pulling that budget together."
- **SECRETARY OF HEALTH AND HUMAN SERVICES TOM PRICE:** "What an incredible honor it is to lead the Department of Health and Human Services at this pivotal time under your leadership. I can't thank you enough for the privilege that you've given me, and the leadership you've shown."

What gives? Trump didn't *make* these people say these things. The sycophancy wasn't forced; it was volunteered!

Former speaker of the House Newt Gingrich, who presents himself as a kind of Trump whisperer these days, offered one explanation. There is no halfway in Trumpism. Gingrich said that Trump's allies had to be with him 110 percent, or else risk being destroyed altogether. He told the *Atlantic*, "You either decide you're going to defend Trump and Trumpism, or you let the left browbeat you into doing stupid things." The reporter asked if Trump supporters could find middle ground with the media. "Not these people," he said.

"You are all so far to the left, so contemptuous to Trump. Trying to conciliate you is silly. It's like trying to pet lions." Gingrich was right. Gaslighting requires total commitment to the lies. Otherwise, it doesn't work.

Other Trump supporters likened their advocacy to selfless acts of religious and political martyrdom. Kayleigh McEnany penned an op-ed about the criticism she faced and said she reassured herself with words written by the late Supreme Court justice Antonin Scalia: "Have the courage to have your wisdom regarded as stupidity. Be fools for Christ. And have the courage to suffer the contempt of the sophisticated."

Trump social media manager Dan Scavino viewed Trump like family, his blood. "It is very personal to me," he said, describing the political attacks on Trump. "I don't like it. None of us like it. It's like you're attacking my own father."

These sentiments begin to explain an extraordinarily important aspect of Trump's gaslighting: why his most prominent surrogates go along with it. They are, for their own various reasons, able to assign a higher value to defending his objectionable statements and behaviors. They rationalize. They have to. Keeping up the lies is a sign of loyalty to Trump—proof that one is fully devoted to him. Is there any way Trump would welcome a lukewarm surrogate into his camp? Heck no. He expects his troops to walk through fire for him.

This is why, while their own personal motivations varied, they all shared one unmistakable quality: lack of shame. Their universal ability to cast aside the embarrassment in sticking to the most fetid of Trump's fake narratives set them apart from previous classes of professional communicators. Memorably, CNN's Anderson Cooper once told Trump surrogate Jeffrey Lord that if Trump "took a dump on his desk, you'd defend him." (Lord laughed in response; Cooper later apologized.) Trump surrogates, as a collective, never let their personal dignity get in the way of flacking for their man.

Even when the campaign was caught red-handed, they went to the camera with full-throated denials, at times saying people who believed otherwise might be "crazy." Take, for example, when Melania Trump plagiarized a portion of her convention speech from First Lady Michelle Obama. Trump campaign manager Paul Manafort assured reporters, "There's no cribbing of Michelle Obama's speech. These were common words and values." He added, "To think that she would be cribbing Michelle Obama's words is crazy." The defense became even more laughable when Trump spokesman Sean Spicer invoked *My Little Pony*. Spicer said:

> *"Melania Trump said, 'the strength of your dreams and willing-ness to work for them.' Twilight Sparkle from 'My Little Pony' said, 'This is your dream. Anything you can do in your dreams, you can do now.' . . . I mean if we want to take a bunch of phrases and run them through a Google and say, 'Hey, who else has said them,' I can do that in five minutes. And that's what this is."*

Hours later the campaign admitted that Melania Trump had pla-giarized Michelle Obama. Nothing about this chain of events was unusual for the Trump campaign, though. Telling lies and watching them be disproven in real time was a run-of-the-mill occurrence. Any-one who publicly defends Trump has to accept that as part and parcel of the job.

As a frequent CNN panelist through the 2016 season I had occasion to debate Trump surrogates and closely observe the various strategies they employed to defend him. Many of them would later be adopted by other Republicans once Trump became president. I became familiar with them and you can, too. Let me reveal to you the tricks they use.

WHATABOUTISM: Trump's allies frequently employed a rhetorical de-vice that comes straight out of the Soviet Union. Known as a type of logical fallacy called tu quoque, or "appeal to hypocrisy," it boils down to answering a tough question with another question: "What about [this]?" Edward Lucas, a former Moscow bureau chief for the *Econo-mist*, is credited with defining the technique of whataboutism, writing in 2008, "Any criticism of the Soviet Union (Afghanistan, martial law in Poland, imprisonment of dissidents, censorship) was met with a 'What about . . .' (apartheid South Africa, jailed trade-unionists, the Contras in Nicaragua, and so forth)."

Trump campaign spokeswoman Katrina Pierson used this as one of her main lines of argumentation in her many television appearances. After Trump criticized the parents of a slain Muslim U.S. soldier, Captain Humayun Kahn, for speaking out against him at the Democratic National Convention, CNN's Wolf Blitzer asked her if he was being "disrespectful" to the Gold Star family. No, Pierson answered. Then, she pivoted directly to Clinton. She said, "Donald Trump never voted for the Iraq war. Hillary Clinton did." When another surrogate, Scottie Nell Hughes, was asked to respond to lewd comments Trump had made toward women, Hughes said, "Donald Trump may be vulgar, but Hillary Clinton is a two-faced liar."

Another time, Trump campaign adviser and former congressman Jack Kingston was questioned why his candidate wouldn't release his tax returns that the candidate claimed were being audited. Hillary was to blame for all the complexity, Kingston said. "Well, let's take a step back," he said. "If there's a problem with the tax code, who has been in office for 30 years? It's Hillary Clinton. She's been a part of that."

Trump himself tapped into the technique so well at times that he sounded like a Russian propagandist. In an interview that aired before the Super Bowl, Fox's Bill O'Reilly described Russian president Vladimir Putin as a "killer," to which Trump appeared to defend the foreign leader with a dose of Soviet-sanctioned whataboutism. "There are a lot of killers," Trump said. "We've got a lot of killers. What do you think—our country's so innocent?"

ANTI-ANTI-TRUMPISM: The natural outgrowth of whataboutism is "anti-anti-Trumpism." It's used by Republicans who are reluctant to align themselves with Trump, but will attack those who attack him in the name of stopping liberalism. Even if it means abandoning conservative values to do it. Talk-radio titan Rush Limbaugh sought sanctuary in this position, changing one of his longest-held approaches to analyzing current events to embrace it. In 2017, he decided to stop spending so much time explaining conservativism to his audience. Limbaugh told his listeners that, in the era of Trump, it was better to just focus on beating liberals. Limbaugh said:

"How many times during the campaign did I warn everybody Trump is not a conservative? Multiple times a day. How many times a day did I tell people that Donald Trump is not even ideological? Multiple times a day. How many times have I told you, do not expect Trump to be a conservative; he isn't one. Why did I change the name of my think tank from the Institute for Advanced Conservative Studies to the Institute for Advanced Anti-Leftist Studies?"

TRUMPSPLAINING: This is the idea that only Trump sympathizers are capable of properly interpreting Trump. Trump's detractors, often derided as an ultraliberal, cocktail-sipping clique of elites inside D.C. and New York, do not have the capacity to correctly analyze Trump, the theory goes. In November 2017, talk-radio host Hugh Hewitt wrote in the *Washington Post* that the only people complaining about a fractured GOP were members of the "chattering Manhattan-Beltway class estranged from President Trump."

Gingrich has even written a book to this effect, *Understanding Trump*. He contended that while the "elites snubbed" Trump for "ad-libbing his speeches, boasting about his wealth, and his theatrics," his messages "resonated with normal Americans."

Similarly, when Trump made a typo in a tweet—writing "Despite the constant negative press covfefe"—his press secretary, Sean Spicer, took this approach to comedic lengths. Rather than admit what was an obvious typo Spicer said, "The president and a small group of people know exactly what he meant."

EVERYONE DOES IT: Occasionally, a Trump supporter will admit to something egregious that Trump has said, but will find a way to blame it on other people and claim he was right to say it. Take this exchange between *The View*'s Joy Behar and former 2016 contender Ben Carson, who, at the time, was acting as a surrogate for the Trump campaign.

Behar asked Carson about Trump's previous comments in which he compared Carson to a child molester.

BEHAR: He's a liar. Unless you say you're a child molester, then he's a liar. Do you want a liar for the presidency?
CARSON: Tell me a politician who doesn't tell lies.

Whoopi Goldberg followed up later in the show:

GOLDBERG: If he had spoken to your wife the way he had spoken to some of these women, would you take that, sir?
CARSON: Let me tell you something. When you're very nice, when you're very respectful, you talk about the real issues and not get into all of these issues, where does that get you? It gets you where it got me. Nowhere.

FIGURATIVELY, NOT LITERALLY: This is the belief that one should always assume the best possible "figurative" interpretation of whatever Trump "literally" says. Shortly before the election, Trump-supporting Silicon Valley giant Peter Thiel spoke at the National Press Club about the unfair treatment he believed his candidate had received. He said:

"I think one thing that should be distinguished here is that the media is always taking Trump literally. It never takes him seriously, but it always takes him literally. . . . I think a lot of voters who vote for Trump take Trump seriously but not literally, so when they hear things like the Muslim comment or the wall comment, their question is not, 'Are you going to build a wall like the Great Wall of China?' or, you know, 'How exactly are you going to enforce these tests?' What they hear is we're going to have a saner, more sensible immigration policy."

A very similar construction about Trump had appeared in a September piece in the *Atlantic* by Salena Zito that theorized that "the press takes him literally, but not seriously; his supporters take him seriously, but not literally." Trump campaign manager Kellyanne Conway adopted the concept in an interview with CNN's host Chris Cuomo. She said:

"Why don't you believe him? Why is everything taken at face value? You can't give him the benefit of the doubt on this and he's telling you what was in his heart? You always want to go by what's come out of his mouth rather than look at what's in his heart."

PLAY PRETEND: Sometimes Trump surrogates would pretend Trump had said something completely different from what he did. Vice President Mike Pence turned this technique into an art form while on the stump for Trump, displaying it exceptionally well during his vice presidential debate against Tim Kaine.

When Kaine listed off the insults Trump had memorably dished out—including the slam that McCain wasn't a war hero, derogatory comments toward women, and the notion that Obama was not a U.S. citizen—Pence pretended like it never happened that way and turned them right back on Kaine. "To be honest with you, if Donald Trump had said all the things you said he did, in the way you said he said them, he still wouldn't have a fraction of the insults that Hillary Clinton leveled when she said that half of our supporters were a 'basket of deplorables.'" (Did you catch the dose of whataboutism in that answer, too?)

Another time, Trump told voters that if Clinton "gets to pick her judges, nothing you can do, folks. Although the Second Amendment people—maybe there is," which some people viewed as a veiled assassination threat, although Trump carefully avoided making such a charge directly. Rather than saying Trump should have chosen his words more carefully, Kayleigh McEnany played pretend, telling CNN's Erin Burnett:

"This is so absurd to me. He said if Hillary Clinton appoints judges, maybe there is nothing you can do, but maybe there is something

*Second Amendment folks can do. Guess what they can do in this
country? You can file amicus briefs, you can bring cases before the
Supreme Court with a friendly set of facts. . . . When I heard it, I
said, oh yeah, file amicus briefs."*

Yeah, that's immediately what people think of when they think
about the right to bear arms. Gun-wielding Americans rapidly filing
amicus briefs. *Yeah.*

PLAY DUMB: Various Trump surrogates would often act as if they
were not aware of events they were called upon to discuss as a means
of burning up time on the TV clock. Their mini-filibusters forced
moderators to use up their precious time explaining to the Trump ally
the very questions the ally was appearing on television to defend. In
one excruciating exchange Trump's lawyer Michael Cohen appeared
on CNN to bat down concerns about the Trump campaign's abrupt
dismissal of campaign manager Paul Manafort. Host Brianna Keilar
said, "You say it's not a shake-up, but you guys are down—"

"Says who?" Cohen interrupted.

"Polls," said Keilar. "Most of them, all of them."

Cohen stared blankly into the camera for an uncomfortable amount
of time. After the long pause he played dumb again. "Says who?"

Keilar replied, "Polls. I just told you—I answered your question."

"Which polls?" Cohen demanded.

"All of them," Keilar said.

"OK, and your question is?" Cohen said. Then Keilar had to go back
to the original question about the shake-up. Cohen looked like an idiot, but he limited the amount of time he had to spend talking about
internal campaign problems. Better for the surrogate to look dumb
than the actual candidate.

Other times, Trump allies would play dumb to give Trump free rein
to tout his conspiracy theories. Sean Hannity did this well during the
primary. In one radio interview Hannity invited Trump to expound
on the JFK conspiracy theory he was touting about Cruz's father. After
letting Trump talk about why it was a legitimate issue, Hannity said,

"You know, I have no idea because I haven't seen it, but I never thought it was going anywhere. I don't know the truth or veracity of it."

THE SNOWFLAKE TREATMENT: Anytime the Trump campaign did something particularly brash, his supporters would act as if critics were too pinheaded and soft to handle it. They called the critics "snowflakes," conjuring up the image of *Fight Club*'s Tyler Durden, who lectured his band of anarchists: "You are not special. You're not a beautiful and unique snowflake. You're the same decaying organic matter as everything else." This was one of Trump-supporting Internet sensation Tomi Lahren's favorite techniques. "If Donald Trump's tweets bother you more than the four Americans we lost in Benghazi, classified information shared on a private server, Saudi-bought influence at the State Department or paid violence at Trump rallies, you might be a snowflake," she said during one of her signature rants.

Those who opposed Trump were nothing but wimps to them. Scottie Nell Hughes flaunted this attitude when she brushed off the bruises *Breitbart News* reporter Michelle Fields sustained after being forcefully grabbed by Trump campaign manager Corey Lewandowski by saying, "I can show bruises having a six-year-old and a seven-year-old that are worse."

CONVERSATION KAMIKAZE: No one employed this technique better than CNN's top Trump defender Jeffrey Lord, who would often reach for historic parallels while making a provocative point that was sure to derail the conversation. Shortly after Trump refused to disavow former KKK grand wizard David Duke, Lord dove into the folds of history to embarrass Democrats. During CNN's Super Tuesday coverage Lord told black liberal commentator Van Jones, "Don't hide and say that's [the KKK] not part of the base of the Democratic Party. They were a military arm, the terrorist arm of the Democratic Party, according to historians. For God's sake, read your history." Needless to say, Democrats living in the year 2016 didn't appreciate the reference. Another time, during a discussion about repealing Obamacare, Lord told liberal black commentator Symone Sanders something he prefaced by saying he knew it would drive her "crazy." He said she should "think of Donald Trump as the Martin Luther King of health care." He explained, "When I was a kid, President Kennedy did not want to introduce the civil rights bill because he said it wasn't popular and he didn't have the votes for it, et cetera. Dr. King kept putting people in the streets in harm's way to put pressure on so the bill would be introduced." Sanders, predictably, didn't appreciate the comparison and the segment disintegrated from there.

Some Trump allies used this tactic in lowbrow ways. In a segment that aired on the Fox Business network, Trump surrogate Omarosa Manigault, a former *Apprentice* star, shut down the discussion with a comment about the size of a fellow panelist's breasts. Democratic contributor Tamara Holder said Trump should spend more time expressing support for Black Lives Matter, but Manigault wanted to focus on Clinton's previous support for the Iraq war. During the discussion, Manigault mispronounced Holder's first name. "It's Tamara," Holder interjected. "It's the same difference, boo," Manigault replied. "You want to come on with big boobs, then you deal with the pronunciation of your name." Holder's mouth dropped open. Host Maria Bartiromo was dumbfounded. "Wait a second," she said. "Why are you bringing up Tamara's boobs?" Bartiromo couldn't contain her laughter and for the next few minutes Manigault dominated the conversation with her talking points unchallenged.

SORE LOSERISM: Anytime someone raised concerns about Trump, Trump's allies could chalk it up to that person's supposed refusal to accept the fact that Trump was leading in the polls and winning. This was a message that came straight from the top. Trump called all the 2016 candidates who didn't endorse him "sore losers" who "should never be allowed to run for public office again." Surrogates used this argument ad nauseam when asked about the internal opposition Trump faced within the party. When the Bush family skipped the convention, Gingrich told reporters in Cleveland, "You have a handful of people who are sort of sore losers. Jeb Bush lost, so the family doesn't want to show up." Hannity took it up as well, telling his Fox News audience:

"I am tired of people—it's everything that is wrong with politicians. The crybaby, sore loser faction. All these guys, 'Oh, will you support the eventual winner? Yes.' Jeb Bush. No. Lindsey Graham. No. John Kasich. No. You know what? Why did you lie to us? And why be the sore loser? Why be the crybaby? The crybaby caucus now that exists out of that."

Former presidential candidate and Trump supporter Herman Cain, who was with Hannity during that segment, agreed. "Here's the only thing I want the Never Trump, anti-Trump, crybaby Trump folk to do," Cain said. "Shut up. Keep quiet. Just keep quiet." Sore loserism is an evergreen debate tactic. After the election Clinton communications director Jennifer Palmieri suggested that Trump appealed to white supremacists. Trump campaign manager Kellyanne Conway would have none of it. "Guys, I can tell you are angry, but wow," Conway said. "Hashtag he's your president. How's that? Will you ever accept the election results? Will you tell your protesters that he's their president, too?"

NONDENIAL DENIAL: The late *Washington Post* editor Ben Bradlee coined this term as a means of explaining the numerous evasions Nixon aides employed during the paper's Watergate investigation. This is a technique that Trump and his surrogates employ as a defensive technique, usually when it comes to some type of legal issue, as Trump's associates did when discussing his divorce with Ivana. The purpose of using a nondenial denial is to give the appearance that an allegation is being denied while not actually denying it. You will see this technique used again later in the book when Trump and his allies want to deflect questions about his personal life, David Duke, and Russia.

NOT HILLARY: If all else fails, Trump supporters will remind Never Trump Republicans that Trump has accomplished one momentous task for which the GOP should be eternally grateful. He beat Hillary Clinton. Take this explanation provided by Sarah Palin:

Remember, those of you who maybe still aren't aboard the Trump Train but know that the Trump movement had to be ushered in, in order to get rid of the status quo that was harming America, keep doing your ABCs and remember what that was: it was Anybody but Clinton. So stick with your little alphabet analogy there. Those who are asking for a grade of this administration, just keep remembering it could have been Clinton.

Similarly, Breitbart senior editor-at-large Joel Pollak tweeted in August 2017 why Trump, warts and all, was worth it. "The worst day of a Trump presidency is still better than the best day of a Clinton presidency."

PUNCH 'EM IN THE FACE

During his ascension to become the GOP nominee, Trump pulled off another incredible gaslighting feat. He lit up the entire American media complex, convincing his base to trust him—and all the conspiracies he espoused—above anyone in the media who may have a negative word to say about him.

At the time of the first GOP 2016 primary debate, hosted by Fox News, Megyn Kelly was one of the most-watched women on the most-influential network to Republican voters. One would have thought that Trump would desire a good relationship with such a powerful woman. But no. Instead he typecast Kelly—a tenacious, impressive broadcaster—as a moody bimbo. Her great offense? She asked questions about Trump's relationship with women that Trump didn't want to answer. Whoosh! Gaslit she got.

Trump's decision to go after Kelly wasn't a fluke. He knew there would be a good chunk of the Fox News crowd who would cheer him on. Her rise to the top of Fox News had been meteoric, but there were constant whispers that she wasn't conservative. The suspicion was that she was giving just enough lip service to the crowd to appease the corporate bigwigs there. And her approach to her show *was* markedly different from that of the other hosts in the prime-time lineup. She didn't tout the Republican party line or berate liberal guests quite like her counterparts. Those who thought all Fox News hosts should exhibit aggressively conservative personas believed she was a poseur and, even worse, a closet liberal.

Taking down Kelly was Trump's first major effort in his war against the media, which makes it well worth examination. How did he do it? It all goes back to an article the *Daily Beast* posted in July 2015 that retold a story about Trump's divorce from his first wife, Ivana, contained in the 1993 book *Lost Tycoon: The Many Lives of Donald J. Trump* by former *Texas Monthly* and *Newsweek* reporter Harry Hurt III. According to sworn divorce deposition papers Hurt had obtained, Ivana claimed Trump raped her after a furious fight they had had over a scalp-reduction surgery Trump underwent to reduce the appearance of a bald spot, performed by one of her recommended plastic surgeons. Hurt said Trump, upset with how the procedure turned out, ripped chunks of Ivana's hair out in retaliation and forced himself on her. Ivana described the incident as a "rape" in the divorce papers, but as the first printing of Hunt's book was awaiting shipment, Hunt's publisher received the following statement from Ivana through Trump's lawyers:

> During a deposition given by me in connection with my matrimonial case, I stated that my husband had raped me.
>
> I wish to say that on one occasion during 1989, Mr. Trump and I had marital relations in which he behaved very differently toward me than he had during our marriage. As a woman, I felt violated, as the love and tenderness which he normally exhibited toward me, was absent. I referred to this as a "rape," but I do not want my words to be interpreted in a literal or criminal sense.
>
> Any contrary conclusion would be an incorrect and most unfortunate interpretation of my statement which I do not want to be interpreted in a speculative fashion and I do not want the press or media to misconstrue any of the facts set forth above. All I wish is for this matter to be put to rest.

Hurt noted that Ivana's statement "does not contradict or invalidate any information" in his book and later told the *New Yorker* that he felt the statement was a nondenial denial used to help settle the divorce amicably; she reportedly received $14 million.

Trump, for his part, has denied both the assault and the surgery. The *Daily Beast* included the response Trump gave to *Newsday* in 1993 when Hurt's account first went public: "It's obviously false. It's incorrect and done by a guy without much talent. He is a guy that is an unattractive guy who is a vindictive and jealous person." When the *Daily Beast* asked the Trump campaign for a fresh comment about the rape accusation in 2015, Trump's lawyer Michael Cohen responded in a way that sounded audacious to those unfamiliar with how Trump's allies operated.

"It's not the word that you're trying to make it into," Cohen told the *Daily Beast*. He said Ivana had "felt raped emotionally . . . She was not referring to it [as] a criminal matter, and not in its literal sense, though there's many literal senses to the word." Then Cohen made a curious claim. "You cannot rape your spouse. There's very clear case law."

Then Cohen started making threats. He said:

"I'm warning you, tread very fucking lightly, because what I'm going to do to you is going to be fucking disgusting. You understand me? You write a story that has Mr. Trump's name in it, with the word 'rape,' and I'm going to mess your life up . . . for as long as you're on this frickin' planet . . . you're going to have judgments against you, so much money, you'll never know how to get out from underneath it."

Needless to say, the *Daily Beast* published the story and all of Cohen's quotes. Megyn Kelly arranged to have one of the reporters, Tim Mak, appear on her program to discuss it on July 28. Trump was infuriated that Fox News had breathed any kind of life into the allegations. Kelly wrote in her 2016 memoir, *Settle for More*, that after the segment aired Trump refused to appear on her program unless she called him personally. When they spoke, he gave her a stern warning. "I almost unleashed my beautiful Twitter account against you," Kelly said Trump told her, "and I still may." According to Kelly, Trump then phoned Fox executives to complain about her and told them that he knew she was preparing "a very pointed question directed at him" for the upcoming debate. She described it as "bizarre behavior, especially for a man who wanted the nuclear codes." And when the debate did take place, Kelly did have a pointed question regarding Trump's treatment of women, although not the one Trump feared. Did he ever call women "fat pigs, dogs, slobs and disgusting animals?" she asked.

"Only Rosie O'Donnell," he deadpanned.

"For the record," Kelly said, maintaining her composure, "it went well beyond Rosie O'Donnell." She reminded him he once told a contestant on his hit program *The Apprentice* it "would be a pretty picture to see her on her knees."

Trump said one of the country's "biggest problems was being politically correct."

Trump said:

"What I say, and oftentimes it's fun, it's kidding. We have a good time. What I say is what I say. And honestly, Megyn, if you don't like it, I'm sorry. I've been very nice to you, although I could probably maybe not be, based on the way you have treated me. But I wouldn't do that."

Then he did exactly what he threatened to do. This is when Trump's gaslighting of Kelly began. Everything that had happened up to this point was only pretext. Step One, he unleashed his "beautiful Twitter account" against her, branding Kelly as "overrated," "crazy," "angry," and "a bimbo" to his millions of followers. He told CNN's Don Lemon that she had acted like a feral animal at the debate, saying there was "blood coming out of her eyes" and "blood coming out of her wherever."

He wanted everyone to believe she was the wrongdoer, the one who had acted unprofessionally and unhinged. (Not him!) Everything he said added up to the mental image that Kelly, an accomplished anchor, was a hysterical woman who couldn't control her emotions, let alone her bodily functions.

Step Two: Trump advanced the story while denying it. While Trump continued to make the rounds in the media to talk about his debate performance, he denied ever referring to Kelly's menstrual cycle, saying only a "sick person" would interpret the comment that way. No matter what outrageous thing he said, his reliable advance-and-deny technique would get him out of the jam.

Trump's antics weren't pleasing the head honchos at Fox News. Then–Fox News CEO Roger Ailes put out a statement that said that Trump's repeated attacks on Kelly were "unprovoked" and that Trump "rarely apologizes, but in this case, he should." Like Bush, Ailes asked Trump for an apology he was never going to get. Trump wasn't done gaslighting Fox News; he needed to get the meganetwork under his control.

Time for Steps Three and Four—the suspense and discrediting. Trump temporarily boycotted the network—there's the suspense—and went right on slamming Fox, saying, "I do not think Megyn Kelly is a quality journalist"—more discrediting.

The boycott represented a new phase of Trump's gaslighting. Like he had to do with Ted Cruz, Trump would need to go through his method more than once to burn up Fox News. He boycotted the next Fox News debate. This was new political territory—Step One. No one boycotts debates, because it means you lose out on all the media coverage. But Trump had a plan for that.

He hosted a separate event that evening, a fund-raiser for veterans, where he claimed he raised $6 million for veterans in one hour. There he was standing alone, on his own stage, making another bold new claim. It was a clever ploy devised to make the executives at Fox News think Trump didn't need the network as much as the network needed Trump. He was gaslighting Fox News to make the executives feel like they were unimportant to him, which couldn't be further from the truth.

When the *Washington Post* followed up later asking him for proof of the funds raised and where they were dispersed, the campaign acted like it was a rude question to ask. This was because raising money for vets wasn't the true purpose of the event. The true purpose was to provide cover for boycotting the Fox News debate. So, the Trump campaign had advanced the story about raising money but then denied that they be responsible for showing the receipts. Step Two.

"If the media spent half as much time highlighting the work of these groups and how our veterans have been so mistreated rather than trying to disparage Mr. Trump's generosity for a totally unsolicited gesture for which he has no obligation, we would all be better for it," spokeswoman Hope Hicks said.

All this created its own suspense—Step Three—as reporters kept badgering him for the receipts. How much was raised and where did it go? Trump put them off, telling them they would find out "soon," one of his favorite ways of keeping the story alive.

But it wasn't very "soon" that the receipts came out. Four months later, after a whole lot more nagging, he finally came forward with the numbers. He'd raised $5.6 million including a $1 million personal donation. Not quite what he'd said originally, but still an impressive amount. Trump chided "sleazy" reporters for having the nerve to ask for documentation. "I don't think it's anybody's business if I want to send money to the vets," he said, as if he had never held a televised fund-raiser and issued press releases for that express purpose.

That was all a sideshow, though. The important thing was that he won his face-off with Fox News, the network idolized by his voter base, receiving no major punishment for skipping their event and lambasting its top anchor. So what if he had to spend and raise a few million to do it? Well worth the money.

In May 2016, Kelly went to Trump Tower to make amends and film an interview with Trump. Then in January 2017, Kelly left her powerful prime-time perch at Fox News to do morning news at NBC. All good for Trump; he'll never have to contend with Kelly at that network again, which remains a major center of influence for GOP voters. Victory.

Remember, the goal of Trump's gaslighting is always to gain the upper hand. Trump gaslit Kelly to gain control over Fox News. He'd need to do much more to gain control over the rest of the media. He needed a big, bold narrative that could carry him through the election and also cast blame upon others in case he lost.

He had just the trick up his sleeve. One he'd already tested out as both a TV star on *The Apprentice* and a political pundit. *The system was rigged.* When his hit TV show failed to win an Emmy in 2012, he tweeted: "The Emmys are all politics, that's why, despite nominations, The Apprentice never won—even though it should have many times over." After Romney lost the 2012 election, Trump tweeted, "This election is a total sham and a travesty. We are not a democracy!"

Step One, the rigged narrative, was airtight; it captured everything Trump wanted. Megyn Kelly and the *Washington Post* weren't his only obstacles. The entire election and media complex was. This created a sense of urgency among his voters.

To carry out Step Two Trump told his supporters things like "We're going to win so much, you're going to be sick and tired of winning," while in the next breath, "The whole system is rigged." He constantly advanced the idea that he was a winner, but that he never had a chance because of the unfair media coverage he was getting. As he tweeted, "This election is being rigged by the media pushing false and unsubstantiated charges, and outright lies, in order to elect Crooked Hillary!"

As Trump gaslit the media, the media had no choice but to cover the story. Every time Trump took the podium there was suspense, Step Three, as no one could figure out what he would say next. Trump came off like a political tightrope walker. Any minute, he could go over the edge. For those who tuned in to hate-watch the rallies, this was half the fun.

The more Trump insulted the media, the less seriously the media took him, which only gave him even more ammunition to use against them. Reporters like the *Washington Post*'s Amber Phillips said things such as, "Let me go on the record saying this right now: Donald Trump will not be our next president. He won't even be the GOP nominee. And I know, I know: We've underestimated him before. But still." Statements like that could be found far and wide. Bloomberg News editor John Heilemann confidently predicted: "Donald Trump will not be the Republican nominee, in almost—almost all certainty." Trump delighted in throwing those statements back in their faces as proof of how wrong they were. This represented Step Four. The discrediting element of Trump's gaslighting of the media was surely his favorite part. Trump delighted in calling the press "scum," "horrible people," "illegitimate," and "terrible," to name only a few of the adjectives he used to describe the reporters writing stories about him.

There was no way the media could ignore Trump's gaslighting. At every step in his gaslighting process, Trump gave them new material. It didn't matter if you were a pro-Trump blogger, a rabid liberal, or a down-the-middle stringer. Each time he engaged in Step One—a new line of attack—there was something new to write about. When Trump advanced and denied his accusations—Step Two—he built interest in their stories. All the suspense—Step Three—only made political coverage more compelling. Step Four, the discrediting, created more controversy for the media to cover. And, the mind-boggling victories Trump kept racking up, Step Five, created even more need for further debate and analysis.

There hasn't been a slow news day since he announced his candidacy. Trump is good for the news business, period. For his efforts, Trump was bestowed with what was estimated by SMG Delta, a firm that tracks television advertising, to be $2 billion in free media coverage. He received coverage even while he insulted the media to their faces, like he so often did to the writers at what he called "the failing *New York Times*." And just what did his insults do for the *New York Times*? Its paid subscriptions *soared*. CEO Mark Thompson even thanked Trump for the boost in an early 2017 conference call with industry analysts. "We absolutely believe the extraordinarily intense news cycle has been a significant factor," Thompson said. ". . . And it's the single most important factor in the scale of the bump we've seen in recent quarters."

While the media honchos could certainly be satisfied with an increase in traffic, it did come with a cost. Trump's ire directed toward the media did have another effect. In September 2016, Gallup found that Americans' trust in the mass media had fallen to its lowest level in its polling history, with Republicans fueling the massive drop. While only 32 percent of Americans overall said they had a "great deal" or "a fair amount" of trust in the media, only a paltry 14 percent of Republicans said the same. The swelling well of anger was revealed at Trump's rallies, particularly when Trump would gesture toward the pool of reporters covering his events and encourage the crowd to yell at them. "See the dishonest people back there?" he would say, prompting his supporters to boo in their direction. At his prompting, they'd shout "CNN sucks!," call reporters "traitors," and spit epithets their way.

You see, Trump was the consummate ringmaster, controlling the media's narrative *and* the emotional response from his supporters. All to his benefit. One embed reporter later reflected:

Perhaps I'd been naïve, but it only now dawned on me, in the final week of the campaign, to my great horror, that the real reason they put us in the pen was so they could turn us into props. We were a vital element in Trump's performance. He never once failed to invite his crowds to heckle us. He was placing us on display like captured animals. And it worked. . . . When the crowds lustily booed us, we'd sit there impassive and stone faced, and this only further served to convince the rally goers that we were snobby, superior pricks. The pen was an amazingly efficient means of othering us. Behold, Trump said to his fans, I've rounded up a passel of those elites you detest. And I've caged them for you! Allow me to belittle them for your delight. Here, now you take a turn—go ahead, have at it! Do it again, don't be shy!

One might think that all the ranting and raving at Trump rallies would be cathartic. Nope. Anger actually *begets anger*. Dr. Brad Bushman, a professor of communication and psychology at Ohio State University, who studied the various ways people have been told to purge anger, said, "Venting anger is like using gasoline to put out a fire. It only feeds the flame by keeping aggressive thoughts active in memory and by keeping angry feelings alive." In a 2002 study on the subject, he concluded:

> *For reducing anger and aggression, the worst possible advice to give people is to tell them to imagine their provocateur's face on a pillow or punching bag as they wallop it, yet this is precisely what many pop psychologists advise people to do. If followed, such advice will only make people angrier and more aggressive.*

But that's the kind of advice Trump gave his supporters.

Psychological researchers at the University of Arizona who studied the effects of anger and anxiety in the presence of a perceived enemy—when it came to Trump rallies, this was the media—found the dynamic can be emotionally rewarding to those feeling insecure. "The feeling of anger along with the identification of an enemy then increases one's sense of control and certainty," the study stated. Trump's attacks on the media gave supporters who were angry and fearful of the future a nice, psychological high. It was like Trump was saying to them, "Look, there is the enemy right there and we will not be afraid to confront them anymore!"

As his campaign progressed, Trump started testing his supporters to see how loyal they were to him. Standing before an audience in Sioux City, Iowa, in late January 2016, he said the polls showed that "I could stand in the middle of Fifth Avenue and shoot somebody and I wouldn't lose voters." He pointed his hands like a gun at them and pulled the trigger at the audience as he said it. They laughed, but he was on to something. To his supporters, it was Trump versus the world and they chose Trump.

At a February 1 stop in Cedar Rapids, he pushed them a little further. Trump instructed attendees to get rough with protesters. "If you see somebody getting ready to throw a tomato, knock the crap out of them, would you? Seriously, OK? Just knock the hell—I promise you, I will pay for the legal fees. I promise. I promise." Then, when a protester was escorted out of a February 22 Las Vegas rally with a smile on his face, Trump talked about his desire to change the pleased expression. "I'd like to punch him in the face," Trump said. "He's smiling, having a good time." He reminisced. "In the old days," he said, protesters would be "carried out on stretchers." "We're not allowed to push back anymore," he lamented.

Trump even promised financial assistance to his supporters who roughed up protesters, something he would later deny. During a March 4 Michigan rally Trump said, "Get him out. Try not to hurt him. If you do, I'll defend you in court, don't worry about it." He then praised his supporters who helped tamp down protesters at a previous rally saying:

"We had one guy in New Hampshire, actually, who was a rough guy and he was swinging and swinging and punching. He was really going down for the count and we had a couple of people in the audience who were equally rough and they took him out. They took him out. No, they took him out and I'll tell you what. It was really amazing to watch."

On March 10, a seventy-eight-year-old white man sucker punched a twenty-six-year-old black protester during a Trump rally in Fayetteville, North Carolina, as police were leading him out of the event. "I was basically in police custody and got hit," the victim said. Trump surrogates toed the line. Andy Dean, a former *Apprentice* star, said, "That guy's 78 and throwing a punch like that . . . at that age, it looks like good exercise."

Trump didn't go out of his way to calm anyone down. He ginned up the atmosphere to make it seem even more dangerous. When a protester rushed the stage during a March 12 event, forcing Secret Service to swarm around Trump onstage, Trump suggested that it was akin to an act of terror. He tweeted that the protester "has ties to ISIS. Should be in jail!" His proof? A video that was later revealed to be a hoax. When asked by MSNBC's Chuck Todd about it, Trump said, "All I know is what's on the Internet." (Do you recognize Steps One and Two of Trump's gaslighting method in this interview? He claimed the protester was a member of ISIS. He advanced the message with a video and then denied any responsibility for it. Touché.)

If you didn't know that advancing and denying a narrative at the same time was one of Trump's staple techniques, you would think that a statement he made on March 14 to be strange. "The press is now calling, they're saying, 'Oh, but there's such violence.' There's no violence," Trump said before hedging a bit. "You know how many people have been hurt at our rallies? I think like, basically none, other than I guess maybe somebody got hit once or something. But there's no violence." Yes, someone maybe got hit, but no violence, no!

Trump surrogates, as always, had his back. The fighting was good, a sign of progress. Scottie Nell Hughes told CNN, "Riots aren't necessarily a bad thing if it means it's because [Trump supporters are] fighting the fact that our establishment Republican Party has gone corrupt and decided to ignore the voice of the people and ignore the process."

The punches really started flying on March 20 when a white supremacist and two others assaulted a black female protester during a Trump rally in Louisville, Kentucky. They were charged with assault after a video of the trio pushing and shoving the woman out of the audience went viral. Their defense? Trump made 'em do it. One of the defendants wrote in a letter: "Trump kept saying 'get them out, get them out' and people in the crowd began pushing and shoving the protesters. I physically pushed a young woman down the aisle toward the exit, an action I sincerely regret." That doesn't change the fact he did it, though. At the request of a presidential candidate. How far would others go? Like his aides?

Look no further than what happened when a reporter from the Trump-friendly *Breitbart News* named Michelle Fields covered one of Trump's press conferences at the Trump National Golf Club in Jupiter, Florida. During that time, she was a well-regarded and welcome guest on many conservative programs. Everything changed the moment she approached Trump after the press conference to ask a question about affirmative action. As she wrote in one of her last pieces for *Breitbart News*:

Trump acknowledged the question, but before he could answer I was jolted backwards. Someone had grabbed me tightly by the arm and yanked me down. I almost fell to the ground, but was able to maintain my balance. Nonetheless, I was shaken. The Washington Post's Ben Terris immediately remarked that it was Trump's campaign manager, Corey Lewandowski, who aggressively tried to pull me to the ground. I quickly turned around and saw Lewandowski and Trump exiting the building together. No apology. No explanation for why he did this.

The Trump campaign flatly denied that any such incident had occurred, calling Fields's account "entirely false." Trump's aides didn't go through the steps, but they did their best to gaslight Fields, making her out to be some crazy woman who had made up the whole story for attention. This wasn't the kind of gaslighting Trump and his team were good at. They weren't controlling the narrative; they were trying to make it go away. Gaslighting never works as well defensively as it does affirmatively.

The Trump campaign issued a statement that questioned Fields's character and said: "In addition to our staff, which had no knowledge of said situation, not a single camera or reporter of more than 100 in attendance captured the alleged incident." To prove her case, Fields took a photo of the bruising on her arm and posted it on social media. Campaign manager Lewandowski questioned her sanity in response, tweeting: "@MichelleFields you are totally delusional. I never touched you. As a matter of fact, I have never even met you." Soon enough, video and audio the Trump campaign claimed did not exist surfaced. C-SPAN video showed Fields approaching Trump and Lewandowski and then falling to the floor. In a separate audio recording Fields could be heard, in real time, expressing shock to the *Post* reporter. "Holy shit," she said. "I can't believe he just did that, that was so hard. Was that Corey?" She called the episode "insane . . . Oh my God, that really spooked me that someone would do that."

"I don't understand," Fields said on the audio. "That looks horrible. You're going after a Breitbart reporter, the people who are nicest to you?"

Pretty much. Trump went so far as to suggest that Fields was a terrorist, tweeting a photo of her approaching him to ask a question. In the photo she was holding a pen in her hand that appeared close to Trump's elbow. Trump tweeted, "Why is this reporter touching me as I leave a news conference? What is in her hand??" When he was asked by CNN's Anderson Cooper about it, Trump said that Fields could have been seeking to do him bodily harm. "She had a pen in her hand, which the Secret Service is not liking because they don't know what it is, whether it's a little bomb." Then he added, "Michelle Fields, by the way, is not a baby." Trump said he was the victim. Cooper asked if he planned to take any kind of legal action. "Maybe I should because you know what, she was grabbing me," Trump replied.

Trump was gaslighting on full blast. Pretty soon, people began to abandon Fields.

Her employer, *Breitbart News*, wouldn't stand by her through the onslaught. Conservative TV hosts who, until then, regularly asked her to contribute to their programs quit calling. Fields gave up her job at *Breitbart News*, and in protest, a few of her colleagues followed her out the door. Her boss, Steve Bannon, eventually left, too . . . to join the Trump campaign as its CEO. No one affiliated with the Trump campaign paid any price for their despicable treatment of Fields.

Fields was no naïf; her eyes were wide open to the reason she was ostracized. Writing in the *New York Times*, she said:

> *Had Hillary Clinton's campaign manager, rather than Mr. Trump's, grabbed my arm, I would not have been abandoned by many of my friends and mentors at Fox News, or my employer, Breitbart News. But I was inconvenient to their political narrative.*

In the early 1960s, Stanford psychologist Albert Bandura carried out experiments to test the effect that violent adult behavior had on children. To do it, he had researchers physically and verbally abuse an inflatable "Bobo doll," the kind that someone can hit and it will pop back up. Not surprisingly, he found that children exposed to the most aggressive behavior by the researchers imitated those responses. It's not that far-fetched to think that future candidates will mimic the Trump campaign's Bobo-like aggressions. It's already happened. During one of the first special election races of 2017, Republican candidate Greg Gianforte punched a *Guardian* reporter in the face, breaking his glasses, an act the campaign vigorously denied before Gianforte apologized and pleaded guilty to misdemeanor assault. The incident had no discernible impact on the voters. Gianforte won his race.

10

KAYFABE

One of Trump's favorite names to call critical media is "fake news." When Trump uses that term, however, what he's really doing is hijacking a term scholars and news observers use to describe something else—the onslaught of hoax news stories flying around the Internet. Fake information on the Internet was nothing new in 2016, but, it became a huge problem for one reason: That year more people were getting their news from social media—Facebook, Twitter, and Instagram—than ever before. Each of them mega-platforms with zero editorial accountability for content, unlike traditional news sources that have layers of researchers, editors, and other people who can be fired for getting information wrong. Almost anything short of direct death threats and pornography is permitted on social media, and yet, these are the places where the majority of Americans get their news. According to the Pew Research Center, most adults in the United States—62 percent—got their news via social media in 2016, a hefty increase over the 49 percent who reported even seeing, not getting, news on social media in 2012 when the last presidential election was held.

During that period, a new genre of "news" was pioneered by individuals with no interest in publishing real news, but rather generating clicks for ad revenue. It's hard to pinpoint its origins, although most people can agree on how it organically began. Web editors who needed to drive traffic to their websites wrote headlines to appeal to what their audience most wanted (or feared). Writers began to follow their lead, exaggerating the story or making it up if they had to for the purpose of being able to attach provocative headlines to their articles. This is how fake news got its start. Pretty soon, fake news writers got so good it was hard to tell the difference between what was real and what was fake.

Many fake news outlets mimick the look and feel of authentic news outlets with slick websites and professional-sounding names such as the *Denver Guardian*. Their stories, however, were wholesale fabrications with fictitious sources and quotes. In 2016, fake news manufacturers discovered that the people most willing to click and spread their fake news stories were those open to supporting Trump. Paul Horner, who died in September 2017, was one of its top purveyors. He created a very successful website that looked very similar to the genuine one maintained by ABC News. Only a careful eye would detect the tell in the domain name. Horner's website was ABCNews.com.co, not ABCNews.com. A sampling of Horner's most successful headlines included:

- "Obama Signs Executive Order Banning the National Anthem at All Sporting Events Nationwide"
- "Ted Cruz: 'I Will Endorse Donald Trump for President If He Makes Masturbation Illegal'"
- "Donald Trump Protester Speaks Out: 'I Was Paid $3,500 to Protest Trump's Rally'"
- "The Amish in America Commit Their Vote to Donald Trump; Guaranteeing Him a Presidential Victory"

His piece about the paid protesters went viral. In it, he used himself as a "source," writing:

"I was given $3,500 to protest Donald Trump's rally in Fountain Hills," Horner said. "I answered a Craigslist ad about a group needing actors for a political event. I interviewed with them and got the part."

All of it was made up, but it was a brilliant fake news story. The Trump campaign had openly speculated protesters were being paid to disrupt their events. Then, miraculously, this story appeared, confirming the rumor the campaign had floated. A lot of people who study media worry about something called "confirmation bias." Meaning, how news consumers look for news that confirms their existing political worldview. This was another level. In this case, Trump had said something not proven to be true and then an item of fake news was created to make it seem true.

Trump campaign manager Corey Lewandowski tweeted Horner's story out. As did Trump's son Eric, who commented, "Finally the truth comes out. #CrookedHillary." Horner, for his part, was dumbfounded. He told the *Washington Post*:

> *"My sites were picked up by Trump supporters all the time. I think Trump is in the White House because of me. His followers don't fact-check anything—they'll post everything, believe anything. His campaign manager posted my story about a protester getting paid $3,500 as fact. Like, I made that up. I posted a fake ad on Craigslist. . . . I thought they'd fact-check it, and it'd make them look worse. I mean that's how this always works: Someone posts something I write, then they find out it's false, then they look like idiots. But Trump supporters—they just keep running with it!"*

He continued:

> *"There's nothing you can't write about now that people won't believe. I can write the craziest thing about Trump, and people will believe it. I wrote a lot of crazy anti-Muslim stuff—like about Trump wanting to put badges on Muslims, or not allowing them in the airport, or making them stand in their own line—and people went along with it!"*

Some of the more successful fake news outlets selling Trump content weren't even based in the United States. Veles, Macedonia, was home to at least 140 websites that produced content about U.S. politics, according to *BuzzFeed News*. "They almost all publish aggressively pro-Trump content aimed at Trump supporters in the US," their analysis found. Why? It was a cash cow. Generating clicks from Facebook users in the United States makes good money in Macedonia. One of the more successful Macedonian stories, from the phony website ConservativeState.com, claimed: "Hillary Clinton in 2013: 'I Would Like to See People Like Donald Trump Run for Office; They're Honest and Can't Be Bought.'" Upon publication, it received almost four times as many clicks as a *New York Times* story about the $916 million loss Trump reported on his 1995 tax returns that was published the same month. Fake news was outcompeting real news. *BuzzFeed News* also found that in the final three months of the presidential campaign, the top stories manufactured by wholly fake news outlets generated more engagement than top stories from real outlets such as the *New York Times* and the *Washington Post*. A gold mine of clicks. *BuzzFeed News* stated:

> *During these critical months of the campaign, 20 top-performing false election stories from hoax sites and hyper partisan blogs generated 8,711,000 shares, reactions, and comments on Facebook. Within the same time period, the 20 best-performing election stories from 19 major news websites generated a total of 7,367,000 shares, reactions, and comments on Facebook.*

How come so many people fell for these stories? After all, there's Snopes and no shortage of other dedicated fact-checkers in the news media, right? There's PolitiFact, FactCheck.org, the International Fact-Checking Network at Poynter, and the Fact Checker at the *Washington Post*, to name a few. There are even partisan fact-checkers keeping tabs on the media, such as the liberally leaning Media Matters and the conservative-leaning Newsbusters. One problem. A lot of people tuned them out. A September 2016 Rasmussen poll found that only 29 percent of Americans trust fact-checking of candidates' comments.

The poll also found that 62 percent believed that news organizations would skew the facts to help candidates they supported.

I'm among the doubters myself. In my experience, many of these so called fact-checkers aren't fact-checkers at all. They're opinion checkers. Let me give you an example from when I was working in Senator Cruz's communications shop and a supposedly reputable fact-checker made urgent inquiries to our office to ask about the veracity of a *joke* Cruz had told. That's right. A *joke*.

PolitiFact—which never misses the chance to remind its readers that it won a Pulitzer—ripped Cruz for a zinger about Iran. During an interview with talk-radio host Hugh Hewitt, Cruz said: "Here, we have Thanksgiving, we have Christmas, we have the 4th of July. Every year in Iran, they celebrate Death to America Day." Again, maybe it's not their idea of humor, but I laughed and I bet Hewitt's listeners did, too. It was a good dig because it had a ring of truth. Every November 4, Iranians commemorate the anniversary of the day Iranians took Americans hostage at the U.S. embassy in 1987. Radio Tehran has referred to it as "Death to America Day." Those are the facts the fact-checker did not dispute.

Instead, PolitiFact demanded that our office show them where exactly on the list of nationally declared holidays "Death to America Day" fell. "A list of Iranian holidays posted online by Iran's office in Washington, D.C., doesn't show a special designation for Nov. 4," the fact-checker huffed. The writer consulted some academics who confirmed as much. Indeed, there was no formally declared "Death to America Day" for which Iranians exchanged pithy cards and chocolates. I tried telling the writer that St. Patrick's Day wasn't on our federal calendar but it's still considered a holiday. It didn't work. "We rate this claim, which has a strand of truth but ignores critical facts, Mostly False," the article stated.

Cue the liberals who would then run with the "mostly false" headline to accuse Cruz of being the lyingest liar who ever was. I could only take heart in what *Breitbart News*, before it became Trump's *Pravda*, enjoyably said about the piece. Their headline said it all: "Fact Check: Ted Cruz Attack Proves PolitiFact Is Run by Gigantic Assholes."

So don't be shocked that conservatives were so quick to dismiss the role of fact-checkers during the election. They were a joke long before Trump started giving them fits.

Fact-checking is never going to stop fake news. That's like trying to put out a raging forest fire with a garden hose. Fake news goes viral. Fact-checks emailed to coworkers with the subject line "SEE I TOLD YOU SO! THIS FACT-CHECK LINK PROVES ME RIGHT" get deleted. The *Washington Post* learned the hard way, with their short-lived Internet fact-checking project. Writer Caitlin Dewey said in her final column that "it's starting to feel a little pointless." She explained:

> *We launched "What was Fake" in May 2014 in response to what seemed, at the time, like an epidemic of urban legends and Internet pranks: light-hearted, silly things, for the most part, like new flavors of Oreos and babies with absurd names. Since then, those sorts of rumors and pranks haven't slowed down, exactly, but the pace and tenor of fake news has changed. Where debunking an Internet fake once involved some research, it's now often as simple as clicking around for an "about" or "disclaimer" page. And where a willingness to believe hoaxes once seemed to come from a place of honest ignorance or misunderstanding, that's frequently no longer the case. Headlines like "Casey Anthony found dismembered in truck" go viral via old-fashioned schadenfreude—even hate.*

There's the rub. A fair amount of people *knew* they were sharing fake news. The Pew Research Center found that nearly a quarter of Americans, 23 percent, knew they had shared "fake news" online; 14 percent said they had shared a story they knew to be fake; and 16 percent said they shared stories they realized later to be fake.

Why? For the same reason Trump says things he must know are not true: because there is something about it he wants to be true, even though he can't prove it. You can see how this works even more easily when people spread fake news that gives the impression things are better than they actually are.

Look at what happened in London after four people were killed in a terrorist attack in March 2017. Someone shared an image of a whiteboard outside a tube station that said: "All terrorists are politely reminded that THIS IS LONDON and whatever you do to us we will drink tea and jolly well carry on thank you." It went viral. BBC Radio broadcaster Nick Robinson read the sign on air thinking it was real. But it wasn't. Still, he stood by the report. Upon finding out it was faked he tweeted: "Well, you learn something every day. That lovely tube sign might be a 'fake' but the sentiment isn't for thousands sharing it."

That kind of thinking explains why people will spread fake information we would like to be true, for whatever altruistic or abominable reasons we have, even when we know it's not. If it feels good, we click it.

When it comes to "going viral" on the Internet, feelings usually matter more than fact. That's because social media is not a passive medium, unlike watching TV or listening to the radio. One must be compelled to act. Writers are judged on the amount of engagement—clicks, shares, and comments—that their pieces generate. To do that, the story must provoke a kind of emotional response that gets the blood pumping in some way. Something that makes you think, "Ooo, I need to see that."

Jonah Berger, a professor of marketing at the Wharton School at the University of Pennsylvania, conducted a study in 2011 to find out what kind of material goes viral on the Internet. He discovered that stories that generate physiological arousal—particularly awe and anger—are much more likely to be shared. When readers experienced those two emotions they felt much more compelled to share the story with others. Keep in mind that the stories that provide "physiological arousal" don't necessarily need to be highbrow intellectual stimulation, either. A magazine photo of Kim Kardashian's giant coconut-oil-slathered booty "broke the Internet" in 2014. People contemplating the picture comprised 1 percent of all web-browsing history in the United States the day her photo hit the web.

The kind of political fodder that the collective American political mind obsesses over tends to be much darker, a phenomenon that's as old as American politics itself. Richard Hofstadter's famous 1964 essay "The Paranoid Style in American Politics" still rings true today. He noted that a strain of conspiracy has always plagued our political thought. Outlandish, mysterious, and even apocalyptic theories have been directed toward everyone—the Masons, the Catholics, the Mormons, shadowy "international bankers," and other groups. The stunning thing is how *normal* it is.

He wrote:

In fact, the idea of the paranoid style as a force in politics would have little contemporary relevance or historical value if it were applied only to men with profoundly disturbed minds. It is the use of paranoid modes of expression by more or less normal people that makes the phenomenon significant. . . . Any historian of warfare knows it is in good part a comedy of errors and a museum of incompetence; but if for every error and every act of incompetence one can substitute an act of treason, many points of fascinating interpretation are open to the paranoid imagination. In the end, the real mystery, for one who reads the primary works of paranoid scholarship, is not how the United States has been brought to its present dangerous position but how it has managed to survive at all.

Enter Hillary Clinton, a case study of how far the imagination of the paranoid American mind can be stretched. Clinton has been a lusty target for the conspiratorial right ever since she came on the national scene.

Understanding how and why conspiracy theories emerge is essential to understanding how Trump's seemingly out-of-the-blue fake narratives are so readily accepted. He is unparalleled in his ability to choose the right kinds of fringe ideas to push into mainstream thought.

The list of conspiracy theories that have dogged Hillary Clinton over the years is legend. The longest-lasting can be traced to an email that has floated through thousands of in-boxes during the past few decades that purports to contain a list of roughly fifty people the Clintons allegedly murdered to cover up unknown crimes. Snopes attempted to debunk the rumor back in 1998 with a lengthy post that fact-checked the circumstances surrounding those who had died. It said:

> *We shouldn't have to tell anyone not to believe this claptrap, but we will anyway.*
>
> *In a frenzied media climate where the Chief Executive couldn't boff a White House intern without the whole world finding out every niggling detail of each encounter and demanding his removal from office, are we seriously to believe the same man had been having double handfuls of detractors and former friends murdered with impunity?*

The answer is yes. Many people do, or at least suspect it's possible. Trump told the *Washington Post* in May 2016 he believed there was "something fishy" about the suicide of Clinton White House aide Vince Foster. Trump said, "He knew everything that was going on, and then all of a sudden he committed suicide." He continued, "I don't bring [Foster's death] up because I don't know enough to really discuss it. I will say there are people who continue to bring it up because they think it was absolutely a murder."

I can testify to the fact that I've had several conversations with Republican voters who by all measures appear reasonable and who will, after a few minutes of talking, lean over and ask me in hushed tones if I've ever seen the list of all the people the Clintons have had murdered.

But the endless speculation about the state of the Clintons' marriage is what sparked the most eye-popping rumormongering. The conspiracy theories took the element of truth about the lack of fidelity within the Clintons' marriage and went much further. The stock lines, fed on websites such as *WorldNetDaily* and *Breitbart News* and on various fringe blogs, were that Hillary was a secret lesbian and that Bill flew around the world with rich billionaires who engaged in pedophilia and sex trafficking for fun.

Fox News and other outlets kept close tabs on Bill's friendship with financier Jeffrey Epstein, who pled guilty in 2008 to underage prostitution charges. Here's one sample from Fox News published in May 2016:

> *Former President Bill Clinton was a much more frequent flyer on a registered sex offender's infamous jet than previously reported, with flight logs showing the former president taking at least 26 trips aboard the "Lolita Express"—even apparently ditching his Secret Service detail for at least five of the flights, according to records obtained by FoxNews.com.*

(Epstein, for those keeping track, also happened to be a longtime friend of Trump's over the years. Trump told *New York* magazine in 2002, "I've known Jeff for fifteen years. Terrific guy. He's a lot of fun to be with. It is even said that he likes beautiful women as much as I do, and many of them are on the younger side. No doubt about it—Jeffrey enjoys his social life." But no one, to date, has developed any kind of conspiracy theory about that.)

Hillary Clinton's health also frequently came into question. Her occasional fainting spells, coughing fits, and wearing of thick glasses fed speculation that she was hiding a severe ailment. *WorldNetDaily*'s Jerome Corsi—who also championed the Obama birther conspiracy—reported that Clinton took special drugs derived from "desiccated pig glands" and "rat poison" to treat her condition. (He was actually describing the popularly prescribed medications Armour Thyroid and Coumadin for which Clinton was thought to have prescriptions. The thought of Clinton consuming dead pigs and rat poison makes for a juicier story.)

These stories apply a heavy artistic license to what is passed off as news but match up exactly with what people know about the Clintons: Bill is not faithful; they both have a vindictive streak, have lots of wealthy friends with questionable histories; and Hillary is intensely secretive about everything, including important details about her health.

Most of this was happening, mind you, before it became known that Hillary Clinton had created a secret communications system while working as secretary of state, which provided an excellent framework for conspiracists to seed theories to explain why.

"What was she hiding?" was the question that launched a thousand new theories. What did she want to keep secret from Freedom of Information Act requests? From her old rivals in Obama world? Was she covering up Clinton crimes? Uranium deals with Russia? More knowledge about the terrorist attack in Benghazi? The list goes on and on.

Even Clinton's most ardent defenders believed she had made a colossal mistake. One of the hacked emails written by the Center for American Progress president Neera Tanden said, "Do we actually know who told Hillary she could use private email? And has that person been drawn and quartered? Like whole thing is fucking insane." Well, yes, it was. But that was just the beginning.

Every persistent conspiracy theory starts with a triggering event that begs for an explanation. In this case, it was the presence of Clinton's secret email system. According to University of Miami political scientists Joseph E. Uscinski and Joseph M. Parent, who wrote the 2014 book *American Conspiracy Theories*, most successful conspiracy theories have a similar narrative—one person or group is working in secret to usurp power at the expense of the common good.

And for those looking for an elegant explanation as to why Clinton was hiding her emails, Trump easily filled in the blanks, which he would use to gaslight Clinton later. For now, the important thing to focus on is how his story captured the imagination of the conspiracy-minded right that was already suspicious of Clinton or looking for a reason to reject her. As Trump explained it to voters, her emails were kept secret because Clinton was doing the bidding of rich liberal donors and globalists who were taking advantage of American blue-collar guys and gals.

Review these portions of Trump's GOP convention speech with

what you now know about persistent conspiracy theories in mind. Standing before the GOP delegation with 32.2 million people watching on TV, Trump said:

> *"Big business, elite media and major donors are lining up behind the campaign of my opponent because they know she will keep our rigged system in place. They are throwing money at her because they have total control over everything she does. She is their puppet, and they pull the strings."*

Trump continued at another point in the speech:

> *"When the FBI Director says that the Secretary of State was 'extremely careless' and 'negligent,' in handling our classified secrets, I also know that these terms are minor compared to what she actually did. They were just used to save her from facing justice for her terrible crimes. In fact, her single greatest accomplishment may be committing such an egregious crime and getting away with it—especially when others have paid so dearly."*

It was a narrative that many Republican voters readily accepted. "Tens of millions of people believe in conspiracy theories," Brendan Nyhan, a political science professor at Dartmouth who studies conspiracy theories, told CNN for a piece that explained why people were so prone to believing these stories about the Clintons. "There's a group of people that believe in a lot of them, but there's a much broader group that is willing to endorse them in certain cases. It's not a reflection of mental illness or pathology. It's a common thing that otherwise smart and well-informed people do."

Hillary Clinton gave Trump a lot of material to work with, though. She stonewalled Congress, handing over some emails in preapproved batches, and appeared unreasonably irritated when the press asked questions about them.

All of this was catnip for the conspiratorial right, with whom

Trump cultivated a strong bond. The most well-known media figure occupying this space was Alex Jones, who obsessed over Clinton and told his listeners that she was a genuine demon. On December 5, 2015, Trump called Jones to deliver strong praise. "Your reputation is amazing," Trump told Jones. "I will not let you down. You will be very, very impressed, I hope. And I think we'll be speaking a lot."

Trump wasn't talking to a typical shock-jock radio host here. The Texas-based podcaster and publisher of InfoWars.com and Prison-Planet.com made a name for himself perpetuating the notion that the U.S. government was responsible for 9/11, school shootings at Sandy Hook and Columbine, and the bombings in Oklahoma City and at the Boston marathon. He also believes that the government is poisoning the population by using airplanes to spread "chem trails" as a means of population control. Jones isn't some local wacko, either. He broadcasts his radio show over 129 stations, and ships his content to millions of followers on his various social media channels.

And, most usefully for Trump, Jones despises Hillary Clinton. In Jones's mind, there is no evil she was not capable of committing. He once described her as an "abject psychopathic demon from hell that as soon as she gets into office is going to try and destroy the planet." One of his most popular videos about her claims to show Clinton "birthing alien life" from her mouth; it generated more than 2 million views. During the campaign, Jones made one especially preposterous claim about the way Clinton and Obama smelled. Jones said:

> "I've been told this by high up folks. They say listen, Obama and Hillary both smell like sulfur. I never said this because the media will go crazy with it, but I've talked to people that are in protective details, they're scared of her. And they say listen, she's a frickin' demon and she stinks and so does Obama. I go, like what? Sulfur. They smell like Hell."

Like the birtherism conspiracy, Democrats believed the more attention they gave to Jones, the more it would play in their favor. Clinton gave a speech in August 2016 that complained about how Trump was easily swayed by the likes of the *National Enquirer* and Jones. While out on the stump for Clinton, Obama said, "There's a guy on the radio who apparently said me and Hillary are demons, and we smell like sulfur. Ain't that something," Obama laughed. He then leaned into his arm to take a sniff. "Now, I mean, come on, people!"

Jones relished the attention and took it as proof that his methods were working. "You can call me a conspiracy theorist all day long," he said. "You can try to use me as the poster boy to say 'Look, people that cover these issues aren't credible.' I'm the poster boy that got all this information out. I'm the person that did it in a theatrical way but always told the truth to break through to the public who was in a coma."

What about those "demon" comments? After receiving a lot of criticism, Jones said he was speaking in "an allegory way" that went to the "edge of satire," but added, "I don't retract the fact that she behaves like the metaphysical historical demons we read about in the history books or the Bible." Then he replayed his previous remarks, a greatest hits of sorts, of all the times he likened Clinton to Satan.

The big question is, did Jones and his followers believe what Jones said? Or was it satire? The authenticity of Jones's statements became a factor in his 2017 divorce proceedings when his wife submitted his irate monologues to the court as proof of his instability. Again, Jones claimed his more objectionable work was satire. "He's playing a character," one of his lawyers told the court. "He is a performance artist."

Sociologist Nick Rogers said Jones's defense reminded him of something out of the professional wrestling world called "kayfabe" that he described as the "unspoken contract between wrestlers and spectators: We'll present you with something clearly fake under the insistence that it's real, and you will experience genuine emotion." He explained:

To a wrestling audience, the fake and the real coexist peacefully. If you ask a fan whether a match or backstage brawl was scripted, the question will seem irrelevant. Kayfabe isn't about factual verifiability; it's about emotional fidelity. . . . Ask an average

Trump supporter whether he or she thinks the president plans to build a giant wall and have Mexico pay for it, and you might get an answer that boils down to, "I don't think so, but I believe so." That's kayfabe. Chants of "Build the Wall" aren't about erecting a structure; they're about how cathartic it feels, in the moment, to yell with venom against a common enemy. . . . Kayfabe isn't merely a suspension of disbelief, it is philosophy about truth itself. It rests on the assumption that feelings are inherently more trustworthy than facts.

The wrestling comparison goes much deeper than that, as we shall see, because Trump didn't only use the conspiratorial right as a convenient R&D department for his fake narratives. They were among his biggest fans and defenders of his brand.

THE CULT OF KEK

A certain segment of Trump supporters known as the alt-right believe that the more offensive Trump is, the better. They cheered
Trump's gaslighting because it represented a blow to the PC culture the alt-right hated. His gaslighting disposed of the conventional
norms of campaigning, media discourse, and political rhetoric. The
alt-right loved it all—the smears, the denials, the suspense, and the
discrediting alike.

Trump was their political savior, dubbed with equal parts sarcasm
and affection their "God Emperor." While many of their beliefs about
the supremacy of the white male identity were beyond the pale, the
desperation of struggling white Americans was begging for attention from someone. The alt-right deserves every bit of criticism it
has received for its hostile acts and offensive ideas. That said, some
consideration for factors contributing to their aggression is needed to
understand the movement. White males in America *are* suffering—
look no further than the research conducted by Princeton economists
Anne Case and Sir Angus Deaton in 2015 that documented a disturbing rise in the mortality rate among middle-aged white males due to
suicide, drugs, and alcohol. Between 1999 and 2013, the death rate
rose by more than 20 percent. The pair described them as "despair
deaths." A generation of white men were killing themselves and barely
a whisper of advocacy was being done on their behalf.

Daniel Sullivan, an assistant professor of social psychology at the University of Arizona, wrote that these individuals were attempting to solidify their own kind of victim status, something Trump tapped into. "The recession, ever-expanding personal debt, and high-profile terrorist attacks have undermined their sense of personal agency, especially for lower-income members of this group," Sullivan said. "Simultaneously, minority groups have achieved more rights and a louder voice, which is generally perceived by conservative white Americans to be an attack on their moral value."

He conducted a series of studies in 2012 that showed that when white American males were told they caused suffering among minorities, they would respond with what Sullivan called "competitive victimhood." This is a mainstay of alt-right ideological thought that Trump consistently appeals to with his talk about the "forgotten man." That psychological connection is paramount. "Even if the economy nosedives back into collapse under Trump's presidency, if he continues to satisfy his supporters' psychological needs better than the Democratic alternatives, he may still have an army of supporters in four years—no matter what chaos ensues," Sullivan said.

That's a very likely scenario. To this day, there is no socially appropriate way for white males to express grievance without the risk of being branded as sexists or racists. Which is why the alt-right was formed and why it continues to exist in such an ugly fashion. If someone is going to be unfairly branded as a bigot, the thinking goes, why not go all in? As detailed in previous chapters, this is the same type of vicious thinking that pushed conservatives to back Trump and his questionable methods. If Mitt Romney was going to be smeared as a greedy money-grubbing bully, what's the downside in nominating someone with those qualities?

The alt-right took this mind-set to another level. The loose conglomeration of online bandits sought to harass the opposition through their social media networks and working mercilessly to mock, scare, and intimidate anyone who stood in their way. Alt-right sympathizers claimed it was all harmless, but anyone who spent time analyzing their chat forums and websites could see how it all stemmed from a disturbing form of white nationalism. Make no mistake about that point. White nationalist Andrew Anglin, who runs the prominent alt-right website Daily Stormer, summarized it thusly:

> *The core concept of the movement, upon which all else is based, is that Whites are undergoing an extermination, via mass immigration into White countries which was enabled by a corrosive liberal ideology of White self-hatred, and that the Jews are at the center of this agenda.*

While most Trump supporters are not anti-Semites like these hardcore alt-rightists, the rest of Anglin's theory resounded among many of Trump's fans. And without ever identifying himself as one of them, Trump spoke their language from the start. His speech announcing his candidacy for presidency was a siren call. "When Mexico sends its people, they're not sending their best," Trump said. "They're sending people that have lots of problems, and they're bringing those problems with us. They're bringing drugs. They're bringing crime. They're rapists."

In fact, Trump's longtime flirtation with white nationalists is one of the biggest cons he's pulled since he became a political candidate. For years, he advanced messages that were happily received and endorsed among that crowd, while coyly denying any association with them.

Take, for example, how Trump declined to denounce David Duke, repeatedly, in a CNN interview. Jake Tapper asked him if he would disavow Duke and Trump replied, "Just so you understand, I don't know anything about David Duke, OK?" Trump was asked three times and each time he demurred. "I don't know anything about what you're even talking about with white supremacy or white supremacists." (He later claimed he had a bad earpiece and couldn't hear the question.) Trump's subsequent "denial" to ABC's *Good Morning America* was a nondenial denial. Read carefully what Trump said:

GEORGE STEPHANOPOULOS: So, are you prepared right now to make a clear and unequivocal statement renouncing the support of all white supremacists?
TRUMP: I mean, there's nobody that's done so much for equality as I have. You take a look at Palm Beach, Florida, I built the Mar-a-Lago Club, totally open to everybody; a club that frankly set a new standard in clubs and a new standard in Palm Beach and I've gotten great credit for it. That is totally open to everybody. So, of course, I am.

Once Stephanopoulos asked Trump to make a "clear and unequivocal statement" it was all but certain that Trump would not. As shown in previous chapters, he will never do something his perceived opponents demand that he do. When ABC's Tom Llamas told Trump the phrase "anchor babies" was offensive, Trump replied, "I'll use the word anchor baby! Excuse me, I'll use the word anchor baby!" This is one of Trump's tried-and-true rules for handling his critics. He will not comply with their requests, even if it means refusing to disavow white supremacists. He'd rather risk being called a racist than weak and subservient.

When it came to Trump's views on David Duke, complying with federal law to ensure that people of all races are welcome at his golf club isn't exactly a disavowal. If anything, Trump was saying that David Duke would be made welcome in his club. For people who are used to speaking to one another with dog whistles, it was as if Trump was yelling into a megaphone. Richard Spencer, white nationalist and alt-right icon, said, "Before Trump, our identity ideas, national ideas, they had no place to go." He runs the National Policy Institute and often repeats the mantra "Race is real, race matters, and race is the foundation of identity." Spencer's fellow alt-right traveler Mike Cernovich said, "I went from libertarian to alt-right after realizing tolerance only went one way and diversity is code for white genocide."

"White genocide" is a significant phrase among the alt-right. It signifies their belief that white culture is being exterminated all across the West. Trump even retweeted a popular alt-right account named WhiteGenocideTM, which also listed its location as "Jewmerica," when that user posted an unflattering image of Jeb Bush.

A small action like this was a gleaming green light to members of the alt-right, who carefully monitored social media. While Trump didn't join arms with white nationalists, he was sending signals that their support was welcome. Their pent-up anger and frustration could be channeled behind a real, viable candidate. They were no longer regulated to the sidelines, a significant development since the political arena has become an increasingly important place to advance their ideas. Especially if they were able to do so under the cloak of opposing Hillary Clinton.

One 2015 study conducted by researchers at Princeton University and Stanford University found that, increasingly, partisan politics have become a venue for people to express views about sexuality and race that were considered taboo. "While Americans are inclined to 'hedge' expressions of overt animosity toward racial minorities, immigrants, gays, or other marginalized groups, they enthusiastically voice hostility for the opposing party and its supporters," the study said. For example, someone may not be able to comfortably say, "I want to restore white culture in America," but they can easily slam Hillary Clinton as corrupt, or worse. Being vehemently against an opposing political party is more socially acceptable than talking about beliefs that animate the objection.

It continued:

Unlike race, gender, and other social divides where group-related attitudes and behaviors are constrained by social norms, there are no corresponding pressures to temper disapproval of political opponents. . . . In contemporary America, the strength of these norms has made virtually any discussion of racial differences a taboo subject to the point that citizens suppress their true feelings. No such constraints apply to evaluations of partisan groups. The

larger animus associated with the party divide is further attribut-
able to fundamental differences between partisan and race-based
identity.

No wonder the alt-right thrived online, where anonymity is prized. Cleverly, the alt-right's most callous messages were masked in memes and jokes. They got a lot of people to contemplate their worldview with things that seemed funny, if a bit weird, until one discovered what it really represented. The veil of humor also provided a degree of plausible deniability about their true intentions. When Spencer led an audience in the Nazi salute at a Washington conference in November 2016, he told reporters who questioned him about the offensive gesture that it was "done in the spirit of irony and exuberance."

Part of the irony included a fake religion alt-rightists invented for which they could claim persecution: "The Cult of Kek." See if you can follow this. For some inexplicable reason, Trump supporters hanging out in political chatrooms began using a green cartoon frog named Pepe as their symbol, pumping out pro-Trump memes with the image. Many of them were also World of Warcraft fans who have long used the word "kek" in place of "lol" for reasons too obscure and nerdy to go into. Then, oddly enough, they found out that there actually was an Egyptian god named Kek who was depicted as a man with a frog's head. Some thought it was a mystical coincidence that shouldn't be ignored, or at least should be made into a delightfully kooky storyline. They decided that Trump was a living version of Kek, hence the nickname "God Emperor." Mostly for fun, a canon was created around the Cult of Kek. Adherents claim heritage to an ancient kingdom called "Kekistan" that was overtaken by "Cuckistan" and "Normistan." They created their own flag, inspired by the German Nazi war flag, which is sometimes spotted at pro-Trump events.

The Southern Poverty Law Center's David Neiwert wrote one of the best explanations on the religious parody. (Yes, SPLC has unfairly labeled some reputable conservative organizations as "hate groups," but they know how to write an explainer about this bizarre subject. So I'm quoting it.) Neiwert wrote:

> *The main point of the whole exercise is to mock "political correctness," an alt-right shibboleth, and deeply reflective of the ironic, often deadpan style of online trolling in general, and alt-right "troll storms" especially. Certainly, if any "normies" were to make the mistake of taking their "religion" seriously and suggesting that their "deity" was something they worshipped, they would receive the usual mocking treatment reserved for anyone foolish enough to take their words at face value.*

So while the alt-right goes on about their fake religion or brandishes Nazi paraphernalia, no one is supposed to say a word. It's all a joke to show that lefty multiculturalists have no sense of humor. That's what people were told anyway. Most people saw through the "humor" and dismissed it. But, that doesn't mean the alt-right's rhetoric hasn't had any effect. Whether influential conservative thought leaders will admit it or not, the alt-right ethos has been absorbed into the vast bloodstream of Trump supporters.

Rush Limbaugh passed along a variation of one of the alt-right's signature disgusting slurs—"cuck"—in a July 22, 2015, broadcast. That was around the time Trump said that 2008 GOP presidential nominee John McCain wasn't a "war hero" and wasn't apologizing for it, either. "If Trump were your average, ordinary, cuckolded Republican, he would have apologized by now, and he would have begged for forgiveness, and he would have gone away," Limbaugh said. "And the establishment would have claimed another scalp, claiming that they had protected the sanctity of campaigns." He used the word "cuckolded" just as the alt-right did—to trash Republicans as being insufficiently moderate. It got at the same idea many Tea Party conservatives threw around, though they used words like "RINO" to describe it. But the alt-right's version had much sleazier roots. "Cuck" refers to a genre of porn in which married white men watch their wives have intercourse with black men.

Why does any of this matter? Because the same kind of freewheeling, moral-free spirits on the Internet who will spread Nazi propaganda are mercilessly trolling for Trump and influencing big conservative media figures. Once someone is comfortable telling a Jewish writer to get into the oven, there is no limit to what else they will say to help their candidate.

12

HACKS

As fake news purveyors and the alt-right were aligning to help Trump, an aggressive group of foreign nationals were doing the same. They'd do it by dumping information that would rock the whole election. It would also accomplish what we now know the Russian government wanted most: pervasive fear among the American people that the political system was rigged and untrustworthy.

On July 22, 2016, mere days ahead of the Democratic National Convention, Russian hackers used the multinational activist organization WikiLeaks to make public thousands of private emails stolen from the Democratic National Committee. A political bombshell, splendidly positioned for Trump to exploit.

Among the thousands of emails posted, the most damaging showed DNC operatives disparaging Clinton's primary rival, Senator Bernie Sanders, roiling the most progressive wing of the party, which was reluctant to support Clinton in the first place. In one email, a staffer wondered if Sanders's Jewish heritage and suspected atheism could hurt his standing among Southern voters. The leaks had major, immediate consequences that cast a shadow of doubt over the convention. Two days later, as the curtains were being raised for the DNC's big event, the woman in charge, DNC chair Debbie Wasserman Schultz, resigned, leaving the party in chaos.

Trump knew how to play it. He used the development to underscore a theme that he already had in the works. He held up the hacked emails as proof the election process was rigged. Trump said the emails showed Sanders never had a fair shot because the DNC party bigwigs were all in lockstep behind Clinton. "Leaked e-mails of DNC show plans to destroy Bernie Sanders," Trump tweeted on July 23. "Mock his heritage and much more. On-line from WikiLeakes [*sic*], really vicious. RIGGED." The Russians had to be cheering. An American presidential nominee was using his massive media microphone to amplify their work. *Score.* Trump wasn't done yet, either. He was taking ownership of the WikiLeaks narrative. He was *going there.* This was Step One of his next gaslighting.

Once his tweet went out into the world, Trump moved on to Step Two—advance and deny. During a July 27 press conference in Doral, Florida, Trump advanced the WikiLeaks story—calling it "very serious . . . horrible, absolutely horrible"—while denying the emails would help him beat Clinton. Before the press conference, Clinton campaign manager Robby Mook told reporters that the Russians put the emails out to help Trump win, something the GOP nominee vociferously denied. When Trump was asked about that specific allegation he said:

"It is so farfetched. It's so ridiculous. Honestly, I wish I had that power. I'd love to have that power, but Russia has no respect for our country. And that's why—if it is Russia, nobody even knows this, it's probably China, or it could be somebody sitting in his bed."

Huh? If you read that carefully, you'll see that Trump's denial about the Russian hacking was a special one—a nondenial denial. (Note: This is a special strategy mentioned in the previous Surrogate Secrets chapter.) Trump said that he didn't carry out the hacking, didn't know who did it, then said, "I wish I had that power. I'd love to have that power." A bit "ridiculous," indeed.

Then, Trump did something unthinkable to kick off the suspense-laden Step Three of his method. He openly called on Russian hackers to obtain and release the emails from Clinton's secret server that she never turned over to Congress in its investigation of Benghazi. "Russia, if you're listening, I hope you're able to find the 30,000 e-mails that are missing," Trump said. "I think you will probably be rewarded mightily by our press. Let's see if that happens. That'll be next."

This would send the media into a frenzy for months to come.

The Clinton campaign said that Trump's call on Russia to produce more stolen emails was equivalent to treason, but for Trump the request had its intended effect. It reminded everyone of Clinton's longstanding email scandal. And he planted the seed that there was more damaging information that would soon come to light. "Let's see if that happens," Trump had said. "That'll be next." He sounded confident. He sounded sure. He had everyone's attention, no doubt. From there, Step Four was simple. Trump would maintain that the WikiLeaks emails proved the election was rigged for Clinton and she didn't deserve to be the Democratic nominee. As you will see, it became one of his biggest closing arguments to voters in the final stages of the campaign. Trump's method was intact.

For their part, the Russians' election-meddling efforts were working out quite nicely. They didn't, after all, dump the emails as an altruistic act in the name of global transparency. They had a deliberate plan, aimed at crippling Clinton's candidacy and sowing distrust in the American electoral process. All messages Trump enthusiastically espoused. No one needs to prove any kind of criminal collusion to see how Trump's arguments and the Russian hacking complemented each other.

The intelligence community noticed the themes. The Senate Intelligence Committee released a bipartisan report in early January 2017 that stated that throughout the election the Russian government had engaged in a campaign to boost Trump over Clinton, who Putin believed was responsible for inciting mass protests against him in 2011 and 2012.

With a "moderate" to "high" degree of confidence, the CIA, FBI, NSA, and Office of the Director of National Intelligence said that Russian president Vladimir Putin had ordered an influence campaign to undermine public faith in the United States' democratic process and to denigrate Clinton and harm her electability and potential presidency. The American intelligence community concluded that to do it, the Russians followed a "messaging strategy that blends covert intelligence operations—such as cyber activity—with overt efforts by Russian government agencies, state-funded media, third-party intermediaries, and paid social media users or 'trolls.'" Analysts assessed with "high confidence" that Russian military intelligence was responsible for leaking the data to WikiLeaks. Trump would maintain throughout the election and his presidency that he didn't know who hacked the emails, but the American intelligence community was crystal clear that it did not harbor such doubts.

Russia also aided Trump's war against American media. According to the Senate report, beginning in March 2016, state-run Russian TV and Sputnik would "consistently cast President-elect Trump as the target of unfair coverage from traditional US media outlets that they claimed were subservient to a corrupt political establishment." Specifically, the report pointed to Putin's chief propagandist, Dmitry Kiselev, who used his weekly news program to cast Trump "as an outsider victimized by a corrupt political establishment and faulty democratic election process that aimed to prevent his election because of his desire to work with Moscow." Russian TV (RT) created English-language videos to echo these messages that generated millions of views online. Some of their more popular RT stories included:

- "Julian Assange Special: Do WikiLeaks Have the E-Mail That'll Put Clinton in Prison?"
- "Clinton and ISIS Funded by the Same Money"
- "How 100% of the Clintons' 'Charity' Went to . . . Themselves"
- "Trump Will Not Be Permitted to Win"

For his part, Putin scoffed at the notion that he had made any attempt to influence the U.S. election despite the fact that his government spends roughly $190 million each year disseminating RT content. Putin said that such thoughts were "fictional, illusory, provocations and lies."

But the Russians have a long history of doing exactly this to great effect. Moreover, they specialize in creating realistic fictions to smear their opponents or, in other cases, throw their lives into chaos. Soviet "dezinformatsiya," or disinformation, existed long before anyone heard the phrase "fake news." Clint Watts, a former FBI agent and cybersecurity expert, watched a disinformation campaign unfold in real time one day in July 2016. He told the sobering story about how Russian operatives spread a fake story about a U.S. airbase in Turkey, where nuclear weapons are stored, being attacked by terrorists. Watts testified:

"On the evening of July 30, my colleagues and I watched as RT and Sputnik News simultaneously launched false stories of the U.S. airbase at Incirlik being overrun by terrorists. Within minutes, pro-Russian social-media aggregators and automated bots amplified this false news story and expanded conspiracies asserting American nuclear missiles at the base would be lost to extremists. More than 4,000 tweets in the first 78 minutes after launching of this false story linked back to the Active Measures accounts we'd tracked in the previous two years. These previously identified accounts, almost simultaneously appearing from different geographic locations and communities, amplified this fake news story in unison. The hashtags incrementally pushed by these automated accounts were #Nuclear, #Media, #Trump and #Benghazi. The most common words found in English-speaking Twitter user profiles were: God, Military, Trump, Family, Country, Conservative, Christian, America, and Constitution. These accounts and their messages clearly sought to convince Americans a U.S. military base was being overrun in a terrorist attack like the 2012 assault on the U.S. consulate in Libya. In reality, a small protest gathered outside the Incirlik gate and the increased security at the airbase sought to secure the arrival of the U.S. Chairman of the Joint Chiefs of Staff the following day."

The story was false, but what could have happened if a government acted as if the information were real and launched military action in response? Consider how quickly a military conflict could begin. This kind of fake news isn't only concerning to national security interests, either. The stock market is even more vulnerable. What's to stop an army of Russian bots from pushing a bigger spoof that would cause traders to act on bad information, potentially triggering an economic crash? In 2012, one Twitter user impersonating Russian interior minister Vladimir Kolokoltsev tweeted that Syrian president Bashar al-Assad was "killed or injured." Crude oil prices went up by more than a dollar before the report was confirmed as false.

Russia's fake news story about Incirlik didn't move markets or start a war, but it did infiltrate the highest levels of the Trump campaign. Trump campaign manager Paul Manafort repeated the falsehood during an August 14 appearance on CNN's *State of the Union*. When host Jake Tapper asked Manafort about controversial comments Trump had made, Manafort asked Tapper why he wasn't covering other, more important news, such as "the NATO base in Turkey being under attack by terrorists." Well, because that attack never happened. Where did Manafort get that information? That wasn't hard to figure out. The only places it appeared were on Sputnik News and RT.

13

BIMBO ERUPTIONS

If there was one thing Republicans remembered from the Clinton White House it was this: how the Clintons got away with lying about Monica Lewinsky. The lowest point of Bill Clinton's presidency was when he looked into the TV camera and told America, "I did not have sexual relations with that woman, Miss Lewinsky." Hillary was equally defiant. "I mean, look at the very people who are involved in this—they have popped up in other settings," she famously said. "This is—the great story for anybody willing to find it and write about it and explain it is this vast right-wing conspiracy that has been conspiring against my husband since the day he announced for president."

We all know now they were blowing smoke. President Clinton personally invited Monica Lewinsky into his private quarters, but when their secret came out, she was depicted as some obsessed groupie. As if there was nothing anyone could do to stop a young woman with an out-of-control crush on the leader of the free world from gaining access to him and the most protected spaces in America. Illogical, yet that was the line they took. In a letter to her friend Diane Blair, Hillary called Lewinsky a "narcissistic loony toon." They gaslit Lewinsky, although few people recognized it at the time. And, hand it to the Clintons, it worked. Bill got to keep on being president and Monica got her life ruined. After suffering through one of the greatest public humiliations of all time, Lewinsky went underground for nearly two decades. She didn't really resurface until 2014, writing in *Vanity Fair*:

> *Sure, my boss took advantage of me, but I will always remain firm on this point: it was a consensual relationship. Any "abuse" came in the aftermath, when I was made a scapegoat in order to protect his powerful position. . . . I was the Unstable Stalker (a phrase disseminated by the Clinton White House), the Dimwit Floozy, the Poor Innocent who didn't know any better. The Clinton administration, the special prosecutor's minions, the political operatives on both sides of the aisle, and the media were able to brand me. And that brand stuck, in part because it was imbued with power.*

The real lesson that Trump, and every other politician who studied the situation, could learn is that full-on denial of reality works when expressed with enough confidence. Especially when so many others are willing to assist. The Clintons had plenty of help. Clinton ally and New York Democratic representative Charlie Rangel said during that time, "That poor child has serious emotional problems. She's fantasizing. And I haven't heard that she played with a full deck in her other experiences." Even liberal feminists were willing to rationalize Bill's womanizing in the name of preserving their political power. Eleanor Smeal, president of the Feminist Majority, stood by Clinton, assuming the anti-anti-Clinton position. "It was a right-wing attack," she said. "We saw it as a right-wing effort to draw out of office a president for ideological reasons." Feminist icon Gloria Steinem did the same, penning a 1998 op-ed in the *New York Times* that said:

> *If all the sexual allegations now swirling around the White House turn out to be true, President Clinton may be a candidate for sex addiction therapy. . . . But feminists will still have been right to resist pressure by the right wing and the news media to call for his resignation or impeachment.*

Some liberal women even said it made Bill hot. In the midst of the scandal, Tina Brown described the president in the *New Yorker* as "a man in a dinner jacket with more heat than any star in the room . . . He is vividly in the present tense and dares you to join him there." At least Brown had some pretense about it, though. White House correspondent Nina Burleigh made her desires explicit. She told the *Washington Post*, "I'd be happy to give him [oral sex] just to thank him for keeping abortion legal."

"Feminism sort of died in that period," *New York Times* columnist Maureen Dowd would later tell Yahoo. "Because the feminists had to come along with Bill Clinton's retrogressive behavior with women in order to protect the progressive policies for women that Bill Clinton had as president." Writer Marjorie Williams, a self-identified Democrat, was one of the few not to go along with such tawdry nonsense. She wrote a barn burner of a piece for *Vanity Fair* in 1998 questioning what the hell had happened to her supposedly feminist liberal friends. "When I look back over my life," she concluded, "I expect to remember Clinton's two terms in the White House as the Gaslight Presidency. . . . But we have no excuse. Denial is insidious; it always claims more than you think you have ceded to it." (Sadly Williams, a maestro profiler, passed away in 2005. She surely would've written some powerhouse pieces documenting Trump's gaslight presidency. She was on to this gambit long before anyone else was.)

Before Monica Lewinsky became a household name in the 1990s, there were four other women who had come forward. The Clintons were able to deny and attack their way out of each of those allegations. However, the Clintons' gaslighting was always *reactive*. They were never in control of the situation. This is the distinction between how previous politicians, including President Richard Nixon, which will be explained later, typically gaslit someone and how Trump did it. The Clintons used gaslighting as a defense mechanism to protect against what the Clinton rapid-response hand Betsey Wright termed "bimbo eruptions." Trump, on the other hand, gaslit proactively. He affirmatively created media firestorms and fanned the flames.

This is the key to understanding why Trump's gaslighting is so different from anyone else's. He took something no one else would contemplate doing unless they were cornered and built a movement out of it. It also explains why Trump was willing to dredge up this scandal and use it against Hillary in 2016.

First, a reminder of who these women were, in no particular order:

- Juanita Broaddrick, who said President Clinton raped her in a hotel room in 1978 while she was doing volunteer work for his first gubernatorial campaign.
- Kathleen Willey, a former White House volunteer who said President Clinton hugged and kissed her against her will when she asked him for a paid job. "His hands were all over me," she testified in 1999. When asked if she tried to resist his advances, Willey said yes.
- Gennifer Flowers claimed she had a love affair with Bill Clinton. Hillary Clinton dismissed her as "some failed cabaret singer who doesn't even have much of a resume to fall back on." In another interview Hillary Clinton talked about her desire to cross-examine Flowers. "I mean, I would crucify her," Hillary Clinton said. (Bill later admitted he did have a sexual encounter with Flowers.)
- Paula Jones, who filed a sexual harassment suit against Bill Clinton in 1994 alleging that while Clinton was the governor of Arkansas and she a state clerk, he asked her up to his hotel suite, lowered his pants, and requested oral sex. Bill Clinton eventually settled the suit in November 1998 for $850,000.

Trump knew their names and stories by heart, as did so many Republicans who had bought books and watched films and endless segments on Fox News detailing the allegations. When Hillary Clinton started holding herself out as a women's icon on the campaign trail, it was too much. The memory of these accusations was far fresher than Clinton anticipated. She seemed to have no clue, issuing a tone-deaf tweet that invited ridicule. Early in the campaign season, in November 2015, she tweeted that "every survivor of sexual assault deserves to be heard, believed, and supported." That tweet immediately brought to mind the names Juanita, Kathleen, and Paula, none of whom, in all the years that had passed, retracted their stories about Bill Clinton's sexual misconduct. And so, during a New Hampshire event the next month someone asked Clinton about her husband's accusers.

"You recently came out to say that all rape victims should be believed? But would you say that about Juanita Broaddrick, Kathleen Willey, and Paula Jones? Should we believe them as well?" an attendee asked.

"Well, I would say that everybody should be believed at first," Clinton said, "until they are disbelieved based on evidence." Broaddrick told *BuzzFeed News* she went "ballistic" when she heard Clinton say that. She logged on to Twitter and typed a message: "I was 35 years old when Bill Clinton, Ark. Attorney General raped me and Hillary tried to silence me. I am now 73. . . . it never goes away."

Just as they did in the 1990s, liberal feminists fell in line to defend the Clintons. "Women know that this is an unfair attack on Hillary, and that's why it continues to exist in this small corner of the right-wing media world," Emily's List vice president of communications Marcy Stech said.

Here was a topic considered off-limits in polite discussions, but was frequently discussed below the mainstream media's radar and represented a huge crack in Clinton's strongest claim to the White House—the notion that, as president, she would be a woman's champion. Moreover, these were all known facts Trump could use to tamp down questions about his own record with women. You know what that means. Let the gaslighting begin!

Trump had laid the groundwork for this early. Step One was already set; he had expressed a willingness to attack Clinton over Bill's accusers early on—something no other candidate had shown the stomach to do. Trump had put out an Instagram video in January that showed photographs of President Bill Clinton and Monica Lewinsky as a clip of Hillary's voice played on a loop in the background. "Women's rights are human rights and human rights are women's rights. Once and for all let's keep fighting for opportunity and dignity." The message wasn't hard to miss. It was a punch straight to the gut of Hillary Clinton's campaign that encouraged voters to "make history again!" by electing her as the first female president after making Barack Obama the first black president.

Fox News's Chris Wallace asked Trump if he thought the ad was too negative. He should have known better. Interviewers keep thinking they can get Trump to recant, but he will always stick to his story. Gaslighting won't work any other way.

Trump stood by the ad, saying that Clinton is "not a victim. She was an enabler. Some of these women have been destroyed . . . I mean, there's no feeling sorry for Hillary in this situation. And all you have to do is look at some of the facts, and look at some of the settlements. There's no feeling sorry for her." It was clear he had absolutely no intention of backing down from this claim.

For a while, Clinton refused to fire back. "I'm going to let him live in his alternate reality," she told Iowa voters. "I'm not going to respond." Trump took that as a free pass to hit her again on the subject. In May, he released a similar video. Like the previous one, it was short, only fifteen seconds. "Is Hillary really protecting women?" it asked, and it featured clips of President Clinton's accusers tearfully telling their stories until Hillary's voice drowned them out.

Trump's attacks were nervy considering that Trump took Bill Clinton's side in the 1990s when all his accusers were coming forward. "It's like it's from hell, it's a terrible group of people," Trump told Fox News's Neil Cavuto in 1998. He went on. "I don't necessarily agree with his victims, his victims are terrible. He is really a victim himself . . . The whole group, Paula Jones, Lewinsky, it's just a really unattractive group. I'm not just talking about the physical."

Cavuto asked, "Would it be any different if it were a supermodel crowd?"

Trump replied, "I think at least it would be more pleasant to watch."

But, when it was convenient for Trump to use those "really unattractive" women for his own purposes, he would. Republicans didn't seem to mind. They were all too content to sit back and watch Trump take shots at their favorite punching bag: Hillary Clinton. After all, the only reason most of them were supporting Trump was to stop her.

Step Two of the method—advance and deny—began ahead of the debates. In September, Trump floated the idea that he might seat Gennifer Flowers in the front row of the first presidential debate. Upset that Clinton was bringing in billionaire and ABC *Shark Tank* star Mark Cuban to support her at the debate, Trump tweeted: "If dopey Mark Cuban of failed Benefactor fame wants to sit in the front row, perhaps I will put Gennifer Flowers right alongside of him!" Then during the actual debate, he denied he would ever bring up such a salacious subject even though he had put out videos and given interviews to that very effect. Feigning he was a man of polite manners, he said: "You want to know the truth? I was going to say something extremely rough to Hillary, to her family, and I said to myself: I can't do it. I just can't do it." In a post-debate interview on CNN, he applauded his supposed restraint. Trump said he was proud of himself because he "was able to hold back on the indiscretions with respect to Bill Clinton, because I have a lot of respect for Chelsea Clinton, and I just didn't want to say what I was going to say." But he wasn't holding back at all. Moreover, behind the scenes his campaign was actively pushing it, sending out a post-debate memo instructing surrogates to talk about the women who had accused President Clinton. The talking points, obtained by CNN, went as follows:

- Mr. Trump has never treated women the way Hillary Clinton and her husband did when they actively worked to destroy Bill Clinton's accusers.
- Hillary Clinton bullied and smeared women like Paula Jones, Gennifer Flowers, and Monica Lewinsky.
- Are you blaming Hillary for Bill's infidelities? No, however,

she's been an active participant in trying to destroy the women who has [*sic*] come forward with a claim.

Then came the opportune moment when Trump would need to bring out some secret weapons to carry out Step Three and create suspense like we've never seen before in a presidential election.

I remember how it all went down in vivid detail.

14

LOCK HER UP

Late Friday afternoon on October 7, 2016, I was in the car with my husband and kids on the way to do a run through Home Depot and grab some Chick-fil-A for dinner. I got a call from a CNN producer; could I come to the studio that evening? She asked that I check my email for a breaking story about something Trump had said on *Access Hollywood* in 2005. When I read the story, I gasped. Silently, I gestured to my husband, who was driving, to turn the car around as I kept reading. I would need to grab my TV clothes and get to the studio fast.

"You aren't going to believe this," I told my husband before reading him the transcript with some key words whispered for the benefit of the kids in the back of the car.

"Okay, you go, but we're getting Chick-fil-A without you," he said, flashing a grin. Fair enough! A few minutes later I was off to the D.C. bureau. On the way in, I listened intently to all the coverage over SiriusXM radio. It seemed like everyone was missing what Trump was really talking about. Sexual assault. On the air that night I said, "If there's any elected Republican official who doesn't know what to say, they should call a rape survivor tonight and ask them what they heard when they heard Donald Trump say these words."

The final presidential debate was scheduled to be held that Sunday and Republicans were scattering fast. Not even Mike Pence, Trump's very own vice presidential pick, would defend him on this one. Pence canceled an event he was scheduled to hold in Wisconsin with House speaker Paul Ryan on Saturday and sent out a solemn statement. "I do not condone his remarks and cannot defend them," Pence said. "We pray for his family and look forward to the opportunity he has to show what is in his heart when he goes before the nation tomorrow night."

Trump realized what trouble he was in. This wasn't part of the narrative he had planned. He didn't create these headlines. His lapdogs were jumping out of his lap.

He then grabbed the most unexpected political territory for himself to date. He apologized. But he had something up his sleeve.

"I've never said I'm a perfect person, nor pretended to be someone that I'm not," Trump said in a short video posted on Facebook. "I've said and done things I regret, and the words released today on this more than a decade-old video are one of them. Anyone who knows me, know these words don't reflect who I am. I said it, it was wrong, and I apologize." He talked about traveling the country and promised his supporters, "I pledge to be a better man tomorrow, and will never, ever let you down."

This seemed significant. Trump never apologizes, right? But, it wasn't a true apology. He was merely continuing to engage Step Two of the gaslighting method. Trump admitted he said the words but denied he was a womanizer. Moreover, he used the "apology" to kick off Step Three—the promise of more to come. Read his statement closely. Without missing a beat, he continued his video monologue and said:

"I've said some foolish things, but there is a big difference between words and actions. Bill Clinton has actually abused women and Hillary has bullied, attacked, shamed and intimidated his victims. We will discuss this more in the coming days. See you at the debate on Sunday."

I, for one, could barely take the suspense. What in the world was this debate going to be like on Sunday? To blow off steam that afternoon, I went lap swimming at my local pool. As I got out, I received a call from a CNN producer. Could I get to St. Louis that night for

State of the Union tomorrow? I'd need to catch the very next flight out of Dulles to make it; I hotfooted it home to pack my bags. When I checked into my hotel in St. Louis that evening, my hair was still wet from the pool.

That morning, Trump campaign officials were nowhere to be seen. Some Republicans, such as New Hampshire Republican senator Kelly Ayotte, were saying that Trump should drop out of the race. RNC chairman Reince Priebus reportedly made a similar request in private. Trump's electoral outlook was dire, which made Democrats all the more determined to keep Trump in the race. He seemed even more beatable than ever.

The GOP was in crisis, I said on TV. We had to look at all possible options.

Trump's big reveal came on Sunday afternoon, right before the scheduled debate that evening. Trump held a press conference with Bill Clinton's sexual accusers, broadcast on Facebook Live. Paula Jones, Juanita Broaddrick, Kathleen Willey, and Kathy Shelton, a woman who was raped by a man Hillary Clinton defended in 1975 while she was working at a legal aid clinic, all appeared by Trump's side to support him.

"Actions speak louder than words," Broaddrick said. "Mr. Trump may have said some bad words, but Bill Clinton raped me and Hillary Clinton threatened me. I don't think there's any comparison." Jones was asked if she agreed with Trump that his "star power" permitted him to touch women without their consent. "Why don't you ask Bill Clinton that?" Broaddrick shot back. "Why don't you ask Hillary as well?" Step Four, the discrediting of Hillary Clinton over her husband's misconduct, was beginning.

The debate began later that evening. When asked about his comments on the *Access Hollywood* tape, Trump was ready. In his characteristically superlative fashion he said, "I have great respect for women, nobody has more respect for women than I do," ignoring the groans from the audience. Then as the debate progressed, Trump lit the place up. Trump said:

"If you look at Bill Clinton, far worse. Mine are words, and his was action. His was what he's done to women. There's never been anybody in the history [of] politics in this nation that's been so abusive to women. So, you can say any way you want to say it, but Bill Clinton was abusive to women.

"Hillary Clinton attacked those same women and attacked them viciously. Four of them here tonight. One of the women, who is a wonderful woman, at 12 years old, was raped at 12. Her client she represented got him off, and she's seen laughing on two separate occasions, laughing at the girl who was raped. Kathy Shelton, that young woman is here with us tonight.

"So, don't tell me about words. I am absolutely—I apologize for those words. But it is things that people say. But what President Clinton did, he was impeached, he lost his license to practice law. He had to pay an $850,000 fine to one of the women. Paula Jones, who's also here tonight.

"And I will tell you that when Hillary brings up a point like that and she talks about words that I said 11 years ago, I think it's disgraceful, and I think she should be ashamed of herself, if you want to know the truth."

People may say they want politicians to apologize when they've done something wrong, but those politicians rarely recover after they do. It shows weakness, but more important it showcases the wrongdoing in a way that it can no longer be brushed aside. Once guilt is admitted, voters feel more responsibility to punish the politician. There's no plausible deniability. Trump knew Republicans would have a hard time voting for an admitted "pussy grabber," but they would pull the lever for someone committed to destroying Hillary Clinton at all costs. Trump had to keep the focus on her by going as negative as he could.

Sounding no different from Alex Jones, Trump poured on the gas. He accused Clinton of having "tremendous hate in her heart" and described her as the "devil." He dangled out the prospect of truly locking her up. "And I tell you what. I didn't think I would say this, but I'm going to say it, and I hate to say it," Trump said. "But if I win, I am going to instruct my attorney general to get a special prosecutor to look into your situation, because there has never been so many lies, so much deception." Another giant dose of suspense.

Clinton protested that "I told people it would be impossible to be fact-checking Donald all the time. I'd never get to talk about anything I want to do and how we're going to really make lives better for people." (Exactly the point!) She then tried talking about the implications of having Trump "in charge of law in our country," but he cut her off with a sharp retort: "Because you'd be in jail." The audience applauded so loudly, the moderator had to ask them to stop to save precious time.

Political commentators widely agreed that Trump's threat to arrest Clinton was out-of-bounds. The jailing of political opponents is a despised practice used by dictators, not U.S. presidents. Still, Trump's voters liked what they heard. That gaslighting was in full effect. The media had a gripping new storyline. His opponents could dish out some legitimate moral outrage. His allies were thrilled to see Trump double down. And his surrogates knew they'd be in high demand, once again, to go out and explain why Trump was justified in saying yet another loathsome thing. (Steve Bannon would later describe a surrogate's willingness to defend Trump's comments on *Access Hollywood* as a "litmus test" of loyalty to Trump.) The gaslighting was obvious—Trump was never going to put Clinton in jail, but he reaped the benefits of forcing everyone to consider the fact that he would.

Trump's performance was good. So good that Pence hopped off the bench and deployed to Liberty University. "There's no place for believers on the sidelines in a time like this," he told the Christian audience. They weren't quite buying it. Pence only garnered some polite applause when he mentioned Trump's name. But when Pence started talking about Clinton, describing her as "unqualified," the mood turned. Pence received a standing ovation for the critique. They may have not been thrilled with Trump, but their distaste for Clinton would work just as well. Trump's gaslighting was working. The campaign found its way forward. They had regained control of the political environment.

The same arguments that worked to get Republicans behind Trump at the convention would work in the general election, too. Voters didn't have to like Trump; they just had to keep on hating Clinton. The only way Trump could win would be to keep torching away at Clinton and the mainstream media he accused of assisting her. At one rally Trump laid it all out. There was a vast left-wing conspiracy afoot to destroy him! He said:

> *"The establishment and their media neighbors wield control over this nation through means that are very well known—anyone who challenges their control is deemed a sexist, a racist, a xenophobe, and morally deformed. They will seek to destroy your career and your family. They will seek to destroy everything about you including your reputation. They will lie, lie, lie, and then again, they will do worse than that. They will do whatever's necessary."*

The crowd went wild. The Trump campaign was roaring back.

In the aftermath of the *Access Hollywood* tape, more than a dozen women came forward to accuse Trump of various forms of sexual misconduct dating back decades. Trump denied the allegations en masse. "Every woman lied when they came forward to hurt my campaign," Trump said during an October stop in Pennsylvania. "Total fabrication. The events never happened. Never. All of these liars will be sued after the election is over." (They weren't.) During one rally in North Carolina Trump said that one of the women who alleged that he molested her wasn't attractive enough for him. "Believe me, she would not be my first choice, that I can tell you," he said. A man in the crowd approvingly chanted, "We don't care! We don't care!" back at Trump. Trump supporters were going to vote for him anyway.

Trump survived his October surprise. Clinton didn't fare so well. All the fires that had been set through the campaign were about to explode in a grand finale of conspiracy and misinformation, as

Trump, the fake news writers, the Russian hackers, and the alt-right simultaneously went into overdrive to discredit Clinton.

On October 7, WikiLeaks started posting new batches of Russian-hacked emails, this time from Clinton campaign chairman John Podesta. The first round of Podesta emails was dumped only an hour after the first story about the *Access Hollywood* tapes was published by the *Washington Post*. Due to all the attention to the tapes, however, these emails gained little notice. But under the radar, the members of the alt-right were poring over them.

Trump knew well enough that most people had never read the emails, which were mostly mundane and tiresome to go through. He could put whatever spin he wanted on them and so he went before large crowds insisting the hacked emails confirmed every evil Hillary had ever been accused of. This was one of his usual tricks used in Step One of his gaslighting method to lay out a new, fake narrative—misquoting sources. Trump regaled crowds with the information he claimed WikiLeaks had produced. At rally stops through October Trump said things such as:

- "I love WikiLeaks."
- "Hillary Clinton, as WikiLeaks proves, is a corrupt globalist."
- "The WikiLeaks revelations have revealed a degree of corruption at the highest levels of our government like nothing we have ever seen as a country before."
- "The WikiLeaks revelations have exposed criminal corruption at the highest levels of our government."

It was all too easy for Trump. He could keep advancing these claims while denying any responsibility for the dumped emails. The suspense of more to come was always looming, and it all served to discredit Clinton and push Trump to his eventual victory. The DNC emails were a perfectly timed gaslighting package, practically gift-wrapped and hand-delivered to Trump by rogue hackers.

The Clinton-friendly Center for American Progress tracked Trump's mentions of WikiLeaks and found that he brought the subject up at least 164 times during the last thirty days of the campaign.

Still, the cosmos really didn't start turning against Clinton until October 28—eleven days before the election. That was the day FBI director James Comey dropped a bombshell. The FBI was re-opening its investigation into Clinton's email practices. Why? Law enforcement found Clinton emails, perhaps the ones missing from her secret server, on Anthony Weiner's computer—the former congressman married to Clinton aide Huma Abedin and who was under investigation for sexting with a minor. These weren't low-level associates, either. Weiner and Abedin were inner circle; Bill Clinton officiated their wedding ceremony. And, it turned out, Abedin had forwarded thousands of work emails to her husband's computer that were now being examined by the feds.

Comey said that normally he would not inform Congress about ongoing investigations, but this time was different. He had repeatedly testified to Congress that the investigation was completed. Now that wasn't true. He said in a letter to FBI employees that "it would be misleading to the American people were we not to supplement the record."

Right-wingers, particularly *Breitbart News* fans, were practically delirious with glee. The idea that Hillary Clinton, who stood by her cheating man, might go to jail because of stories pushed by self-declared members of the vast right-wing conspiracy about *another* sleazy guy in her inner circle sent jolts of glee through their systems. Weiner's undoing was already cherished as treasured folklore among *Breitbart News* fans, as their writers were the first to raise questions about his communications with young women and girls. The idea that it could take down Clinton's campaign was mind-blowing in the most gratifying way imaginable.

Clinton was helpless. She gave in to Trump's gaslighting at every step, thinking the smears and smut would all backfire on him and work in her favor eventually. He kept talking about things she didn't want to talk about, mainly her emails and her husband's infidelity.

She thought it best to quietly endure the onslaught. She bet voters would admire her stoicism. Wrong. All that did was allow Trump to drown the airwaves with his label of choice for her: Corrupt Hillary.

Which brings us back to October 28, that fateful day when these strange events came together in an exquisitely dire scenario for Clinton. On that day, the whole country learned that Hillary Clinton, the Democratic nominee for president, was under FBI investigation. A conspiracypocalypse was about to rain down on her. Using this information, Trump, his allies, the hackers, the fake news producers, and the alt-right would take their final shots discrediting Clinton. The gaslighting was near completion, all of them working toward their shared goal of defeating her.

Step Five was achieved in early morning hours on November 9, when the race was called and Donald J. Trump was named the next president of the United States. He had succeeded in the biggest gaslighting of his life. Clinton never knew what hit her.

PRESIDENT TRUMP

The bulk of this book is focused on what Trump said and did that helped him win the presidential contest because the campaign is where Trump's gaslighting showed itself in its purest form. The gaslighting looks a little different now that he's president, but if you look with a keen eye, you'll see him blazing away. Learn his methods now. The next campaign isn't far off. The 2018 midterms will present plenty of gaslighting opportunities, and before you know it, Trump's 2020 re-election campaign will be under way.

The difference is that Trump will have far more support among Republicans in 2018 and 2020 than he did when he announced his long-shot bid in 2015. I've felt the pressure.

After Trump's shocking victory, the questions started coming at me fast. "Will you finally support Trump now?" people asked me. I found the inquiries confusing. What did that mean, would I "support" Trump? He was the president. Of course I wanted him to do well. What on earth would obligate me to pledge my political allegiance to him, though? Like the magic of his win could cast a spell over me where I would now be willing to do his dirty work? If anything, I felt it was more important than ever that some Republicans hold the line. That's what I'd been doing during the whole election, my whole career, in fact. And people thought I would change? Washington was now an all-Republican town. If some of us Republicans weren't willing to exercise some much-needed discipline over President Trump and his allies, who would?

Even though Trump once told voters he would change—"I'm going to be so presidential you"—most people knew he never would. He was a seventy-year-old man who had gaslit his way to fame, fortune, and the most powerful elected office in the world. There would be no pivot to a more ethical, more presidential version of Donald Trump. He now had the government at his disposal, not merely a bunch of bungling freelance surrogates. That only meant more people would be working to spin his fabrications into truth, not fewer. He would have much smarter, more experienced people working for him than he had during the campaign.

The gaslighting would continue.

Before he was inaugurated, President-elect Trump tweeted, "In addition to winning the Electoral College in a landslide," he said, "I won the popular vote if you deduct the millions of people who voted illegally." Like every other conspiracy he touted, he didn't have any evidence for this, but it sounded like one of those things that could be true. Most of his followers were deeply suspicious of voter fraud by illegal aliens and Democratic party operatives anyway. It was an easy sell.

Per usual, Trump's media dittoheads got themselves booked to explain away his claim with their characteristically logic-free aplomb. "Everybody has a way of interpreting the truth, or not truth. There's no such thing, unfortunately, anymore of facts," Trump surrogate Scottie Nell Hughes said in an interview on *The Diane Rehm Show*. "And so Mr. Trump's tweet amongst a certain crowd, a large—a large part of the population—are truth. When he says that millions of people illegally voted, he has some—amongst him and his supporters, and people believe they have facts to back it up. Those that do not like Mr. Trump, they say that those are lies, and there's no facts to back it up." You might be inclined to dismiss Hughes's analysis, but Trump would later give a very similar assessment in an interview with ABC News anchor David Muir.

DAVID MUIR: Do you think that your words matter more now?

PRESIDENT TRUMP: Yes, very much.

DAVID MUIR: Do you think that talking about millions of illegal votes is dangerous to this country without presenting the evidence?

PRESIDENT TRUMP: No, not at all. Not at all because many people feel the same way that I do.

Feelings, not facts, are essential to a good gaslighting.

After well establishing his claim (Step One) and advancing the narrative in many more interviews and tweets (Step Two), Trump, predictably, upped the suspense (Step Three) with the announcement of a handpicked voter fraud commission in May 2017. But, its members couldn't obtain proof of millions of people voting illegally or of any policies that could create such a circumstance. No report was ever issued. Instead, Trump axed the commission in early January 2018. In an early-morning tweet the president said, "Many mostly Democrat States refused to hand over data from the 2016 Election to the Commission On Voter Fraud. They fought hard that the Commission not see their records or methods because they know that many people are voting illegally. System is rigged, must go to Voter I.D." See? The Democrats were to blame (Step Four). And, yes, Trump did claim victory (Step Five). An official White House statement announcing the elimination of the commission said, "Rather than engage in endless legal battles at taxpayer expense, today President Donald J. Trump signed an executive order to dissolve the Commission, and he has asked the Department of Homeland Security to review its initial findings and determine next courses of action." The defunct voter commission was an embarrassing failure, yet, in the Trumpian telling of these events, Trump was saving taxpayer money and moving on to something more effective. "Next courses of action" can mean only one thing: More rounds of gaslighting on this topic are ahead.

Trump lit another minifire—not a true gaslight; just a presidential warm-up—on his first day in office, prompting his top White House staff to rely on some of their surrogate secrets to try to keep up. The day after his inauguration, Trump complained that one of the TV networks had shown a photo that didn't adequately represent the size of his inauguration crowd. "It's a lie," Trump said, claiming that somewhere between 1 million and 1.5 million people attended and that his crowds extended from the U.S. Capitol all the way to the Washington Monument.

Press secretary Sean Spicer, plainly put up to it by his boss, summoned the press corps to the briefing room for the Trump administration's first official White House press conference. Armed with photographs that showed the crowd size from Trump's vantage point at the U.S. Capitol, Spicer went through the motions of berating the press pool for not recognizing it as "the largest audience to witness an inauguration—period—both in person and around the globe."

Spicer was trying to reframe Trump's argument into something more plausible—by pretending Trump said more people "witnessed" the inauguration, a figure that could feasibly include anyone who saw photos or videos of it on television or online, than actually attended it. (Remember the "play pretend" strategy in the Surrogate Secrets chapter?) After resigning from his White House job, Spicer said that he "absolutely" regrets telling this lie. That doesn't negate the fact, however, that during that time, the White House team was totally committed to spreading it. White House senior adviser Kellyanne Conway went to work next, trying to trumpsplain why MSNBC's Chuck Todd was not qualified to question their crowd estimates.

> **TODD:** What was the motive to have this ridiculous litigation of crowd size?
> **CONWAY:** Respectfully, your job is not to call things ridiculous that are said by our press secretary and our president. That's not your job. You're supposed to be a news person. You're not an opinion columnist.
> **TODD:** Can you please answer the question? Why did he do this? You have not answered it.

CONWAY: I'll answer it this way: Think about what you just said to your viewers. That's why we feel compelled to go out and clear the air and put alternative facts out there.

Alternative facts. Trump backers now felt entitled to their own set of facts when interpreting Trump. A sign of what was to come.

Then the president really outdid himself early one Saturday morning.

On March 4 at 6:35 a.m., President Trump began pounding out some alarming tweets. "Terrible! Just found out that Obama had my 'wires tapped' in Trump Tower just before the victory. Nothing found. This is McCarthyism!" Another tweet at 7:02 a.m.: "How low has President Obama gone to tapp [*sic*] my phones during the very sacred election process. This is Nixon/Watergate. Bad (or sick) guy!" He posted four tweets on the topic, ensuring that no one would miss the message.

Trump's tweets came against a backdrop of ongoing government inquiries about the Trump campaign's possible coordination with Russia during the election. Trump was again taking something that did contain a grain of truth—intelligence agents were investigating Trump associates, namely former campaign manager Paul Manafort—and twisting it into a much more scandalous narrative that would benefit him and impugn his critics. Step One.

Not missing a beat, Trump spokeswoman Sarah Huckabee Sanders went on ABC's *This Week* the next morning and said that Trump made the charge based on sources "that have led him to believe there was potential" of surveillance. By now the team was on to Trump's game. They were in sync. "Everybody acts like President Trump is the one that came up with this idea and just threw it out there," Sanders said. "There are multiple news outlets that have reported this." Trump was only repeating what *other people were saying*, you see. She offered no hard sources. You know how this goes. Step Two.

When Conway was asked directly if there was any evidence Trump Tower had been wiretapped, she offered some alternative facts of her own. "There was an article this week that talked about how you can surveil someone through their phones, certainly through their television sets, any number of different ways," she told a reporter. "And microwaves that turn into cameras, et cetera. So we know that that is just a fact of modern life."

To throw off the tough questions and buy some time, Trump needed to engage Step Three—some suspense. On March 15 Trump told Fox's Tucker Carlson, "Wiretap covers a lot of different things. I think you're going to find some very interesting items coming to the forefront over the next two weeks."

Trump's allies tried hard to produce some evidence.

Press secretary Spicer attempted to pass off a conspiracy—that President Obama used British spies to surveil Trump—espoused by Fox News pundit Judge Andrew Napolitano. After the White House spokesman referenced Napolitano's story, however, Fox News wouldn't back up their contributor. The network temporarily suspended him for spouting the misinformation. "Fox News cannot confirm Judge Napolitano's commentary; Fox News knows of no evidence of any kind that the now President of the United States was surveilled at any time in any way," anchor Shepard Smith said on the air. "Full stop."

When asked why the White House would reference false material, Trump denied responsibility. "All we did was quote a certain very talented legal mind, who was the one responsible for saying that on television," Trump said. "I didn't make an opinion on it. That was a statement made by a very talented lawyer on Fox. So you shouldn't be talking to me. You should be talking to Fox."

They dropped this storyline soon enough.

Trump then moved on to his next gaslight, on to a much bigger target. On May 9, he abruptly fired FBI director James Comey. Trump was on a mission, to turn Comey into the figurative poster boy of the Deep State. He was setting a new narrative to offset the idea that his campaign had colluded with Russia to win the election. Comey would be his villain.

Step Two came next. Trump simultaneously said he fired Comey because of the Russia investigation and had nothing to hide at the same time. During a discussion about it with NBC's Lester Holt, Trump said, "And in fact when I decided to just do it, I said to myself, I said you know, this Russia thing with Trump and Russia is a made-up story, it's an excuse by the Democrats for having lost an election they should have won." He advanced the story that the firing was all about Russia but denied there was anything substantive to it. Incredible.

Trump then executed Step Three, injecting lots of suspense and drama into the new narrative he had created. On May 12 Trump tweeted: "James Comey better hope that there are no 'tapes' of our conversations before he starts leaking to the press!" Soon enough, Washington tongues were wagging about the prospect of a secret taping system in the White House, à la Richard Nixon. From that point on Trump referred to Comey as a "leaker"—Step Four, the discrediting of Comey. Trump wanted everyone to believe that Comey was someone who couldn't be trusted.

Amazingly, Trump's tweet had the effect of compelling Comey *to* leak. Comey, the diligent agent, had created a paper trail to protect himself after an uncomfortable conversation that the president alluded to. Comey had documented the contents of the conversation in a memo and, through a friend, leaked it to the *New York Times* to get his side of the story out. Trump would later admit there were no "tapes, but he got what he wanted. He had made Comey into a leaker, a symbol of a nefarious Washington culture that was out to destroy Trump's presidency from within. Exactly the kind of storyline that would thrill, enrage, and rally his supporters to his side.

Trump's gaslighting of Director Comey was his way of gaining control over a story he had no control over. If the press was going to write damaging stories about his campaign's connections to Russia, he would do whatever it would take to flip the script and create more favorable headlines for himself. Russia was, he loved to say, "fake news." He gaslit Comey to convince his supporters that the real crimes were being committed by the people inside the government who were telling the media about those connections. Trump turned reality on its head.

His supporters inhaled his conspiracy theories on all counts.

Boston Herald writer Adriana Cohen was furious with the "fake news" about the Russia investigation that had "no proof." She wrote a piece that said: "The days of honest ethical journalism guided by fact, not political motives, have been replaced by agenda-driven activism by political operatives masquerading as mainstream journalists." Yes, my dears, you read that right. The Trumper who used the *National Enquirer* to smear me on live television was upset about the lack of "honest, ethical journalism in America." The schadenfreude would have been delicious had it not been so gagworthy.

Sean Hannity went on the air and told his millions of viewers that a "soft coup is under way right here in the United States, in an attempt to overturn November's election results and forcibly remove a duly elected president from office. Sinister forces quickly aligning, in what is becoming now, in my mind, a clear and present danger." For those living in Trumpland, black helicopters were flying everywhere. Fox Business's Lou Dobbs was similarly alarmed. "Our president is under constant barrage from all quarters, by the vapid but still venomous Dems on Capitol Hill, the left-wing national media, the toxic GOP elites and much of the orthodoxy who hate almost as much as the left and the deep state denizens," he said during one May broadcast. "That includes some of the wealthiest and most powerful people in this nation."

Trump's flacks became fully immersed in an alternative reality of Trump's making. After Special Counsel Robert Mueller was appointed to take over Comey's investigation, some insisted the development was, somehow, positive for Trump. "Sure," I thought to myself. "Like getting a cancer diagnosis is terrific news because it means you can look forward to chemotherapy—*SAID NO ONE EVER.*"

I had to object.

"Can we just cut through the crap!" I said to two Trump boosters—Kayleigh McEnany and Jack Kingston—during an appearance on Anderson Cooper's evening CNN program. "There's no rational world where this was good news for the Trump administration." As I had maintained since Trump burst on the political scene, he wasn't solely responsible for his missteps. His apologists were as well. "I want to know who's going to hold the Republicans accountable who enabled this man to go this far," I said to them directly. I told them:

"We knew from day one what kind of person Donald Trump was. We knew he had no respect for anyone, let alone the rule of law. So, I want to know what's going to happen to people like Reince Priebus who demanded everyone in the GOP pledge loyalty to this guy. And now all these Republicans are handcuffed to Trump. Where has this gotten us? Where are the people, the surrogates, that barked and clapped like circus seals in praise of everything this man did that was bad?"

I reminded the Trump supporters that their blind faith in Trump had led to "investigations as far as the eye can see!" It was stupefying. They were so loyal to Trump, even though he showed them no loyalty at all in acting so recklessly. "What has he done for you?" I said, turning to McEnany. "He's dragged you to a terrible place!" Couldn't they see what was happening? Couldn't they, for once, admit the truth of the situation? They could not. They were too far down the rabbit hole to ever get out.

16

NIXON'S SHADOW

One distinction between Trump's gaslighting as a candidate and his gaslighting as president is that when he was a candidate, there were no serious consequences for his fabrications. Being president is different. Lying and bullying can potentially become serious legal matters, such as perjury and obstruction of justice. The very same troubles that President Bill Clinton and President Richard Nixon learned can lead to impeachment or resignation.

While many were quick to draw the comparisons between Trump's Russia troubles and Nixon's Watergate scandal, the two men share much more than one name-brand controversy. Both presidents possessed some of the same stubborn qualities that, unfortunately, led them straight into scandal.

To start with, both men harbored deep resentments toward the press and rallied their base against it. What Nixon once described as the "silent majority" ignored by the press became Trump's "forgotten man." As Nixon wrote in one 1971 memo to H. R. Haldeman, "I cannot emphasize too strongly my feeling that much more than any single issue that we are going to emphasize, the discrediting of the press must be our major objective over the next few months." Trump discredited the press throughout his campaign and, as president, said "fake news" was the "enemy of the American people."

Like Nixon, Trump despises government leaks. Remember what

led Nixon to create the "plumbers unit" that was caught breaking into DNC headquarters at the Watergate Hotel in June 1972. That team was put together to hunt down and smear the leaker of the so-called Pentagon Papers to the *New York Times*. Had Nixon not taken such drastic action, Watergate might never have happened.

Perhaps most important, both men were able to inspire their aides to cast aside integrity to please the president. Seemingly unthinkable acts were easily justified, in their minds, in the name of loyalty and service to the commander in chief.

Anger at the press, hatred of government leaks, and an army of aides who blindly did their bidding—that's the toxic triad of qualities that led to Nixon's resignation and could doom Trump, too. Just as Nixon had his plumbers, Trump has his firemen, who are all too eager to assist in his gaslighting of America.

The similarities between their White Houses practically jump off the pages of Watergate history.

The head of Nixon's so-called plumbers unit, Egil "Bud" Krogh, who went to prison for his role, described the decision to break into the California office of the Pentagon Papers' leaker Daniel Ellsberg's psychiatrist as the "seminal event in the chain of events that led to Nixon's resignation on August 8, 1974." He said that Nixon's men were convinced that Ellsberg "was very likely at the center of a Soviet-sponsored conspiracy to diminish U.S. influence in the critical theater of Vietnam."

"It was an easy conclusion to reach, somehow made all the easier by the complete lack of corroborating evidence," Krogh wrote. Of the West Coast burglary, Krogh said, "Once undertaken, it was an action that could not be undone or explained away." There was no going back.

Nixon got away with that burglary, which made it all that much easier to carry out more. The Ellsberg break-in and the first bugging of DNC headquarters remained secret until the men returned to the Watergate *a second time* to adjust the devices and search for more files. That's when the arrests happened and the disastrous cover-up began.

As reporters investigated the story, Nixon's men defended their president to the hilt. His men used many of the very same words and phrases Trump would later employ himself as president—including the notion that government investigations into his activities were a "witch hunt." (One of Trump's preferred terms for describing the Russia investigation.)

Nixon re-election campaign chairman Clark MacGregor said, "Using innuendo, third-person hearsay, unsubstantiated charges, anonymous sources and huge scare headlines, the *Post* has maliciously sought to give the appearance of a direct connection between the White House and the Watergate." Now reread MacGregor's line, this time subbing the word "Russia" for "Watergate" and tell me if you don't think the exact same statement couldn't be issued from Trump's communications team.

Just as Trump has with the Russia investigation, Nixon expressed the belief that Watergate was an inside-the-Beltway scandal that only D.C. insiders cared about. "The reaction is going to be primarily in Washington and not the country because I think the country doesn't give much of a shit about bugging," Nixon told his aides four days after the final break-in. "Most people around the country think it's probably routine; everybody's trying to bug everyone else. It's politics."

The courts, as we all know, didn't take Nixon's view. What the Nixon White House tried to toss off as a "third-rate burglary" ultimately led to sixty-nine people being charged with crimes, forty-eight guilty pleas, and the resignation of an otherwise successful president. Without Watergate and the subsequent cover-up, Nixon would probably have become a GOP hero. He'd have been praised in the history books for his winning elections and foreign policy vision. Instead, he's the most disgraced president in American history. He blew it. All because of his irrational measures to retaliate against the *New York Times* and government leakers.

How on earth could it go so wrong? He didn't do it by himself. Nixon surrounded himself with yes-men. For a better understanding of those aides, one could not do any better than to examine the case of operative G. Gordon Liddy, who proposed far worse than what other aides were prosecuted for. Namely, the murder of a journalist, the kidnapping of protesters attending the 1972 Republican convention, sabotaging facilities used for the Democratic convention, the employ of women to sexually exploit Democratic operatives, and the firebombing of the Brookings Institution, where Nixon believed copies of the Pentagon Papers were housed.

Liddy is often depicted as a man alone, but Nixon pushed his staff to such lengths. One conversation captured on the Nixon tapes in which Nixon urged his staff to break into the Brookings Institution is deeply insightful to his reasoning. "Do you think, for Christ sakes, that the *New York Times* is worried about all the legal niceties?" he fumed. "Those sons of bitches are killing me. . . . We're up against an enemy, a conspiracy. They're using any means. We are going to use any means. Is that clear?"

Liddy bought into it all, explaining in his 1980 autobiography, *Will*, how committed he was to Nixon's view. His words show just how unglued someone can become in his loyalty to a president. When he accepted the job with Nixon's Committee for the Re-election of the President, unironically known as CREEP, he viewed it as if he were going to battle. Liddy explained:

> [T]he traditional backers of the Democratic Party among the media—The New York Times, The Washington Post, and networks—made it plain that we weren't in for a campaign in '72; it would be war. . . . I certainly had no reluctance to go to war. But it would be an undeclared war and what I would be doing was certainly illegal. I had no intention of failing any more than I would intend to be killed in a shooting war; the risk was there and in the event of failure, I would have to be prepared to accept the consequences.

He went on:

I knew exactly what had to be done and why, and I was under no illusion about its legality. Although spies in the enemy camp and electronic surveillance were nothing new in American presidential politics, we were going far beyond that. As far as I was concerned, anything went if it were merely malum prohibitum. There is a law of physics that every action has an equal and opposite reaction. I was ready to break that one, too, in reaction to the radical left and the whole drug-besotted 1960s "movement" that was attacking my country from within.

Liddy, however, took his loyalty to a murderous level. In another portion of the book, Liddy spoke frankly about plans he considered to kill columnist Jack Anderson, the recipient of government leaks. It was necessary to protect national security, he wrote: "As a direct result of an Anderson story, a top US intelligence source abroad had been so compromised that if not already dead, he would be in a matter of days. . . . That was too much. Something had to be done. . . . How many of our people should we let him kill before we stop him?"

Over lunch one day in the basement of the Hay-Adams Hotel, Liddy, Watergate mastermind E. Howard Hunt, and a retired CIA physician contemplated options. They debated the pros and cons of powdering the steering wheel of Anderson's car with LSD, poisoning his aspirin at home (Liddy called it "aspirin roulette"), staging a fatal hit-and-run, and a murderous mugging that could be chalked up to a local D.C. street crime. "If necessary, I'll do it," Liddy offered.

Hunt didn't take him up on it, but Liddy was so devoted that when the White House started taking heat for Watergate, he offered himself as a sacrificial lamb. Liddy told Nixon White House attorney John Dean, "If someone wants to shoot me . . . just tell me what corner to stand on and I'll be there, OK?" No one took Liddy up on his unsettling offer. Instead he was sentenced to twenty years in prison. He ultimately served fifty-two and a half months; his sentence was commuted to eight years by President Jimmy Carter and he was released on parole. From there Liddy went on to have a successful twenty-year career in conservative radio, retiring in 2009.

I had occasion to visit Liddy's radio studio once while promoting my 2006 book about Hillary Clinton. I'm embarrassed to admit it, but I had no clue how deeply he'd been involved in Watergate. My publisher's publicity department arranged for the interview. They preferred me to be in-studio, I was told. Dutifully, I reported to their offices in Ballston, Virginia, not having the slightest idea I would soon be sharing close quarters with a convicted felon who once plotted to kill a member of the media. Welcome to Washington.

Like Trump, Nixon also dabbled in gaslighting. Not many knew what gaslighting was at the time, though, and Nixon lacked a deliberate method like Trump's. But the lengths to which Nixon and his men went to tarnish one of their own as a mentally unstable woman when she tried to warn the press of what was happening behind closed doors needs airing.

Her name was Martha Mitchell. She was an insider, married to John Mitchell, Nixon's 1968 presidential campaign manager and attorney general. Unlike her law-and-order husband, however, she was a notorious gossip who enjoyed a drink and phoning reporters, often at the same time. In the beginning, the White House used her to their advantage. She was much more of a right-winger than Nixon and they would trot her out to rev up conservative audiences, content that her message would be accepted but confident that they wouldn't be held responsible for anything she said since she wasn't serving in any official capacity. In other words, she was an ideal surrogate. They called her their "secret weapon."

But then Martha started telling reporters that people were up to no good in the Nixon White House. While traveling with the Nixon campaign on a California fund-raising trip the weekend of the Watergate break-in, she picked up the phone with a really hair-raising story to tell. "That's it, I've given John an ultimatum," United Press International reporter Helen Thomas recalled Martha telling her in Thomas's

1999 book, *Front Row at the White House*. "I'm going to leave him unless he gets out of the campaign. I'm sick and tired of politics. Politics is a dirty business."

"Then suddenly, her voice became more agitated and she yelled, 'You get away. Just get away,' and the line went dead," Thomas wrote. She tried calling Mitchell back. A switchboard operator informed her, "Mrs. Mitchell is indisposed and cannot talk." Thomas then phoned John Mitchell in Washington to see what he thought had happened. "That little sweetheart," he told her. "I love her so much. She gets a little upset about politics but she loves me and I love her and that's what counts." Thomas thought his remarks were "bizarre." She wrote that other Nixon aides "began hinting that Martha was hallucinating, that she was deranged or that she was just drunk."

Upon arriving back at her apartment in New York City, Martha told Thomas what had happened. She had gone to California the weekend of June 16, 1972, for a campaign fund-raiser. That Saturday morning, June 17, Nixon staffers learned about the botched Watergate break-in and were quickly assembling to respond to the crisis. Rather than bring Martha back home to Washington, John Mitchell told her she deserved a restful stay. In reality, the campaign didn't want her to know what was unfolding. Instead of getting a vacation, she was being kept under close watch by FBI agents at the hotel. Nixon's staff knew she was an eavesdropper who sometimes rifled through her husband's work materials. They wanted her kept away, quarantined.

She said she opened up to Thomas because "I want to make sure my side is revealed and people know I'm not sitting here a mental case or an alcoholic." While in California, Martha eventually figured out what was going on and called Thomas. But the security detail watching over Martha caught her and ripped her phone out of the wall, causing the call to drop. That's why her initial call to Thomas ended so abruptly. Martha tried to escape but was put back into her room by FBI agents, cutting her hand so badly in one scuffle involving a glass door that she required stitches. Yes, Martha had been drinking; still, she was sure of what happened next. She was drugged. "They threw me down on the bed—five persons did it . . . pulled my pants down and stuck a needle in my behind, the longest needle you ever saw," Martha told Thomas. "I've never been treated like this before."

It all sounded too unbelievable to be true. FBI agents confining the attorney general's wife in a hotel? Pulling a phone out of the wall? Manhandling her? Injecting her with a sedative? But it was. Nixon aide H. R. Haldeman can be heard in the Nixon tapes that later went public confirming Martha's whole sordid story. In a June 29 conversation Nixon asked Haldeman if Martha had advance knowledge of her husband's role in the Watergate break-in. Haldeman said:

> No. That's part of what caused his problem, is that she found out. John didn't tell her that weekend about the fact that it was out in the papers, and after he left, she found it on television and read about it in the papers, and she blew her stack about that. That was what caused the tantrum, and she started drinking Kahlua, putting her hand through a window in the hotel, cut her hand all up. They did call a doctor, and they did throw her down in the bed and stick a needle in her ass, because they had to. She was demolishing the hotel.

Dr. Dan Kirkham, who treated Martha, said he was told she was an alcoholic who had gone into hysterics. He thought it reasonable she was heavily guarded "because you can't let the attorney general's wife go out and let everyone know she is an alcoholic." *Washington Post* publisher Ben Bradlee later recalled during a 1997 forum held to discuss the twenty-fifth anniversary of Watergate, "They tried to make her look like a 'nut case' and they succeeded to some extent." Harvard psychologist Brendan A. Maher later dubbed this the "Martha Mitchell effect" in a 1988 study about delusional thinking. Maher wrote that it was "an apt label to describe those people who correctly report what seem to be improbable events, and are judged to be deluded for doing so."

Like Trump, Nixon never gave up on his narrative. He never took responsibility for drugging Martha or for anything else to do with

Watergate. In fact, in the years after his resignation he blamed *her* for Watergate! "If it hadn't been for Martha, there'd be no Watergate because John wasn't mindin' that store," Nixon told British journalist David Frost in a series of TV interviews that aired in 1977. "You see, John's problem was not Watergate," Nixon said. "It was Martha. And it's one of the personal tragedies of our time." Even though his presidency was dead and Martha Mitchell was, too, Nixon never stopped gaslighting her.

Nixon knew the same thing Trump does. Gaslighting, that dirty trick, works. Even in the middle of the Watergate investigations Nixon won a convincing re-election in November 1972, in part by denying any and all wrongdoing. Nixon whipped Democratic candidate George McGovern by one of the largest margins in presidential history. He earned 61 percent of the vote, took 49 states, and won 520 Electoral College votes.

Nixon wasn't impeached, either. He resigned before the House Judiciary Committee could send its articles of impeachment to the full House for a vote and he could face trial in the Senate. A more stubborn president, less affected by the humiliation of public shaming, could have forced a standoff, daring members of his own party to impeach him in the House and convict in the Senate. Would Republicans have actually thrown Nixon out of office? We'll never know for sure.

Not long after being sworn in as president, Trump agreed to do an interview with *Time* magazine about his loose relationship with the truth. Most politicians, let alone a sitting president, would never agree to such a premise. Trump wasn't like them. He cared much more about Americans seeing his mug on the cover of the widely circulated publication than anything the actual story on the inside of its pages may say. He was so enamored with making the cover of *Time* that fake copies of the magazine's cover with Trump on it were hung in a number of his golf clubs for many years. (That is, until the *Washington Post* outed him and then *Time* officials asked him to remove them in June 2017.) In his real interview, however, Trump complained about how bad *Time* was to him. *Time*, he said, "treats me horribly, but obviously I will sell, I assume this is going to be a cover, too, have I set the record? I guess, right? Covers, nobody's had more covers."

"I think Richard Nixon still has you beat," the reporter replied. "But he was in office longer, so give yourself time." Nixon, indeed, had scored the most covers—fifty-five in total. Trump was oblivious to the fact that Nixon had done so largely because of his scandal-ridden presidency.

"Okay, good," Trump said. "I'm sure I'll win." He just might.

AFTERWORD: FIREPROOFING

Typically, gaslighting is a type of manipulation that takes place in one-on-one romantic relationships. Think of a cheating boyfriend who calls his girlfriend a "psycho" when she becomes suspicious about his late-night text messages from other women. Or the woman who convinces her husband that the leaky faucet, broken-down car, and inability to live out her dream lifestyle of the rich and famous is all his fault. In the worst cases, it becomes a debilitating form of mental abuse. Victims find themselves forced to defend themselves from outlandish accusations, trapped in unwinnable circular arguments, and apologizing for circumstances they have no control over. Victims live in a constant state of uncertainty and lose confidence in their ability to react to events. They become dependent on their gaslighters and unwilling to object to their statements and actions.

A psychologist would advise these victims to terminate the toxic relationship or, if it involves a family member, limit contact. Unfortunately, none of us have this choice when it comes to Donald Trump. He's the president. We're stuck.

I know. You still think there is a way out of this, don't you?

"Impeachment!" you say. I hate to break it to you, but even if Trump is impeached—a slim possibility historically—he's not going to give up his media megaphone. Doesn't matter if he's impeached, if he's censured, or if he loses his 2020 re-election in a landslide; he's not going to go away.

Don't believe me? Close your eyes and try picturing Donald Trump going gently into retired life to spend the rest of his days quietly playing golf and enjoying his two scoops of ice cream after dinner at the country club each night. Ha! I couldn't even write that sentence without laughing. Trump has never been content to fade into the background. There is no way, short of a straitjacket, ball gag, and padded room, that Trump is giving up the power and influence he has gained since becoming president.

In fact, he's already taken steps to ensure he'll have a voice on anything and everything to come: TrumpTV. Its short, low-quality commentaries from Trump supporters, spouting pro-Trump propaganda, regularly net 2 million views per video. Moreover, Trump will write books (or, more accurately, have them written for him), dabble in more reality TV, hit the speaking circuit, build more hotels, build his children up for their own careers; he'll do it all! He's Donald Trump! Wrap your head around the fact that he is a permanent fixture in the American landscape. Resistance is futile.

More imminently, there is the 2020 election and he will have more influence than ever. As president, he controls one of the most powerful platforms in the world. He's bigger than Fox News, bigger than Facebook, bigger than the *New York Times*. During the 2016 campaign, the *Huffington Post* attempted to confine Trump to its entertainment section, refusing to acknowledge him as a serious candidate. No one has that option this time around.

He will soon begin laying the groundwork for his re-election campaign. So, as much as I hate to tell you this, the gaslighting will continue. It won Trump the 2016 election. Why wouldn't he use the same playbook in 2020?

What are we going to do about it? Well, reading this book is a good start! You can't tackle a problem until you know exactly what it is. You recognize what he's doing now. You've felt crazy, confused, fed up, flustered, and all bejiggity for a reason. It's not you, it's him. Truly. Now the hard part. (Take a deep breath.) Accept the fact that Trump's gaslighting cannot be stopped. Yes, that's right. The. Gaslighting. Cannot. Be. Stopped.

Listen to me. If he wants to keep doing it—practically guaranteed—who is going to prevent him from doing so? No one is going to run to the podium and throw his or her body between him and a media microphone as a human sacrifice to block him from spreading the next big lie. No number of liberal pundits rocking themselves in a corner and muttering "This is not normal" to themselves will have any impact on him. Trump is not going to wake up one day and have an epiphany and think, "Gee, maybe now I will refrain from my wicked ways." Forget it.

Trump's gaslighting is something you, and the rest of America, will have to endure for the foreseeable future. What I can tell you is how to cope. I can tell you how to stay sane and think through this.

To start, I need to talk to you about how we, as people, need to adapt to this environment. Then we have to consider how candidates who compete directly in this new political world Trump created will need to change, too.

First, us. The people and the media.

Let go of the outrage already. It's too exhausting to keep up and it plays right into Trump's (imaginarily large) hands anyhow. Pushing people to the point of hysterics is the goal of gaslighting. Don't give in to it. Be concerned, be engaged, be vigilant but don't flip out. Take another deep breath. Take many.

Go back to Step One of Trump's gaslighting method: the narrative. When Trump blurts out something new about the next off-the-wall subject, ask yourself what his objective might be. Why is he focusing on this particular person or thing? What he's saying may not be the real message he's pushing.

When Trump floated the birther theory against Obama, it was not to make him produce a paper documentation of his citizenship, but to tap into the idea that Obama was not a legitimate president. Remember, Trump didn't lean into birtherism during Obama's first presidential election when the theory presented itself. Trump dove into the fever swamp in 2011, during Obama's re-election when Republicans were infuriated with what they viewed as constitutional overreaches and were willing to get rid of him at any cost—even if it meant going along with a smear. Trump embraced birtherism to signal to the Republican base that he was willing to beat the Democrats using any and all tools available. The same was true when it came to his eagerness to talk about President Clinton's infidelity.

Trump will need new narratives for the 2020 campaign. What he comes up with will be wholly dependent on the candidates, interest groups, and media entities that stand in his way. But if you want to try predicting what issues Trump will attach himself to next, look for controversial issues that present a clear dividing line among the public and an upside for Trump's coalition. (Confederate memorials and NFL protests are good examples.) The possibilities are endless once you begin thinking outside of the typical political box of Republican versus Democrat and liberal versus conservative.

Blunting the effectiveness of Step Two—the advance-and-deny stage—is more complicated. Voters and media professionals especially should question Trump's references to "what other people are saying." He's the president. What are his actual sources? He doesn't rely on government statistics, academic reports, and RAND studies for research. He, like a lot of other people, surfs social media, consumes cable-TV news, and talks to his buddies. Sometimes his information can be pinpointed to an actual piece—say, a segment on *Fox & Friends*, a rogue tweet, or a blaring headline from the *National Enquirer*. Other times, he's repeating something somebody told him on the golf course. The key is pinning him down on where he's getting the information. Trump's critics often accuse him of "making things up," but he rarely does. He's passing along gossip that's already making its way through the grapevine. Next, stop asking Trump to retract or apologize. He never will. Ask him to explain himself. That's where he struggles. No interviewer should waste his or her breath attempting to get Trump to take back something he said or did. He will always double down and reap the benefit of demonstrating to his supporters, yet again, the strength of his convictions, however misguided they may be.

When Trump engages the advance-and-deny stage of his gaslighting, feel free to tune out. This is usually the point where the media goes bananas, endlessly speculating and debating what exactly it is that Trump is saying. This is where far too much of Trump's dirty work is done for him. One comment will explode into hundreds of breathless clickbait articles. Think of it as Trump spam and most of it is unsolicited, worthless junk.

Try to add some substance to your media diet. For every article you are tempted to share about something Donald Trump said or did, try to share a couple of articles about something else. You have other hobbies, yes? Cooking, gardening, automotive repair? Okay, I see you rolling your eyes. You are reading this book. Politics is your hobby. Mine, too. So, a more practical suggestion: If you are only posting about politics, at least balance out Trump-centric news with posts about real legislation or local elections. Be conscious of falling into Trump's trap. It's not all about him unless you make it all about him.

If you can identify a good clickbait headline, you are more than capable of fireproofing yourself from Trump's Step Three, the suspense building. His favorite words to use are: "We'll see." The information is always coming "soon," usually in "two weeks." It's cookie cutter. Most of the time, he's stalling and buying time, waiting for some turn of events to give the story more oxygen. It's a headline that goes nowhere. Informed news consumers—you!—should realize this is when Trump's story deserves to die. Ideally, members of the media should resist the temptation to speculate about what the promised information may say or be and let the story expire. (Unlikely.) But, Trump's narratives would be more effectively countered if voters and the media mounted heavy pressure on Trump to deliver the goods. He rarely does. Boxing him in at this step and making it well known that he cannot prove his allegations to be true offers the best chance of mitigating Trump's gaslighting.

By the time Trump gets to Step Four—the discrediting—people are usually fully engulfed in his gaslighting. The best one can do is try to see what's coming next. Twitter is his tool of choice for this stage. It's the platform where he tests his jabs. (The *New York Times* maintains a list of all the people, places, and things Trump has insulted on Twitter since becoming president. Last time I checked, he was up to 650.) A lot of people think Trump flings barbs for sport and to satisfy his ego, but you know otherwise because you're reading this book. He tests a lot of words and phrases on Twitter to see what gains traction. The Twitter metrics are like ratings. He can see in real time what branding is working.

It may feel good to support and defend the object of his attacks, but many times he's only finding a way to make you spread the gaslighting flames for him. He loves making people pick sides and fight one another. You have to examine whether the choice he's asking you to make is a false one before rushing to a corner and lacing up your boxing gloves.

Finally, there is Trump's last step: winning. Trump has convinced many of his most hard-core supporters that even the worst kind of political news is, somehow, sunshine and roses for Trump. Case in point, after CNN reported that Trump campaign manager Paul Manafort had been wiretapped by federal investigators, *Breitbart News* ran the following headline: "Trump Vindicated: Shock Report Says Obama Government Wiretapped Trump Campaign." It should not have to be said, but it does: News that someone's campaign manager was under federal investigation is not a selling point for that candidate. Somehow, this still became a relatively popular talking point among the pro-Trump media. Yes, Trump was right! He does hire extremely questionable people with a considerable lack of ethical bounds. That's . . . a good thing? Give me a break.

When someone says Trump is winning or "vindicated," consider this. Would that source suffer any consequences if they admitted otherwise? Or are they somehow invested, either monetarily or psychologically, in his success? Is his loss their loss as well? Therein lies the difference between a passionate Trump superfan and an aspiring Trump cultist. (Okay, I'm only halfway joking about the cult, although I am pretty sure some kind of blood-oath ceremony is required to

write for *Breitbart News* these days.) But there is a way to tell if someone is a real conspiracist.

The test, for all conspiracy theories, comes down to a scientific concept called "falsifiability." It sounds counterintuitive, but for a scientific theory to be true, there must be something that could prove it
untrue. The same goes for conspiracies. Like, say, the political system
is controlled by lizard people, which a 2013 Public Policy Polling survey found 12 million Americans believe.

The thing that makes the conspiracy theory successful is that there
is no way to disprove it. Supposed signs of being a lizard person are
said to include having low blood pressure, light-colored eyes, and the
ability to shape-shift. The fact that no one has been caught transform-
ing into reptilian form only deepens the conspiracy. The cover-up is
bigger than you could ever know! Everyone is in on it. The CIA, the
United Nations, the Illuminati—and they're all out to get us!

You see how this goes. Every successful conspiracy requires that
the lack of proof for the theory also be proof of the theory. This is why
they persist. There is no way to prove them wrong.

One question can determine whether you are dealing with either
a conspiracy theorist or someone who may be able to explain some
questionable phenomena. "What evidence would prove this isn't
true?" If the answer is nothing, back away slowly. You're dealing with
a full-blown conspiracy theorist! There's no use in the conversation
aside from the entertainment value. If you take it seriously, you'll only
spin around in dizzying logic circles until you fall flat on your face.

The same goes for Trump's die-hard defenders who keep telling us
that every setback he suffers is, somehow, evidence of his divine genius that most people are incapable of comprehending. He's playing
4D chess, while everyone else is playing checkers, they say. It's just not
true. For all things regarding Trump and his die-hard adherents, you
have to keep your sense of perspective. Picture them saying the same
things with big, red clown noses on their faces if that helps. Resist the
strong temptation to shout "THAT IS WRONG" or "YOU ARE IN-
SANE" from the rooftops, because you'll only make yourself look nuts

in the process. Meaning, Trump wins. Thanks to the wisdom of our Founding Fathers, Trump doesn't have that much control over our lives. Don't give him any more than he already has.

Now for the second part of this discussion: how political candidates can fireproof themselves in this new gaslit America. There are three things that must be done.

In the past, candidates were praised for their ability to stay on message. They had "message discipline." I've sat through media training classes and campaign schools where a consultant will instruct people that when they are being interviewed by a reporter, they should completely ignore the question asked and instead deliver the answer they'd like people to hear. It would go something like this.

> **REPORTER:** When are you going to release your tax returns?
> **CANDIDATE:** I believe in world peace.
> **REPORTER:** Huh? I asked you about your tax returns.
> **CANDIDATE:** I said I believed in world peace.
> **REPORTER:** But when are you going to release your tax returns?
> **CANDIDATE:** If I am elected, I will work tirelessly to secure world peace.

A successful interview! The reporter didn't knock the candidate off message! The candidate got his or her message out. Er . . . and the candidate sounded like a doofus. This kind of advice may have worked in the past, but the bar for authenticity is much higher today. Those who insist on such message discipline are taking a sitcom-script approach to a reality TV–obsessed world. These sorts of answers are as artificial as a laugh track. To see how such a strategy turns out in real actual life, look at Marco Rubio's New Hampshire debate performance, widely credited with dooming his presidential candidacy and earning him the moniker "Robot Rubio."

> **RUBIO** (13 minutes and 56 seconds into the debate): And let's dispel once and for all with this fiction that Barack Obama doesn't know what he's doing. He knows exactly what he's doing.

RUBIO (16 minutes and 24 seconds): But I would add this. Let's dispel with this fiction that Barack Obama doesn't know what he's doing. He knows exactly what he's doing. He is trying to change this country.

At this point, Chris Christie smelled blood in the water and hammered Rubio for using the "memorized 25-second speech that is exactly what his advisers gave him." The audience applauded. Still, Rubio couldn't drop it.

RUBIO (18 minutes and 03 seconds): Here's the bottom line. This notion that Barack Obama doesn't know what he's doing is just not true. He knows exactly what he's doing.

"There it is, there it is!" Christie interjected. "The memorized 25-second speech. There it is, everybody." Yet Rubio painfully stuck to the script.

RUBIO (18 minutes and 20 seconds): We are not facing a president that doesn't know what he's doing. He knows what he is doing. That's why he's done the things he's done.

Groan. Worse, the talking point Rubio was so faithfully delivering was confusing. What was he trying to say, exactly? That Obama was intentionally destroying the country because of some deep-seated hatred of America? Because of his secret desire to turn the United States of America into a socialist nation? What? Out with it already!

Now look how Trump stepped in to clarify the garble and say exactly what he thought in a way everyone could understand.

TRUMP (28 minutes and 5 seconds): Marco said earlier on that President Obama knows exactly what he's doing. Like we have this president that really knows. I disagree respectfully with Marco. I think we have a president who, as a president, is totally incompetent, and he doesn't know what he's doing. I think he has no idea what he's doing. And our country is going to hell. So I just want to say we disagree on that.

Well, gee, that makes sense, doesn't it? Trump didn't spend hours dreaming up the line in hours of debate prep, either. Here lies the key to the first way candidates are going to have to change. This is going to sound simple, but it's not. CANDIDATES HAVE TO TALK AND ACT LIKE REAL PEOPLE.

Yes, this is very hard. Because politicians are, by and large, not normal people. They don't even dress normal. The idea of message discipline has been overapplied to image discipline, too. How did it come to be that every male politician doesn't leave the house without a blue suit, red tie, flag pin, and gelled side part? Recall the Romney-Ryan 2012 GOP presidential ticket. Both of them fit. Model hair. Twinkly eyes. Chiseled features. Orthodontic-commercial-worthy gleaming teeth. It was like they came out of some Republican prototype factory. (Steve Bannon once complained that Ryan was created "in a petri dish by the Heritage Foundation.") Looking a little disheveled once in a while can be endearing to the rest of us schlubs. Because the contrast between the D.C. stiff-suit crowd and the rest of America walking around in Under Armour athleisure is jarring. Trump's red MAGA hat does more than showcase his slogan and keep his elaborate hairdo in place on windy days. It keeps him real.

Female politicians have a uniform, too. Jewel-toned dress or pantsuit, one monochrome color from head to toe, with a carefully planned piece of flair, whether it be scarf, chunky necklace, or drop earrings. (I call Hillary Clinton's particular ankle-to-neck look "Mao chic.") Only the most risk-taking female politicians will dare to wear an open-toe shoe or (gasp!) leather knee boots. Orthopedic heels for everyone else. Mix it up. There are, I'm sure of this, thousands of other fashion options for women and style blogs dedicated to accessorizing professional women. Give them a look. If that's too much work, ladies, do this. Google "Nikki Haley." She brings plenty of approachable style to work and never sacrifices an ounce of professionalism doing it.

Or just put on some comfortable clothes. Maybe that will help. Go ahead and sit through your prep sessions with the policy nerds and lawyers. Then go to the local bar and chug a couple of alcoholic beverages of your choice and try explaining your platform to some people on barstools.

When people are polled about politicians they would like to have a beer with, what they are really being asked is who could they hang out with and talk about politics with in a way that is not painful, boring, or, worse, annoying. Trump, who doesn't even drink, passes the beer-hall test. Hillary Clinton, no matter how many vodka shots she did with John McCain, could not walk into a watering hole without a $100,000 speaking fee, Huma, Secret Service protection, and a list of preapproved questions. Part of appearing as "a normal" means being able to go to places and do normal things. Donning blackout sunglasses as if you're on a secret special-ops mission to a Midwest Chipotle, as Hillary Clinton did on the campaign trail, is not normal. Not driving yourself in a car, which Clinton has reportedly not done since 1996, is not normal. Meanwhile, Trump happily tweets photos of himself enjoying a taco bowl on Cinco de Mayo and the liberals work themselves into a huffing, puffing political outrage. (Haven't they ever gone out for tacos and margaritas on Cinco de Mayo? No wonder they're so uptight!)

How desperate are voters for politicians who come close to understanding the actual American culture we all live in? For the time, Kid Rock is a plausible Republican candidate for the United States Senate. Moreover, his messaging on health care wasn't all that bad.

ROCK: It seems the government wants to give everyone health insurance, but wants us all to pay. And to be very frank, I really don't have a problem with that, since God has blessed me and made my pockets fat. But redistribution of wealth seems more like their plan. And I don't believe you should save, sacrifice, do things by the book and then have to take care of some deadbeat, milking the system, lazy a** mother****ing man.

Sure, he needs some editing, but understanding his message didn't require an internship with the Joint Committee on Taxation.

My second piece of advice for candidates: Talk big. Be fresh. Sell the dream.

The concept was once explained to me like this. When someone says to you, "Let me take you on a trip to Hawaii!" what do you imagine? You see yourself sitting on the beach, putting your toes in the sand, and taking a dip in the water, right? Of course. What if someone says, "Let's spend hours coordinating our calendars, searching for affordable flight tickets, packing our bags, parking at the airport, going through security, having our flight delayed, going through turbulence, losing our luggage, waiting for a taxi, arriving at the hotel, and then go to the beach, put our toes in the sand, and take a dip in the water"? Eh, doesn't sound so fun.

There is the reason why the saying goes "the devil is in the details." That's where all the trouble happens. So, a successful politician usually avoids talking about them at all costs. President Obama knew this when he was running on "universal health-care coverage" in 2008. He had no preset legislative plan and CBO score for it. We didn't have any idea what Obamacare would look like until years later when Congress hammered it all out. (Congress didn't even understand what the bill was. Before voting, Speaker of the House Nancy Pelosi said, "We have to pass the bill so you can find out what is in it.") But he was the candidate promising something big and fresh. I'm not saying Obamacare worked out beautifully or this is an upstanding way to campaign. What I'm saying is that Obama got it passed. Mostly because he didn't box himself into anything specific early on.

Trump did the same in his announcement speech. He said, "I would build a great wall—and nobody builds walls better than me, believe me, and I'll build them very inexpensively. I will build a great, great wall on our southern border. And I will have Mexico pay for that wall." "But how! There's no plan!" the media hollered. Trump didn't care. He just kept saying "I will build the wall and Mexico is going to pay for it." The thousands of people coming to his rallies didn't care how. They just wanted to hear the wall was getting built. Trump was taking them to Hawaii! *Whoo-hoo* let's go!

Contrast that with how Jeb Bush explained his position on immigration during the first Republican debate.

> **BUSH:** I believe that the great majority of people coming here illegally have no other option. They want to provide for their family. But we need to control our border. It's our responsibility to pick and choose who comes in. I've written a book about this and yet this week I did come up with a comprehensive strategy that really mirrored what we said in the book. . . .

Zzzzz . . . Book?! This is the Republican debate where Bush was asked a question about his immigration plan and he referenced a book he wrote on the subject? Props to him for thinking through the issue, but for heaven's sakes, don't do it in real time with voters.

He isn't the only one to make this mistake. Many politicians will often reference their mountains of white papers, books, and previous speeches as a means of answering questions instead of actually answering the question. I get that it's tiresome to have to repeat something you may have previously stated in a thoughtful and eloquent way somewhere else, but that's too bad. A candidate can't expect people to go look it up when the candidate is right there in the flesh for the very purpose of answering questions.

Hillary Clinton tells a sad little story, mainly because of how tone-deaf it is, in her book *What Happened* about how she was eviscerated for some poorly chosen remarks at an Ohio town hall event. When asked about the loss of jobs in the area, she said:

> *I'm the only candidate who has a policy about how to bring economic opportunity using clean renewable energy as the key into*

*Coal Country. Because we're going to put a lot of coal miners and
coal companies out of business.*

Her plan for green energy is so great that coal miners are going to
lose their jobs? Say that again? Obviously, that answer didn't go over
well with coal miners. Yet in the book she lamented, "I had proposed a
comprehensive $30 billion plan to help revitalize and diversify the
region's economy. But most people had never heard of that. They
heard a snippet that gave the impression that I was looking forward to hurting miners and families." Yep. She actually thought
coal miners were going to go online and read her policy plan after
she threatened to put them out of work standing right there on live
TV? No way. Forget it, they are going to the Trump rally instead.
MAGA!

Clinton didn't know how to go big. Honestly, not many people do,
but I can tell you two people who did. Obama and Trump—the two
most recent winning presidential candidates. You can't lose by going
too big. It's impossible. President Obama sold "hope," for goodness'
sakes. How much bigger can you get than that? Trump, "Make America Great Again."

If a candidate can't go big with a simple slogan, there's a major mal-
function somewhere in the wires. Here's a test. Take a look at these
2016 presidential campaign slogans.

HILLARY CLINTON: *Stronger Together.*

BERNIE SANDERS: *A Political Revolution Is Coming.*

TED CRUZ: *Courageous Conservative: Reigniting the Promise of America.*

JOHN KASICH: *K for US.*

RAND PAUL: *Defeat the Washington Machine. Unleash the American
Dream.*

JEB BUSH: *Jeb Can Fix It.*

MARCO RUBIO: *A New American Century.*

BEN CARSON: *Heal. Inspire. Revive.*

BOBBY JINDAL: *Tanned, Rested, Ready.*

MIKE HUCKABEE: *From Hope to Higher Ground.*

CHRIS CHRISTIE: *Telling It Like It Is.*

CARLY FIORINA: *New Possibilities. Real Leadership.*

SCOTT WALKER: *Reform. Growth. Safety.*

RICK SANTORUM: *Restore the American Dream for Hardworking Families.*

LINDSEY GRAHAM: *Ready to Be Commander-in-Chief on Day One.*

GEORGE PATAKI: *People over Politics.*

RICK PERRY: *We Must Do Right and Risk the Consequences.*

Only one of these slogans, arguably, went big, although the underlying weakness in the country it implied was rather depressing (Clinton). Some mistook ambiguity for bigness (Rubio, Carson, Fiorina). Too many were too hung up on trying to sell the candidate instead of an overarching cause (Cruz, Kasich, Christie, Bush). Some were too narrow (Santorum, Graham). Some sounded scary (Sanders, Paul, Perry). Some were just dumb (Jindal, Pataki). There are lots of ways to screw this up and not many candidates get it right. It's not easy. But if the slogan doesn't inspire and invite the largest possible number of your voters to place the campaign's sign in their yards or wear the campaign's T-shirt, I can tell you you're doing it wrong.

My third and last piece of advice: Start gaslighting a little. No, I do not mean making up deranged stories to smear your opponents. What I mean is, take control of the narrative. That's what Trump does best.

There is no "24/7" media anymore. It is now the "86,400 second, 1440 minute, 24 hours a day, 7 days a week" media. Network TV, cable TV, Twitter, Facebook, Instagram, YouTube, newspapers, radio, magazines, websites, blogs, and podcasts are churning out political content second by second, minute by minute, hour by hour, day by day. You must feed the beast, or you will be eaten by it.

I knew this back when Cruz's presidential campaign was being launched. We had a big meeting where it was somewhat agreed upon, not by me, that he would roll out his announcement with a *Wall Street Journal* op-ed and then do a normal round of TV interviews the next morning. After already having lost the argument about his slogan, I figured I didn't have anything to lose and roasted this approach in front of everyone. Why would we trust the *WSJ*, which had spent many an editorial trashing Cruz, with the announcement? Of course he should do the interviews, but why would we let morning TV hosts who weren't all that friendly to Cruz shape the story in those first critical hours?

My idea was to instead let it leak on early Sunday evening that an "announcement was coming" and to get social media fired up in anticipation. We would get the benefit of having all our friends online tweeting out the story rather than having some huffy journalists do it for us. I knew the headlines they would write. Stuff like "Washington's Most Hated Man Announces Bid to Run Washington." Uh-uh. We had to go around them. We could do it with a tweet, posted late in the evening when most of them were sleeping, with the big news. At 12:09 a.m. on March 23, 2015, Ted Cruz announced. Our friends stayed up to get it firsthand and Twitter exploded, in the best way possible. When the press caught up to it in the morning, part of the story was the merry reception Cruz had received online the previous night.

On Monday, he was off to make it official in a speech at Liberty University (another surprise!), which was carried live by most of the networks largely because of the sneaky nature of the announcement. Another unfiltered opportunity for Cruz to get his message out. No media sit-down required. It all worked like a charm. Cruz had a fabulous rollout. All on his terms, not on the mainstream media's. That's how you create a narrative. *No lies required.*

Of course, not everyone has a presidential announcement to make. But there are a few gaslighting tricks candidates can use guilt-free.

GET PEOPLE TALKING: Don't be afraid to stoke speculation, whether it be about an announcement, a press event, or a policy plan. Let a press person leak to the media that you are thinking about something and then, *whoosh*, let them do some of the thinking for you. Buzz is good and it can be okay to let people spitball about what's coming. Watch what happens. See if it catches how you'd like. You might even get some ideas about how to improve it or, even better, it could save you from making a major mistake. Far easier to kill a bad idea before it turns into something real.

PLAN SOME SURPRISES: People love a curveball. Bring some unexpected guests to an event. Give people some insight into your personality with a few social media posts. Even some hokey Instagram shots of food from your favorite restaurants, parks, and shops (nothing too swanky!) will do to break up the political monotony. Do some interviews with unlikely media figures. If President Obama can sit down and talk with everyone from the green-lipstick-wearing, cereal-bathing GloZell to Anthony Bourdain, you can, too. Get out of your safe spaces.

FIGHT BACK!: While most people don't like candidates who go around picking fights, they expect candidates to stand up for themselves. Trump often went around (rhetorically) punching people by claiming he was a victim. "I'm a counterpuncher!" he'd say. That's because one can get away with almost anything (even shooting people in the middle of Fifth Avenue) if it's done in self-defense.

If you are attacked, fairly or unfairly, come back swinging. You should be secretly thankful for a cheap shot. It gives you the moral high ground to give a bully a well-deserved smack in the face. What red-blooded American doesn't cheer that? We relish a good political fight and hate it when someone walks away from one. A word of caution, though. An all-out counterassault is almost never necessary. Many times a well-placed jab will do the job. One of my favorites came recently when Chris Christie slammed Ted Cruz for criticizing the wasteful spending in the 2010 Hurricane Sandy bill while Texas was dealing with the aftermath of Hurricane Harvey. When asked for a comment Cruz kept it short. He told a reporter that Christie should "go back to the beach," reminding everyone where Christie was found sunning himself during his own state's budget crisis earlier that summer. In other words, "Shut up, punk."

GO ALL IN: Whatever you are selling, commit to it 100 percent. If you cannot project total confidence in your plans, why would anyone else? Trump's overuse of superlatives invites eye-rolls but remains effective. It piques curiosity and imagination and, most important, conveys a sense of success. Enthusiasm is contagious. If you say you have the biggest, greatest ideas about how to change Washington, there must be something to it, right? Tell me more. We want to believe. We are drawn to people who chase dreams, however deluded they might be. We can't help it! We are moths drawn to the gaslighting flame. Use it to your advantage!

APPENDIX I

O nce you are familiar with Trump's gaslighting method, you'll see how Trump uses it all the time. Not only that, you won't be able to unsee it in his interviews, speeches, press conferences, and rallies. The steps of his method will keep jumping out at you. Go ahead, apply the following ripped-straight-from-the-headlines template below to whatever he is messaging and amaze your friends with your ability to predict what the president of the United States says and does next!

STEP ONE

Trump sets the narrative by appearing on *Fox & Friends*, or a similarly unchallenging outlet, to float a wild claim uncontested. He tells the anchors, "I'm starting to wonder about [INSERT CLAIM]." Alternatively, he will tweet the new narrative sometime between 6 a.m. and 9 a.m. to drive the day's news cycle. For this option, Saturday mornings, when there is little other major news to compete with, are preferable.

STEP TWO

Once reporters start making incredulous inquiries about whether Trump really believes what he just said, Trump will advance and deny the story, preferably in a sit-down with a mainstream reporter such as ABC News's Jonathan Karl, where the question is posed to him directly. Trump will respond, "You know, some people say [INSERT

CLAIM]. I'm saying I don't know. Nobody knows and you don't know, either." He will often vaguely reference unverified tabloid news stories, Internet rumors, or YouTube videos. If Trump is feeling particularly cheeky, he may even hold a rally and shout out something such as "I'm not going to say [THE CLAIM] because I'm not allowed to say it, because I want to be politically correct. So, I refuse to say [THE CLAIM]."

STEP THREE

To maintain interest in his implausible story, Trump will promise that more information will soon be produced to prove that [INSERT CLAIM] is correct. "I will tell you about that sometime in the very near future," he might say during a Rose Garden press conference or other media availability. His preferred time frame is "two weeks." He will vow to share the information "as soon as I can, as soon as possible with the American people so the full truth will be known and exposed."

Trump will lead people to believe the missing information may come in the form of an email, a video, a pending announcement, or a report. To avoid answering questions at this step, Trump may even say, "I'll keep you in suspense."

STEP FOUR

Whenever anyone poses some kind of threat to Trump's contention that [INSERT CLAIM], he will take to Twitter to discredit them. His favorite adjectives include, but are not limited to, "loser," "sad," "weak," "dumb," "failing," "overrated," "phony," and "crazy." Name-calling will be repeated in interviews, at rallies, and in other public forums as desired. The verbal assaults will cease only when and if the target of the insults recants and pledges support to Trump.

STEP FIVE

Trump will say he won the argument about [INSERT CLAIM]. He may tell those who say otherwise about [INSERT CLAIM] by saying, "I can't be doing so badly, because I'm the President and you're not." Trump will brag about his ability to command a large crowd, win polls, and net big TV ratings to prove his wisdom about [INSERT CLAIM]. Any data showing otherwise will be dismissed as being "dishonest" or "rigged" against him.

APPENDIX II

Trump's *Art of the Deal* ghostwriter came up with the phrase "truthful hyperbole" to help gloss over Trump's obvious fibbing, but the broader explanation of why Trump exaggerates so much applies now more than ever. Take a look at this passage from the 1987 bestseller.

> *The final key to the way I promote is bravado. I play to people's fantasies. People may not always think big themselves, but they can still get very excited by those who do. That's why a little hyperbole never hurts. People want to believe that something is the biggest and the greatest and the most spectacular. I call it truthful hyperbole. It's an innocent form of exaggeration, and a very effective form of promotion.*

As president, Trump frequently uses hyperbole to play up his accomplishments and attack critics, often invoking the words "never before" and "in history" to dramatize his acts. Below is a compilation of how he has done so since taking office. Some of the views expressed are solely his opinion; most are demonstrably false. The takeaway, however, is how well Trump plays up his meager accomplishments. *The Art of the Deal*'s foundation is wholly dependent on Trump's eagerness to *sell*. And, in every deal he makes, he claims all of the upside and none of the downside.

"I have been on their cover, like, 14 or 15 times. I think we have the all-time record in the history of Time Magazine. Like, if Tom Brady is on the cover, it's one time, because he won the Super Bowl or something, right? I've been on it for 15 times this year. I don't think that's a record, Mike, that can ever be broken."
>—Trump speaking to Vice President Mike Pence during an address to the Central Intelligence Agency, January 21, 2017

"I got a standing ovation. In fact, they said it was the biggest standing ovation since Peyton Manning had won the Super Bowl and they said it was equal."
>—Trump describing his address to the Central Intelligence Agency to ABC News on January 25, 2017 (Note: President Trump never invited them to take a seat after he entered the room. As a matter of respect, they stood for his entire remarks.)

"I have been given as President tremendous taxation powers for trade and for other reasons—far greater than anybody understands."
>—Trump speaking to Mexican president Enrique Peña Nieto, January 27, 2017

"It is a disgrace that my full Cabinet is still not in place, the longest delay in the history of our country. Obstruction by Democrats!"
>—Trump tweet, posted February 7, 2017

"We got 306 because people came out and voted like they've never seen before so that's the way it goes. I guess it was the biggest Electoral College win since Ronald Reagan."
>—Trump speaking in his first White House press conference, February 16, 2017

"Elijah Cummings [a Democratic representative from Maryland]

was in my office and he said, 'You will go down as one of the great presidents in the history of our country.'"

> —Trump in an interview with the *New York Times*, published
> April 5, 2017 (Cummings later denied saying this.)

"No administration has accomplished more in the first 90 days."

> —Trump at a rally in Kenosha, Wisconsin, April 18, 2017

"I don't think anybody has ever done this much in a hundred days."

> —Trump to Fox News, April 28, 2017

"The Fake News media is officially out of control. They will say or do anything in order to get attention - never been a time like this!"

> —Trump tweet, posted May 4, 2017

"We have to prime the pump. . . . Have you heard that expression used before? Because I haven't heard it. . . . I came up with it a couple of days ago and I thought it was good."

> —Trump in an interview with the *Economist*, May 11, 2017

"No politician in history, and I say this with great surety, has been treated worse or more unfairly."

> —Trump addressing the United States Coast Guard Academy
> graduates, May 18, 2017

"They said there's never been anything like it in our history. In the history of this world, there has never been anything like what took place two weeks ago in Saudi Arabia."

> —Trump speaking in Cincinnati, Ohio, June 7, 2017

"The Fake News Media has never been so wrong or so dirty. Purposefully incorrect stories and phony sources to meet their agenda of hate. Sad!"

> —Trump tweet, posted June 13, 2017

"You are witnessing the single greatest WITCH HUNT in American political history - led by some very bad and conflicted people! #MAGA"

—Trump tweet, posted June 15, 2017

"This is the greatest Witch Hunt in political history. Sad!"

—Trump tweet, posted July 12, 2017

"We have done more in five months than practically any president in history."

—Trump in an interview with Reuters, July 12, 2017

"We've signed more bills—and I'm talking about through the legislature—than any president, ever."

—Trump at a "Made in America" White House event on
July 17, 2017

"And by the way, under the Trump administration, you'll be saying Merry Christmas again when you go shopping. Believe me. Merry Christmas. They've been downplaying that little, beautiful phrase. You're going to be saying, Merry Christmas again, folks."

—Trump speaking to the National Boy Scout Jamboree,
July 24, 2017

"That was a standing ovation from the time I walked out to the time I left, and for five minutes after I had already gone. . . . I got a call from the head of the Boy Scouts saying it was the greatest speech that was ever made to them, and they were very thankful."

—Trump speaking to the *Wall Street Journal* on July 25, 2017

"Just think of the amazing moments in history you will witness during your lifetime. Well, you saw one on November 8th, right? That was a pretty amazing moment we have—and we're doing a

good job. Our country is doing so well now. We're doing a good job. You all happy?"
  —Trump speaking to the American Legion Boys Nation and the
American Legion Auxiliary Girls Nation,
July 26, 2017

"With the exception of the late, great Abraham Lincoln, I can be more presidential than any president that's ever held this office."
  —Trump at a rally in Youngstown, Ohio, July 26, 2017

"Business spirit is the highest it's ever been according to polls—if you look at the polls—the highest it's ever been in the history of these polls."
  —Remarks by President Trump after swearing in General John
Kelly as White House chief of staff, July 31, 2017

"Nobody has greater respect for intelligence than Donald Trump."
  —Trump speaking to reporters on August 10, 2017

"The Obstructionist Democrats have given us (or not fixed) some of the worst trade deals in World History. I am changing that!"
  —Trump tweet, posted August 14, 2017

"We have the highest employment numbers we've ever had in the history of our country. We're doing record business. We have the highest levels of enthusiasm. . . . We're doing far more than any-body's done with respect to the inner cities. . . . We have the highest employment numbers we've ever had in the history of our coun-try. . . . The people are going to be working, they're going to be mak-ing a lot of money—much more money than they ever thought possible. . . ."
  —Trump's remarks about infrastructure on August 15, 2017

"Few, if any, Administrations have done more in just 7 months

than the Trump A. Bills passed, regulations killed, border, mili-
tary, ISIS, SC!"

—Trump tweet, posted August 25, 2017

"Nobody could have done what I've done for #PuertoRico with so
little appreciation. So much work!"

—Trump tweet, posted October 8, 2017

"I didn't have a schedule, but if I did have a schedule, I would say
we are substantially ahead of schedule."

—Trump talking about the progress he made as president to the
Values Voter Summit, October 13, 2017

"I'm not going to blame myself, I'll be honest. They are not getting
the job done."

—Trump complaining about the lack of progress Congress had
made on his agenda during a cabinet meeting on October 16, 2017

APPENDIX III

Trump's official spokespersons and media friends go to such extreme measures to prove their loyalty to the president that their statements are often difficult to take seriously. So don't. Laugh at it. Mock it. Roll your eyes. They signed themselves up for it. Read this compendium of greatest hits since he became our forty-fifth president and have a good chuckle. (While you still can.)

> *"It's so great our enemies are making themselves clear so that when we get into the White House, we know where we stand . . . let me just tell you, Mr. Trump has a long memory and we're keeping a list."*
>
> —Omarosa Manigault, *Independent Journal Review* interview, November 8, 2016

> *"I've never met anyone more dedicated to the safety and security of the people of the United States of America, or anyone who is a greater strategic thinker about how we accomplish that for this nation. In fact, to understand the life of our new President is—his whole life was strategy. He built an extraordinary success in the private sector, and I know he's going to make America safe again. And lastly, I can honestly tell you, for all my years serving in the Congress, serving as governor of my home state, traveling cross-country and seeing the connection that he's made to men*

*and women who serve and protect in every capacity in this coun-
try, I've never met anyone with a greater heart for those who every
day, in diverse ways, protect the people of this nation through their
character and their service and their sacrifice."*
  —Vice President Mike Pence, CIA headquarters, January 21, 2017

*"I want to begin by recapping the incredible, historic trip that the
President and the First Lady have just concluded, because it truly
was an extraordinary week for America and our people. In just
nine days, the President traveled across Europe and the Middle East
and interacted with nearly 100 foreign leaders. It was an unprece-
dented first trip abroad, just four months into this administration,
and it shows how quickly and decisively the President is acting to
strengthen alliances, to form new partnerships, and to rebuild America's standing in the world. We've never seen before at this point in a
presidency such sweeping reassurance of American interest, and the
inauguration of a foreign policy strategy designed to bring back the
world from growing dangers and perpetual disasters brought on by
years of failed leadership. . . . The President's address to the leaders
of more than 50 Arab and Muslim nations was a historic turning
point that people will be talking about for many years to come. He
did exactly as he promised in his inaugural address: united the civilized world in the fight against terrorism and extremism. . . . The
President's historic speech was met with near universal praise. . . .
He accomplished the return of a strong America to international
affairs, rallied civilized nations of the world against terrorism, took
real steps towards peace in the Middle East, and renewed our alliances on the basis of both shared interest and shared burdens. The
trip sets the stage for a much more safe and more prosperous nation
here at home and a more peaceful world for all."*
  —Sean Spicer, White House press briefing, May 30, 2017

*"And this president deserves the full commitment of his White
House staff, who should be fighting as hard as the president for*

him, his agenda, and this country. The all-too-civil, low-energy Trump White House communications [sic] remains flatfooted and failing. They need to change that. They aren't obviously fighters, they obviously aren't street smart and they haven't been strategic. And they must change all of that. They must become all of that and much more. Because the determined forces of evil that surround this White House are trying to destroy the Trump presidency. This is a war, dammit, so go to war now."

—Lou Dobbs, *Lou Dobbs Tonight*, May 16, 2017

"President Trump has a magnetic personality and exudes positive energy, which is infectious to those around him. He has an unparalleled ability to communicate with people, whether he is speaking to a room of three or an arena of 30,000. He has built great relationships throughout his life and treats everyone with respect. He is brilliant with a great sense of humor . . . and an amazing ability to make people feel special and aspire to be more than even they thought possible."

—Hope Hicks, White House spokeswoman, May 30, 2017

"I will always be loyal to President Trump, I would take a bullet for him."

—Carl Higbie to White House chief of staff Reince Priebus in a July 2017 email obtained by Real Clear Politics

"Somebody has to be the president's pit bull, and I'm ready."

—Sebastian Gorka on Fox News, July 14, 2017

"If the president asks you, you don't say no. I have rocks in my head and steel balls."

—Ty Cobb, Trump's lawyer, July 21, 2017

"I think there has been at times a disconnect between the way we see the President and how much we love the President, and the

way some of you perhaps see the President. . . . But I love the Pres-
ident, and I'm very, very loyal to the President. And I love the
mission that the President has, okay? . . . I've seen this guy throw a
dead spiral through a tire. I've seen him at Madison Square Gar-
den with a topcoat on. He's standing in the key and he's hitting
foul shots and swishing them, okay? He sinks 30-foot putts. . . . I
love the President, and I think a lot of you guys know in the me-
dia, I've been very, very loyal to him. . . . The American people are
actually playing a long game, and I think they really, really love
the President. And when you look into the individual state-by-
state polls, you can see the guy is doing phenomenally well. So, it's
indicating to me at least—me personally—that the President is
really well loved."

—Anthony Scaramucci, White House communications director,
July 21, 2017

"I'd like to read you a letter from 9-year-old Dylan: 'My name is
Dylan Harbin, but everybody calls me Pickle. I'm nine years old,
and you're my favorite President. I like you so much that I had a
birthday about you. My cake was the shape of your hat.' . . . 'I don't
know why people don't like you.' Me either, Dylan."

—Sarah Huckabee Sanders, White House press secretary, White
House press briefing, July 26, 2017

"Hey, everybody. I'm Kayleigh McEnany. Thank you for joining
us as we provide the news of the week from Trump Tower here in
New York. More great economic news on Friday: The July jobs
report added a better-than-expected 209,000 jobs. Overall, since
the president took office, President Trump has created more than
1 million jobs, the unemployment rate is at a 16-year low, and
consumer confidence is at a 16-year high—all while the Dow
Jones continues to break records. President Trump has clearly
steered the economy back in the right direction. On Wednesday,
the president introduced the Raise Act. For decades, a steady rise

in immigration has depressed the wages of American workers. The Raise Act will increase wages, decrease poverty and save the taxpayers billions. Americans deserve a raise, and President Trump is finally putting the American worker first. . . . Thank you for joining us everybody. I'm Kayleigh McEnany, and that is the real news."

—Kayleigh McEnany, Trump TV, August 7, 2017

"Anybody who thinks they are gonna change the President is not going to because he is the greatest communicator we have ever seen as an elected official. There is no question about it."

—Corey Lewandowski, Fox News, August 1, 2017

"President Trump is the most gifted politician of our time and he's the best orator to hold that office in generations."

—Stephen Miller, White House policy adviser, Fox News, August 8, 2017

"I stand before you today deeply humbled—deeply humbled to be able to continue to serve this state as the 48th Vice President of the United States. And I owe it all—I owe it all to the confidence of the 45th President of the United States, President Donald Trump."

—Vice President Mike Pence, August 11, 2017

"Ladies and gentlemen, I was told this by high level sources and it was evident and especially after [Ronald] Reagan was shot in his first year in office when he was acting like Trump, and doing the right things, that he never really recovered. They gave him cold blood, and his transfusion that causes brain damage. They slowly gave him small amounts of sedatives. It's known that most presidents end up getting drugged. Small dosages of sedatives till they build it up, Trump's such a bull he hasn't fully understood it yet. But I've talked to people, multiple ones, and they believe that they

are putting a slow sedative that they're building up that's also ad-dictive in his Diet Cokes and in his iced tea and that the president by 6 or 7 at night is basically slurring his words and is drugged. Now first they had to isolate him to do that. But yes, ladies and gentlemen, I've talked to people that talk to the president now at 9 at night, he is slurring his words. And I'm going to leave it at that. I've talked to folks that have talked to him directly. So notice, 'Oh, he's mentally ill. Oh, he's got Alzheimer's.' They isolate him then you start slowly building up the dose, but instead of titrating it like poison, like venom of a cobra, or a rattlesnake, or a water moccasin where you build it up slowly so that you get an immu-nity to it, you're building it slowly so the person doesn't notice it. First, it's almost zero, just a tiny bit and then a little more and then your brain subconsciously becomes addicted to it and wants it and so as the dose gets bigger and bigger you get more comfort-able in it. The president is about two months into being covertly drugged. Now I'm risking my life, by the way, to tell you all this. I was physically sick before I went on air. Because I'm smart. And I don't mean that in a braggadocious way. I mean I'm not dumb. The information you're going to get today is super dangerous. In fact, I'm tempted just to let it out now so they don't cut the show off or something before this goes out. I mean this is the kind of thing that gets you killed."

—Alex Jones, September 11, 2017

MARTHA RADDATZ: The president is calling them SOBs. Is that the kind of language, no matter how you feel about the issue, that he should be using?

TREASURY SECRETARY STEVE MNUCHIN: I think the president can use whatever language he wants to use.

> —A September 24, 2017, exchange between ABC's Martha Raddatz and Treasury Secretary Steve Mnuchin over President Trump's remarks that NFL owners "get that son of a b**** off the field right now" in reference to NFL players who protest during the national anthem

"I think Donald Trump has the potential to be the greatest President since Abraham Lincoln."

> —Jerry Falwell Jr. on *Fox & Friends*, October 15, 2017

PETER ALEXANDER: "What are President Trump's flaws?"
WHITE HOUSE PRESS SECRETARY SARAH HUCKABEE SANDERS: "Probably that he has to deal with you guys on a daily basis."

> —White House press briefing, November 1, 2017

ACKNOWLEDGMENTS

This book would not have been possible without my husband, Chris. Throughout my career, he has given me invaluable advice and supported me every step of the way. I've pursued stressful jobs that require being on call at all times and he's offered nothing but love and encouragement as I rushed away for emergency conference calls and television hits, or barricaded myself behind closed doors to write the next big piece.

I thank my two young children for motivating me to write this book. President Trump is the first president they have been able to recognize. One day they'll ask me what his presidency was like. Knowing this, I felt an urgency to capture the disorienting quality of this election before those memories fade into history. Kids, I pray this book helps guard your generation from falling for any kind of similar con.

My manager, Josanne Lopez, is a rock. I am indebted to her not only for her help guiding my career, but for her friendship. 2016 was an emotional roller coaster and she was an unwavering source of refuge where I could turn to in times of need.

Working with my editor, Eric Nelson, to bring this book from my proposal to print has been a delight. From the start, he believed in the vision I had and made it a reality. The entire team at HarperCollins is stellar and made the writing process, widely known to induce ulcers and tears, enjoyable and fun.

My work at CNN informed a significant part of this book. I am deeply thankful for the opportunity to be part of their incredible team of executives, anchors, producers, and assistants.

Lastly, I thank Jim DeMint and Ted Cruz for allowing me to assist them in the United States Senate and contribute, in my small way, to this unique chapter in American political history. Both men possess the exceedingly rare capability to put principle over party and pulled together teams of dedicated patriots willing to do the same. It was an honor to be included with them.

God bless each and every one of you.

NOTES

CHAPTER 1: BIRTHING A PRESIDENT

2 Ted Cruz, endorsed: David Wright, Tal Kopan, Julia Manchester, "Cruz Unloads with Epic Takedown of 'Pathological Liar,' 'Narcissist' Donald Trump," CNN, May 3, 2016, http://www.cnn.com/2016/05/03/politics/donald-trump-rafael-cruz-indiana /index.html.

4 "I'd rather have 30 Marco Rubios than 60 Arlen Specters": Jim DeMint, Conservative Political Action Speech, February 18, 2010, https://www.senateconservatives .com/print/148.

6 Jonah Goldberg wrote: Jonah Goldberg, "In a Slow-Motion *Invasion of the Body Snatchers*, Media Figures Embrace Trump One by One," *National Review*, March 12, 2016, http://www.nationalreview.com/article/432708/donald-trumps-media-supporters -principles-dont-matter-them.

10 "Everybody that even gives a hint of being a birther": Ashleigh Banfield, Nah McHugh, Suzan Clarke, "Exclusive: Donald Trump Would Spend $600 Million of His Own Money on Presidential Bid," ABC News, March 17, 2011, http://abcnews.go.com /Politics/donald-trump-president-trump-weighs-sheen-palin-obama/story?id=13154163.

11 "Why doesn't he show his birth certificate?": Gabriella Schwarz, "Trump Again Questions Obama's Birthplace," CNN, March 23, 2011, http://politicalticker.blogs.cnn .com/2011/03/23/trump-again-questions-obamas-birthplace/.

11 [H]e told Fox News: Interview, "Trump on Birth Certificate: Obama Spent Millions to Get Away from This Issue," Fox News, March 28, 2011, http://nation.foxnews .com/donald-trump/2011/03/28/trump-birth-certificate-obama-spent-millions-get -away-issue.

11 He told *Morning Joe*: Evan McMorris-Santoro, "Trump Promises to Reveal Secrets of Obama's Birth Before Summer," *Talking Points Memo*, April 7, 2011, http:// talkingpointsmemo.com/dc/trump-promises-to-reveal-secrets-of-obama-s-birth-be fore-summer-video.

11 He pointed out: Brian Montopoli, "Obama: I Released Birth Certificate Because Media Has Been 'Distracted by Sideshows and Carnival Barkers,'" CBS News, April 27,

2011, http://www.cbsnews.com/news/obama-i-released-birth-certificate-because-media -has-been-distracted-by-sideshows-and-carnival-barkers.

12 Obama vented: Ibid.

12 Perry told CNBC: Paul Steinhauser, "Perry on Obama: It's Fun to Poke at Him," CNN, October 25, 2011, http://politicalticker.blogs.cnn.com/2011/10/25/perry-on -obama-its-fun-to-poke-at-him/.

12 In August 2012: Donald J. Trump, Twitter, August 6, 2012, https://twitter.com /realdonaldtrump/status/232572505238433794?lang=en.

12 ABC's Jonathan Karl asked Trump: Jonathan Karl, "The Last Time Donald Trump Talked About 'Birtherism,'" ABC News, September 7, 2016, http://abcnews .go.com/Politics/time-donald-trump-talked-birtherism/story?id=41927366.

12 In 2014, Trump was still pushing it: Donald J. Trump, Twitter, September 4, 2014, https://twitter.com/realDonaldTrump/status/508194635270062080.

12 A poll conducted by Fairleigh Dickinson University: Poll, "Fairleigh Dickinson University's PublicMind Poll Finds Trump Supporters More Conspiracy-Minded Than Other Republicans," May 4, 2016, http://view2.fdu.edu/publicmind/2016/160504/.

13 Trump made his long-awaited statement: Katie Reilly, "Read Donald Trump's Speech Finally Admitting President Obama Was Born in the U.S.," *Time*, September 16, 2016, http://time.com/4497626/donald-trump-birther-address-transcript/.

14 CNN's Jake Tapper lamented: Louis Nelson, "Jake Tapper Calls Trump Event a 'Political Rick-Roll,'" *Politico*, September 16, 2016, https://www.politico.com /story/2016/09/jake-tapper-trump-political-rick-roll-228281.

CHAPTER 2: WINNING UGLY

18 Harry Reid took to the Senate floor: Congressional Record, August 2, 2012, https://www.gpo.gov/fdsys/pkg/CREC-2012-08-02/pdf/CREC-2012-08-02-pt1 -PgS5901-5.pdf#page=1.

18 [T]he *Wall Street Journal* conceded: *Wall Street Journal* Editorial Board, "Hope over Experience," *Wall Street Journal*, November 8, 2012.

19 Rick Reed wrote: Rick Reed, "Maybe the Romney Campaign Was Just Too Nice," *Daily Caller*, November 13, 2012, http://dailycaller.com/2012/11/13/maybe-the -romney-campaign-was-just-too-nice/.

19 "[I]t turns out that people want their politicians to lie to them": Jesse Singal, "3 Insights About Donald Trump's Constant Lying," *New York*, March 29, 2016, http:// nymag.com/scienceofus/2016/03/3-insights-about-donald-trumps-constant-lying.html.

20 [S]enator Jay Rockefeller said: David Jackson, "Senator: Race Is Part of Criticism of Obama Health Law," *USA Today*, May 22, 2014, https://www.usatoday.com/story /theoval/2014/05/22/obama-health-care-jay-rockefeller-ron-johnson/9434021/.

20 One *Huffington Post* headline: Samanta Honigman, "'Kate's Law' and the License to Hate," *Huffington Post*, April 27, 2016, https://www.huffingtonpost.com/samanta -honigman/kates-law-and-the-license_b_9789508.html.

21 Beck told viewers: Media Matters Staff, "Beck Imitates Obama Pouring Gasoline on 'Average American,'" Media Matters, April 9, 2009, https://www.mediamatters.org/video/2009/04/09/beck-imitates-obama-pouring-gasoline-on-average/149059.

21 One pre-2016 election comment from HBO's Bill Maher was telling: Oliver Darcy, "Bill Maher: Democrats 'Made a Big Mistake' When We 'Cried Wolf' on Other Republicans," *Business Insider*, November 5, 2016, http://www.businessinsider.com/bill-maher-democrats-trump-romney-mccain-2016-11.

CHAPTER 3: #WAR

24 "We didn't declare war on the Left, they declared war on us": "Andrew Breitbart: We Didn't Declare War on the Left. They Declared War on Us!" *The Right Scoop*, April 9, 2010, http://therightscoop.com/andrew-breitbart-we-didnt-declare-war-on-the-left-they-declared-war-on-us/.

24 I also had the occasion to meet James O'Keefe: "Acorn Investigation," Project Veritas, http://projectveritas.com/acorn/.

24 Breitbart lectured members of the Conservative Political Action Conference in 2012: "Full Speech: Andrew Breitbart at CPAC in 2012," *The Right Scoop*, February 10, 2012, http://therightscoop.com/full-speech-andrew-breitbart-at-cpac-2012/.

27 Philadelphia abortionist Dr. Kermit Gosnell: Jon Hurdle, Trip Gabriel, "Philadelphia Abortion Doctor Guilty of Murder in Late-Term Procedures," *New York Times*, May 13, 2013, http://www.nytimes.com/2013/05/14/us/kermit-gosnell-abortion-doctor-found-guilty-of-murder.html.

27 [T]he Philadelphia district attorney's office found: Sarah Kliff, "The Gosnell Case: Here's What You Need to Know," *Washington Post*, April 15, 2013, https://www.washingtonpost.com/news/wonk/wp/2013/04/15/the-gosnell-case-heres-what-you-need-to-know/?utm_term=.0bbf67a76587.

27 [A] number of conservative senators: Press release, "Lee Introduces Resolution to Review Illegal Abortion Practices," www.lee.senate.gov, May 6, 2013, https://www.lee.senate.gov/public/index.cfm/press-releases?ID=de392285-b2d1-44fd-ac79-d2cb7a5a3342.

27 One *Washington Post* reporter: John Sexton, "Post Reporter: Gosnell Is Just a Local Crime Story," *Breitbart News*, April 11, 2013, http://www.breitbart.com/blog/2013/04/11/post-reporter-gosnell-is-just-a-local-crime-story/.

28 *Goonies* actress Martha Plimpton: Jennifer Smith, "Goonies Actress Martha Plimpton Is Slammed After Boasting at a Pro-Choice Event That She Had Her 'Best Abortion' in Seattle When She Was 19," *Daily Mail*, September 6, 2017, http://www.dailymail.co.uk/news/article-4858556/Martha-Plimpton-says-best-abortion-Seattle.html#ixzz4rvKb8CYo.

29 [A] solar panel start-up that went bankrupt: Tom Hals, "U.S. Solar Firm Solyndra Files for Bankruptcy," Reuters, September 6, 2011, https://www.reuters.com/article/us-solyndra/u-s-solar-firm-solyndra-files-for-bankruptcy-idUSTRE77U5K420110906.

30 Charlie Sykes wrote: Charlie Sykes, *How the Right Lost Its Mind*, St. Martin's Press, 2017, pg.16.

31 Texas governor Greg Abbott had to ask the Texas State Guard: Dan Lamonthe, "Texas State Guard Ordered to Monitor Military's Operation Jade Helm 15," *Washington Post*, April 29, 2015, https://www.washingtonpost.com/news/checkpoint/wp/2015/04/29/as-conspiracy-theories-persist-governor-asks-texas-state-guard-to-monitor-militarys-operation-jade-helm-15/?tid=a_inl&utm_term=.060ec0016c4a.

31 The *Texas Tribune* commissioned a poll: Ross Ramsey, "UT/TT Poll: Texans Skittish About Domestic Use of U.S. Military," *Texas Tribune*, June 25, 2015, https://www.texastribune.org/2015/06/25/uttt-poll-texans-wary-domestic-use-military/.

31 Daron Shaw: Ibid.

CHAPTER 4: TERRORIZED

33 She released a statement that evening: Reuters staff, "U.S. Confirms Death of Official in Benghazi Attack," *Reuters*, September 11, 2012, http://www.reuters.com/article/libya-usa-clinton/u-s-confirms-death-of-official-in-benghazi-attack-idUSL1E8KC0G120120912.

34 "Two of our officers were killed": Justin Fishel, "Hillary Clinton's Long-Awaited Hearing Marked by Testy Exchanges," ABC News, October 22, 2015, http://abcnews.go.com/Politics/hillary-clintons-long-awaited-benghazi-testimony-set-begin/story?id=34574693.

34 According to State Department notes: Lawrence Randolph email, State Department, September 12, 2012, https://benghazi.house.gov/sites/republicans.benghazi.house.gov/files/documents/Tab%2079.pdf.

35 In his farewell address, President Obama sought: Transcript, "Read the Full Transcript of President Obama's Farewell Speech," *Los Angeles Times*, January 10, 2017, http://www.latimes.com/politics/la-pol-obama-farewell-speech-transcript-20170110-story.html.

38 Writing for the *Claremont Review of Books*: Publius Decius Mus, "The Flight 93 Election," *Claremont Review of Books*, September 5, 2016, http://www.claremont.org/crb/basicpage/the-flight-93-election/.

38 Rush Limbaugh spent an extensive amount of time: Transcript, "The Shaming of the Never Trumpers," *The Rush Limbaugh Show*, September 7, 2016, https://www.rushlimbaugh.com/daily/2016/09/07/the_shaming_of_the_never_trumpers/.

38 Trump campaign strategist Steve Bannon later said: Susan B. Glasser, "Does Trump Still Believe in Trumpism?" *Politico*, April 17, 2017, https://www.politico.com/magazine/story/2017/04/michael-anton-donald-trump-foreign-policy-215036.

39 One postelection study: Bobby Azarian, "Research Suggests Anxiety over Terrorism Helped Trump Win," *Psychology Today*, December 30, 2016, https://www.psychologytoday.com/blog/mind-in-the-machine/201612/research-suggests-anxiety-over-terrorism-helped-trump-win.

CHAPTER 5: INSIDE JOB

43 Bush turned to Trump and began lecturing him: Stephanie Condon, "Republican Debate: Jeb Bush Asks Donald Trump to Apologize to Bush's Wife, Trump Refuses," CBS News, September 16, 2015, https://www.cbsnews.com/news/gop-republican

-debate-2015-jeb-bush-asks-donald-trump-to-apologize-to-bushs-wife-trump
-refuses/.

44 Trump started his taunts in the fall: Jordan Frasier, "Bush Defends Brother Against Donald Trump's 9/11 Charges," NBC News, October 16, 2015, http://www.nbcnews.com/politics/2016-election/bush-defends-brother-against-donald-trumps-9-11-charges-n446201.

45 He used the smooth, poll-tested line: Byron York, "Team Jeb Poll-Tested 'W Kept Us Safe' Line," *Washington Examiner*, October 30, 2015, http://www.washingtonexaminer.com/team-jeb-poll-tested-w-kept-us-safe-line/article/2575315.

45 "Does anybody actually blame my brother": Transcript, *State of the Union*, CNN, October 18, 2015, http://cnnpressroom.blogs.cnn.com/2015/10/18/jeb-bush-on-trump-having-hand-on-nuclear-codes-i-have-grave-doubts-to-be-honest-with-you/.

45 Trump told *Fox News Sunday*: Daniel Strauss, "Trump-Bush Feud Fires Up over 9/11," *Politico*, October 18, 2017, https://www.politico.com/story/2015/10/trump-immigration-terror-attacks-214905.

45 [D]uring a February 13 debate: Transcript, "Read the Full Transcript of the Ninth Republican Debate in South Carolina," *Time*, February 16, 2016, http://time.com/4224275/republican-debate-transcript-south-carolina-ninth/.

46 Trump had tweeted earlier: Donald J. Trump, Twitter, February 6, 2016, https://twitter.com/realdonaldtrump/status/695979656617578496?lang=en.

46 "The World Trade Center came down during your brother's reign": Katie Glueck, "Trump Blames George W. Bush for 9/11," *Politico*, February 13, 2016, https://www.politico.com/blogs/south-carolina-primary-2016-live-updates-and-results/2016/02/gop-debate-2016-trump-911-219260.

46 Mark Levin said Trump's remarks were a "disgrace": Ian Schwartz, "Mark Levin: Trump Sounded Like 'Radical Kook,' Pretty Damn Close to Being 9/11 Truther," Real Clear Politics, February 15, 2016, https://www.realclearpolitics.com/video/2016/02/15/mark_levin_donald_trump_sounded_like_radical_kook_pretty_damn_close_to_being_911_truther.html.

47 He went on *The Mike Gallagher Show* to keep driving the point home: Ian Schwartz, "Trump: I Didn't Say George Bush Lied to Invade Iraq, but It's a Fact He Did Not Keep Us Safe on 9/11," Real Clear Politics, February 15, 2016, https://www.realclearpolitics.com/video/2016/02/15/trump_i_didnt_say_george_bush_lied_to_invade_iraq_but_its_a_fact_he_did_not_keep_us_safe_on_911.html.

48 "[Y]ou will find out who really knocked down the World Trade Center": Tim Hains, "Donald Trump on 9/11: 'You Will Find Out Who Really Knocked Down the World Trade Center,'" Real Clear Politics, February 17, 2016, https://www.realclearpolitics.com/video/2016/02/17/trump_you_will_find_out_who_really_knocked_down_the_world_trade_center_secret_papers_may_blame_saudis.html.

48 "This is Michael Moore talk!": MJ Lee, "How Donald Trump Blasted George W. Bush in S.C.—and Still Won," CNN, February 21, 2016, http://www.cnn.com/2016/02/20/politics/donald-trump-south-carolina-military/index.html.

49 "It's hard to argue with the results": Tim Miller, "'Winning' Is Trump's Only Value—but Can a Value-less Country Win?" *Daily Beast*, May 15, 2017, http://www.thedailybeast.com/winning-is-trumps-only-valuebut-can-a-value-less-country-win.

50 I publicly called for a blacklist of Republican politicians who endorsed Trump: Leon Wolf, "Amanda Carpenter Is Right. Blackball the Trump Endorsers," *RedState*, March 18, 2016, https://www.redstate.com/leon_h_wolf/2016/03/18/amanda-carpenter-right.-blackball-trump-endorsers./.

CHAPTER 6: BURNED

57 "These stories have been swirling around Cruz for some time": *National Enquirer* Staff, "5 Romps That Will Destroy Ted Cruz!" *National Enquirer*, April 4, 2016.

58 *Salon* posted a story describing the clamor: Brendan Gauthier, "Internet Scrambles to Identify Women Described in National Enquirer's 'Bombshell' Report Alleging Ted Cruz Had Five Affairs," *Salon*, March 25, 2016, https://www.salon.com/2016/03/25/internet_scrambles_to_identify_women_described_in_national_enquirers_bombshell_report_alleging_ted_cruz_had_five_affairs/.

61 The transcript gives me chills to this day: Callum Borchers, "The Remarkable CNN Exchange That Took the Ted Cruz Affair Rumors from the Tabloids into the Mainstream," *Washington Post*, March 25, 2016, https://www.washingtonpost.com/news/the-fix/wp/2016/03/25/this-remarkable-cnn-exchange-took-the-ted-cruz-affair-rumors-from-the-tabloids-into-the-mainstream/?utm_term=.95fdb84e6399.

62 The segment continued: Ibid.

64 [T]he Cruz campaign blasted out a statement calling the story "garbage": Maya Rhodan, Philip Elliott, "Ted Cruz Blames Donald Trump for 'Garbage' National Enquirer Story," *Time*, March 25, 2016, http://time.com/4272519/ted-cruz-national-enquirer-affairs-donald-trump/.

65 "[P]erfectly Trumpian": Chris Cillizza, "Donald Trump's Statement on the Ted Cruz Affair Story Is Perfectly Trumpian," *Washington Post*, March 25, 2016, https://www.washingtonpost.com/news/the-fix/wp/2016/03/25/donald-trumps-statement-on-the-ted-cruz-affair-story-is-perfectly-trumpian/?utm_term=.8afd6188f044.

65 Jonathan Karl asked: Transcript, *This Week*, ABC News, May 27, 2016, http://abcnews.go.com/Politics/week-transcript-donald-trump-sen-bernie-sanders/story?id=37949498.

66 Scavino posted a reply on Twitter: Dan Scavino Jr., Twitter, March 28, 2016, https://twitter.com/DanScavino/status/714556330921627650.

68 I explained the professional conundrum the allegations had put me in: Transcript, *The Lead with Jake Tapper*, CNN, March 29, 2016, http://transcripts.cnn.com/TRANSCRIPTS/1603/29/cg.01.html.

69 Tapper brought her up to speed: Ibid.

CHAPTER 7: THE PLEDGE

73 [C]onservatives represented the largest ideological group in America: Lydia Saad, "Conservatives Hang On to Ideology by a Thread," Gallup, January 11, 2016, http://www.gallup.com/poll/188129/conservatives-hang-ideology-lead-thread.aspx.

73 [V]oters who identified as Republicans was near record lows: Jeffrey M. Jones, "Democratic, Republican Identification Near Historical Lows," Gallup, January 11, 2016, http://www.gallup.com/poll/188096/democratic-republican-identification-near-historical -lows.aspx.

73 Fox News anchor Brett Baier sought to peg Trump on the question: Transcript, "Read the Full Text of the Primetime Republican Debate," *Time*, August 11, 2015, http:// time.com/3988276/republican-debate-primetime-transcript-full-text/.

73 "You can't say tonight that you can make that pledge?": Ibid.

74 Rand Paul told CNN: Robert Costa, "Trump's Party Loyalty Pledge Ends One GOP Problem, Brings Others," *Washington Post*, September 3, 2015, https://www .washingtonpost.com/politics/trump-to-sign-gop-pledge-commit-to-back-party -nominee/2015/09/03/c5d9ea7c-5242-11e5-9812-92d5948a40f8_story.html?utm_term =.ded3712b62de.

74 Priebus buttered Trump up: Brianna Ehley, "RNC Chair Priebus: Trump a 'Net Positive' for GOP," *Politico*, August 24, 2015, https://www.politico.com/story/2015/08 /reince-priebus-donald-trump-net-positive-121669.

75 "The best way for Republicans to win is if I win the nomination": Tran- script, *Anderson Cooper 360°*, CNN, September 3, 2015, http://transcripts.cnn.com /TRANSCRIPTS/1509/03/acd.01.html.

75 "We were absolutely furious": Eli Stokols, "Reince Priebus' Surrender," *Politico*, July 21, 2016, http://www.politico.com/magazine/story/2016/07/2016-gop-convention -reince-priebus-donald-trump-214078.

75 In one barrage of anger Trump accused: Phillip Stucky, "Trump Hasn't Met an Election He Didn't Think Was Rigged," *Daily Caller*, August 8, 2016, http://dailycaller .com/2016/08/02/trump-hasnt-met-an-election-he-didnt-think-was-rigged/.

76 The Democrats believed: Gabriel Debenedetti, "They Always Wanted Trump," *Politico*, November 7, 2016, http://www.politico.com/magazine/story/2016/11/hillary -clinton-2016-donald trump-214428.

76 Jonathan Chait, of *New York* magazine, assured his fellow liberals: Jonathan Chait, "Why Liberals Should Support a Trump Republican Nomination," *Daily Intel- ligencer*, February 5, 2016, http://nymag.com/daily/intelligencer/2016/02/why liberals -should-support-a-trump-nomination.html.

77 Sherman called the tactic "nounism": Jeremy Sherman, "Trump's Name-Calling a Symptom of Nounism," *Psychology Today*, May 2, 2011, https://www.psychologytoday .com/blog/ambigamy/201105/trumps-name-calling-symptom-nounism.

78 "[Y]ou know what they say about men with small hands?": Sophie Tatum, "Trump: People Say I 'Have the Most Beautiful Hands,'" CNN, March 1, 2016, http:// www.cnn.com/2016/03/01/politics/donald-trump-marco-rubio-beautiful-hands/index .html.

78 *Vanity Fair* editor Graydon Carter called him a "short-fingered vulgarian": Graydon Carter, "Steel Traps and Short Fingers," *Vanity Fair*, November 2015, https:// www.vanityfair.com/culture/2015/10/graydon-carter-donald-trump.

78 "Trump Defends Size of His Penis": Gregory Krieg, "Donald Trump Defends Size of His Penis," CNN, March 4, 2016, http://www.cnn.com/2016/03/03/politics /donald-trump-small-hands-marco-rubio/index.html.

78 Trump boasted later: Ashley Parker, Maggie Haberman, "Donald Trump, After Difficult Stretch, Shows a Softer Side," *New York Times*, April 20, 2015, https://www .nytimes.com/2016/04/21/us/politics/donald-trump-interview.html?_r=0.

79 [H]e said in an interview with CNN's Wolf Blitzer: Theodore Schleifer, Eric Bradner, "Birtherism Is Back," CNN, January 7, 2016, http://www.cnn.com/2016/01/06 /politics/ted-cruz-birthplace-donald-trump/index.html.

80 Trump tweeted to his millions of Twitter followers that Cruz must: Ibid.

80 Liberal writers celebrated: Ryu Spaeth, "Donald Trump Is a Ted Cruz Birther and It's Fantastic," *New Republic*, https://newrepublic.com/minutes/127114/donald -trump-ted-cruz-birther-its-fantastic.

80 "BOTH Cruz AND Rubio are ineligible to be POTUS!": Donald J. Trump, Twitter, February 20, 2016, https://twitter.com/realdonaldtrump/status/701045567783219201 ?lang=en.

81 He was later questioned by: Callum Borchers, "Donald Trump Won't Say That Marco Rubio Is Eligible to Be President," *Washington Post*, February 21, 2016, https:// www.washingtonpost.com/pb/news/post-politics/wp/2016/02/21/donald-trump-wont -say-that-marco-rubio-is-eligible-to-be-president/.

81 He said that Cruz must take down all negative ads against him or he would "bring a lawsuit": Statement by Donald J. Trump, "Response to the Lies of Senator Cruz," Facebook, February 15, 2016, https://www.facebook.com/DonaldTrump /posts/10156647104280725.

81 Cruz told him to bring it on: Emily Schultheis, "Ted Cruz to Donald Trump: Go Ahead and Sue Me," CBS News, February 17, 2016, https://www.cbsnews.com/news /cruz-to-trump-go-ahead-and-sue-me/.

82 A 2003 Gallup poll: Lydia Saad, "Americans: Kennedy Assassination a Conspiracy," Gallup, November 21, 2003, http://www.gallup.com/poll/9751/americans -kennedy-assassination-conspiracy.aspx.

82 The front-page story said: J. R. Taylor, "World Exclusive! Ted Cruz's Father—Caught with JFK Assassin," *National Enquirer*, April 20, 2016, https://www .nationalenquirer.com/celebrity/ted-cruz-scandal-father-jfk-assassination.

83 Trump was determined to make it a topic of conversation that morning: Nolan D. McCaskill, "Trump Accuses Cruz's Father of Helping JFK's Assassin," *Politico*, May 3, 2016, https://www.politico.com/blogs/2016-gop-primary-live-updates-and -results/2016/05/trump-ted-cruz-father-222730.

83 Cruz unleashed: Ian Schwartz, "Cruz Explodes 'Pathological Liar' Trump 'a Narcissist at a Level I Don't Think This Country Has Ever Seen,'" Real Clear Politics, May 3, 2016, http://www.realclearpolitics.com/video/2016/05/03/cruz_explodes_pathological_liar _trump_a_narcissist_at_a_level_i_dont_think_this_country_has_ever_seen.html.

83 Trump responded thusly: Kyle Cheney, "Trump: We Will Win," *Politico*, May 3, 2016, https://www.politico.com/story/2016/05/ted-cruz-braces-losses-indiana-222745.

84 They gasped in shock when Cruz told them: Katie Glueck, Shane Goldmacher, "Ted Cruz Drops Out of Presidential Race," *Politico*, May 3, 2016, https://www.politico .com/story/2016/05/ted-cruz-drops-out-of-presidential-race-222763.

84 [S]till pushing the JFK conspiracy: Elise Viebeck, "'You Can't Knock the National Enquirer': Trump Doubles Down on Oswald-Cruz Conspiracy Theory," *Washington Post*, May 4, 2016, https://www.washingtonpost.com/news/post-politics /wp/2016/05/04/you-cant-knock-the-national-enquirer-trump-doubles-down-on -oswald-cruz-conspiracy-theory/?utm_term=.7087a89c999f.

85 Cruz had, in fact, said it all was "nuts": Donovan Slack, "Trump Bizarrely Links Cruz's Father to JFK Assassin; Cruz Goes Ballistic," *USA Today*, May 3, 2016, https:// www.usatoday.com/story/news/politics/onpolitics/2016/05/03/trump-bizarrely-links -cruzs-father-jfk-assassin-cruz-goes-ballistic/83874972/.

CHAPTER 8: SURROGATE SECRETS

88 "If I accepted all the requests": Tessa Berenson, "Meet the Members of Donald Trump's Television Army," *Time*, April 5, 2016, http://time.com/4281934 /donald-trump-tv-supporters-katrina-pierson-omarosa-jeffrey-lord/.

88 "When Donald says, 'I think you're great'": Ben Schreckinger, Katie Glueck, "Trump's New Face," *Politico*, November 18, 2015, https://www.politico.com /story/2015/11/donald-trump-katrina-pierson-216005#ixzz3wJuQPWj8.

88 "It's definitely boosted my profile": Olivia Nuzzi, "The Desperate Gamble of Scottie Nell Hughes, World's Most Loyal Trump Surrogate," *GQ*, October 19, 2016, https://www.gq.com/story/desperate-gamble-of-scottie-nell-hughes-trump-surrogate.

88 It's like the song from journey": That

88 Ivanka Trump said: Transcript, *Early Start*, CNN, July 22, 2016, http://www .cnn.com/TRANSCRIPTS/1607/22/es.05.html.

88 "If elected, Mr. Trump, I can state unequivocally": Jessica Taylor, "Doctor: Trump Would Be 'Healthiest Individual Ever Elected' President," NPR, December 14, 2015, http://www.npr.org/2015/12/14/459700154/doctor-trump-would-be-healthiest -individual-ever-elected-president.

88 [T]he "Ernest Hemingway of Twitter": Meera Jagannathan, "President Trump Is the 'Ernest Hemingway of Twitter,' Says Corey Lewandowski," *New York Daily News*, July 2, 2017, http://www.nydailynews.com/news/politics/trump-ernest-hemingway-twitter -lewandowski-article-1.3295526.

89 During the introductions: Tina Nguyen, "Trump Appointees Take Turns Praising Him in Bizarre Cabinet Meeting," *Vanity Fair*, June 12, 2017, http://www.vanityfair .com/news/2017/06/donald-trump-cabinet-meeting.

89 Gingrich said: Molly Ball, "Kellyanne's Alternative Universe," *Atlantic*, April 2017, https://www.theatlantic.com/magazine/archive/2017/04/kellyannes-alternative -universe/517821/.

90 [S]he reassured herself: Kayleigh McEnany, "Why I Am Backing Donald Trump," CNN, May 11, 2016, http://www.cnn.com/2016/05/11/opinions/donald -trump-support-mcenany/index.html.

90 "It is very personal to me": Ben Terris, "Inside Trump's Inner Circle, His Staffers Are Willing to Fight for Him. Literally," *Washington Post*, March 10, 2016, https:// www.washingtonpost.com/lifestyle/style/inside-trumps-inner-circle-his-staffers-are -willing-to-fight-for-him-literally/2016/03/10/4b2b18e8-e660-11e5-a6f3-21ccdbc5f74e _story.html?utm_term=.78b6cafc14da.

90 CNN's Anderson Cooper once told Trump surrogate Jeffrey Lord: Chris Ariens, "Anderson Cooper: 'If He Took a Dump on His Desk, You Would Defend Him,'" *TV Newser*, May 20, 2017, http://www.adweek.com/tvnewser/anderson-cooper-if-he-took-a -dump-on-his-desk-you-would-defend-him/329803.

91 Trump campaign manager Paul Manafort assured reporters: Gregory Krieg, Eric Bradner, Eugene Scott, "No One to Be Fired After Melania Trump Speech Plagiarism Episode," CNN, July 19, 2016, http://www.cnn.com/2016/07/19/politics/melania-trump -michelle-obama-speech/index.html.

91 The defense became even more laughable when: Sophie Tatum, "RNC Official Cites 'My Little Pony' to Defend Melania Trump," CNN, July 19, 2016, http://www.cnn .com/2016/07/19/politics/sean-spicer-melania-trump-my-little-pony/index.html.

91 Edward Lucas, a former Moscow bureau chief for the *Economist*, is credited: "Whataboutism," Europe.view, *Economist*, January 31, 2008, http://www.economist .com/node/10598774.

92 Blitzer asked her if he was being "disrespectful" to the Gold Star family: Transcript, *The Situation Room*, CNN, August 2, 2017, http://transcripts.cnn.com /TRANSCRIPTS/1608/02/sitroom.02.html.

92 Hughes said: Transcript, *CNN Tonight*, CNN, October 7, 2016, http:// transcripts.cnn.com/TRANSCRIPTS/1610/07/cnnt.01.html.

92 Kingston said: Transcript, *CNN Newsroom*, CNN, October 2, 2016, http:// www.cnn.com/TRANSCRIPTS/1610/02/cnr.04.html.

92 "What do you think—our country's so innocent?": Rebecca Morin, "Trump Defends Putin, Says US Has 'A Lot of Killers,'" *Politico*, February 5, 2017, https://www .politico.eu/article/trump-defends-putin-says-us-has-a-lot-of-killers/.

93 Limbaugh said: Transcript, "Limbaugh: Media Are Jealous as They Can Be That Trump Responded to Criticism from Me," DailyRushbo, May 3, 2017, http:// dailyrushbo.com/limbaugh-media-are-jealous-as-they-can-be-that-trump-responded -to-criticism-from-me/.

93 Hugh Hewitt wrote: Hugh Hewitt, "There's No Republican Civil War," *Washington Post*, November 2, 2017, https://www.washingtonpost.com/opinions/theres -no-republican-civil-war/2017/11/02/023c860e-bdc2-11e7-959c-fe2b598d8c00_story .html?utm_term=.b7ac0caa81ad.

93 Gingrich has even written a book: Newt Gingrich, *Understanding Trump*, Hachette Book Group, 2017, pg. 3.

93 "The president and a small group of people know": Jessica Estepa, "Sean Spicer Says 'Covfefe' Wasn't a Typo: Trump Knew 'Exactly What He Meant,'" *USA Today*, May 31, 2017, https://www.usatoday.com/story/news/politics/onpolitics/2017/05/31/sean spicer-says-covfefe-wasnt-typo-trump-knew-exactly-what-he-meant/102355728/.

93 Take this exchange between *The View*'s Joy Behar and former 2016 contender Ben Carson: Nick Gass, "Whoopi Presses Carson on Trump: 'He's a Racist,'" *Politico*, March 24, 2016,

94 Trump's previous comments in which he compared Carson to a child molester: Gregory Krieg, "Trump Likens Carson's 'Pathology' to That of a Child Molester," CNN, November 12, 2015, http://www.cnn.com/2015/11/12/politics/donald-trump-ben -carson-child-molester/index.html?eref=rss_topstories.

94 Peter Thiel spoke: Jay Yarow, "Peter Thiel Perfectly Summed Up Donald Trump in a Few Sentences," CNBC, November 9, 2016, http://www.cnbc.com/2016/11/09/peter -thiel-perfectly-summed-up-donald-trump-in-one-paragraph.html.

94 A very similar construction: Salena Zito, "Taking Trump Seriously, Not Literally," *Atlantic*, September 23, 2016, https://www.theatlantic.com/politics /archive/2016/09/trump-makes-his-case-in-pittsburgh/501335/.

95 She said: Louis Nelson, "Conway: Judge Trump by What's in His Heart, Not What Comes Out of His Mouth," *Politico*, January 9, 2017, http://www.politico.com /story/2017/01/trump-statements-kellyanne-conway-233344.

95 "To be honest with you, if Donald Trump had said": Henry C. Jackson, "6 Things Trump Definitely Said That Pence Claimed He Didn't," *Politico*, October 5, 2016, https://www.politico.com/story/2016/10/trump-said-mike-pence-claimed-did -not-229171.

95 Another time, Trump told voters that if Clinton: Nick Corasaniti, Maggie Haberman, "Donald Trump Suggests 'Second Amendment People' Could Act Against Hillary Clinton," *New York Times*, August 9, 2016, https://www.nytimes.com/2016/08/10 /us/politics/donald-trump-hillary-clinton.html?_r=0.

95 McEnany played: Transcript, *Erin Burnett OutFront*, CNN, August 9, 2016, http://www.cnn.com/TRANSCRIPTS/1608/09/ebo.01.html.

96 "Says who?": Rachel Chason, "Trump's Lawyer Asks 'Says Who' When Told Trump Is Losing," CNN, August 18, 2016, http://www.cnn.com/2016/08/17/politics /donald-trump-michael-cohen-polls/index.html.

96 Hannity said: Josh Feldman, "'Neutral' Hannity Allows Trump to Get Away with Pushing Rafael Cruz Conspiracy Crap," *Mediaite*, May 3, 2016, http://www.mediaite .com/online/neutral-hannity-allows-trump-to-get-away-with-pushing-rafael-cruz -conspiracy-crap/.

97 "You're not a beautiful and unique snowflake": Jon Miltimore, "Love or Hate the Term 'Snowflake'? Thank 'Fight Club,'" Intellectual Takeout, January 25, 2017, http:// www.intellectualtakeout.org/blog/love-or-hate-term-snowflake-thank-fight-club.

97 "I can show bruises": Transcript, *Legal View with Ashleigh Banfield*, CNN, March 29, 2016, http://transcripts.cnn.com/TRANSCRIPTS/1603/29/lvab.01.html.

97 "For God's sake, read your history": Transcript, *New Day*, CNN, March 2, 2016, http://www.cnn.com/TRANSCRIPTS/1603/02/nday.03.html.

98 "[T]hink of Donald Trump as the Martin Luther King of health care": Eugene Scott, "CNN Commentator: Trump Is MLK of Health Care," CNN, April 13, 2017, http://www.cnn.com/2017/04/13/politics/jeffrey-lord-donald-trump-martin-luther-king-cnntv/index.html.

98 "Why are you bringing up Tamara's boobs?": "Former Trump 'Apprentice' Omarosa Manigault Brings Up Fox Business Channel Contributor's 'Big Boobs,'" Real Clear Politics, February 16, 2016, https://www.realclearpolitics.com/video/2016/02/16/trump_supporter_omarosa_brings_up_fox_business_channel_contributors_big_boobs.html.

98 Trump called: Ali Vitali, "Donald Trump Wants Consequences for GOP Rivals Not Endorsing Him," NBC News, June 30, 2016, http://www.nbcnews.com/politics/2016-election/donald-trump-wants-consequences-gop-rivals-not-endorsing-him-n601406.

98 Gingrich told reporters in Cleveland: Kaitlyn Schallhorn, "Gingrich Blasts Kasich, Bushes as 'Sore Losers' for Skipping RNC," *The Blaze*, July 18, 2016, http://www.theblaze.com/news/2016/07/18/gingrich-blasts-kasich-bushes-as-sore-losers-for-skipping-rnc/.

99 "The crybaby caucus": Ian Schwartz, "Hannity Rips Anti-Trump Crybaby Caucus: Why Did You Lie to Us? 'I'm Sick of Them,'" Real Clear Politics, July 19, 2016, https://www.realclearpolitics.com/video/2016/07/19/hannity_rips_anti-trump_crybaby_caucus_why_did_you_lie_to_us_im_sick_of_them.html.

99 Trump campaign manager Kellyanne Conway would have none of it: Karen Tumulty, Philip Rucker, "Shouting Match Erupts Between Clinton and Trump Aides," *Washington Post*, December 1, 2016, https://www.washingtonpost.com/politics/shouting-match-erupts-between-clinton-and-trump-aides/2016/12/01/7ac4398e-b7ea-11e6-b8df-600bd9d38a02_story.html?utm_term=.bb84ada1cdd4.

99 Take this explanation provided by Sarah Palin: John Hayward, "Exclusive: Sarah Palin on Donald Trump's First 100 Days," *Breitbart News*, April 27, 2017, http://www.breitbart.com/radio/2017/04/27/exclusive-sarah-palin-trumps-first-100-days/.

100 Breitbart senior editor-at-large: Joel B. Pollak, Twitter, August 18, 2017, https://twitter.com/joelpollak/status/898611991580770305.

CHAPTER 9: PUNCH 'EM IN THE FACE

102 According to sworn divorce deposition papers: Harry Hurt III, *Lost Tycoon: The Many Lives of Donald J. Trump*, Echo Point Books and Media, October 16, 2016, Kindle loc. 897–948 of 9275.

102 [L]ater told the *New Yorker*: Jane Mayer, "Documenting Trump's Abuse of Women," *New Yorker*, October 24, 2016, https://www.newyorker.com/magazine/2016/10/24/documenting-trumps-abuse-of-women.

103 "It's obviously false": Brandon Zadrozny, Tim Mak, "Ex-Wife: Donald Trump Made

Me Feel 'Violated' During Sex," *Daily Beast*, July 27, 2015, https://www.thedailybeast.com /ex-wife-donald-trump-made-me-feel-violated-during-sex.

103 Kelly wrote in her 2016 memoir: "Megyn Kelly Opens Up About Donald Trump's 'Bizarre Behavior' in New Memoir," CBS News, November 11, 2016, https:// www.cbsnews.com/news/megyn-kelly-opens-up-about-donald-trump-in-memoir -settle-for-more-new-york-times-review/.

104 Kelly did have a pointed question regarding: Transcript, "Read the Full Text of the Primetime Republican Debate," *Time*, August 11, 2015, http://time.com/3988276 /republican-debate-primetime-transcript-full-text/.

104 "[B]lood coming out of her eyes": Holly Yan, "Donald Trump's 'Blood' Comment About Megyn Kelly Draws Outrage," CNN, August 8, 2015, http://www.cnn .com/2015/08/08/politics/donald-trump-cnn-megyn-kelly-comment/index.html.

105 Ailes put out a statement: Chris Ariens, "Roger Ailes: Trump Should Apologize to Megyn Kelly; Fox News Won't Be 'Bullied by Anyone,'" *TVNewser*, August 25, 2015, http://www.adweek.com/tvnewser/roger-ailes-trump-should-apologize-to-megyn -kelly-fox-news-wont-be-bullied-by-anyone/270344.

105 Trump temporarily boycotted the network: Erik Wemple, "Donald Trump Is Boycotting Fox News," *Washington Post*, September 23, 2015, https://www.washingtonpost .com/blogs/erik-wemple/wp/2015/09/23/big-news-donald-trump-boycotting-fox -news/?utm_term=.e32bf08ff143.

105 [W]ent right on slamming Fox: Hadas Gold, "Roger Ailes: Donald Trump Should Apologize to Megyn Kelly," *Politico*, August 25, 2015, https://www.politico.com/blogs /media/2015/08/roger-ailes-donald-trump-should-apologize-to-megyn-kelly-212934.

106 [S]pokeswoman Hope Hicks said: Drew Griffin, "What Happened to Trump's Donations to Veterans?" CNN, April 22, 2016, http://www.cnn.com/2016/03/03/politics /donald-trump-veterans-donations/index.html.

106 Trump chided "sleazy" reporters: Eli Stokols, Nolan D. McCaskill, "Trump Taunts Media to Its Face," *Politico*, May 31, 2016, https://www.politico.com/story/2016/05 /trump-veterans-donations-223730.

107 Reporters like the *Washington Post*'s Amber Phillips: Amber Phillips, "Can Donald Trump Win? Here Are 5 Things He Needs to Do—but Probably Won't," *Washington Post*, August 10, 2015, https://www.washingtonpost.com/news/the-fix /wp/2015/08/10/can-donald-trump-win-here-are-5-things-he-needs-to-do-but-probably -wont/?utm_term=.df8efac6d9f3.

108 John Heilemann confidently predicted: Transcript, *Face the Nation*, CBS News, July 26, 2015, http://www.cbsnews.com/news/face-the-nation-transcripts-july-26-2015 -paul-perry-jindal-manchin/.

108 For his efforts: Nicholas Confessore, Karen Yourish, "$2 Billion Worth of Free Media for Donald Trump," *New York Times*, March 15, 2016, https://www.nytimes .com/2016/03/16/upshot/measuring-donald-trumps-mammoth-advantage-in-free -media.html?_r=0.

108 CEO Mark Thompson even thanked Trump for the boost: Etan Vlessing, "N.Y. Times CEO Thanks Trump for Boosting Subscription Growth," *Hollywood Reporter*, May 3, 2017, http://www.hollywoodreporter.com/news/ny-times-ceo-thanks-trump -boosting-subscription-growth-999914.

108 Gallup found that Americans' trust in the mass media had fallen: Art Swift, "Americans' Trust in Mass Media Sinks to New Low," Gallup, September 14, 2016, http:// www.gallup.com/poll/195542/americans-trust-mass-media-sinks-new-low.aspx.

109 One embed reporter later reflected: Seth Stevenson, "How Trump Conned America," *Slate*, November 11, 2016, http://www.slate.com/articles/news_and_politics /politics/2016/11/on_the_trail_for_the_final_week_of_the_trump_campaign.html.

109 Dr. Brad Bushman: Ryan Martin, "Four Questions on the Catharsis Myth with Dr. Brad Bushman," *All the Rage* (podcast), October 26, 2011, https://blog.uwgb.edu /alltherage/four-questions-on-the-catharsis-myth-with-dr-brad-bushman/.

110 In a 2002 study on the subject: Dr. Brad Bushman, "Does Venting Anger Feed or Extinguish the Flame? Catharsis, Rumination, Distraction, Anger, and Aggressive Responding," *Personality and Social Psychology Bulletin*, 2002, http://www-personal.umich .edu/~bbushman/PSPB02.pdf.

110 Psychological researchers at the University of Arizona: Daphna Motro, Daniel Sullivan, "Could Two Negative Emotions Be a Positive? The Effects of Anger and Anxiety in Enemyship," *Journal of Experimental Social Psychology*, 2016, http://rcgd.isr.umich .edu/seminars/Winter2017/Motro_Sullivan_2016.pdf.

110 "I could stand in the middle of Fifth Avenue and shoot somebody": Jeremy Diamond, "Trump: I Could 'Shoot Somebody and I Wouldn't Lose Voters,'" CNN, January 24, 2016, http://www.cnn.com/2016/01/23/politics/donald-trump-shoot-somebody -support/index.html.

110 Trump instructed attendees: Becket Adams, "Trump Tells Crowd to 'Knock the Hell' out of Protesters," *Washington Examiner*, February 1, 2016, http://www .washingtonexaminer.com/trump-tells-crowd-to-knock-the-hell-out-of-protesters/article /2582102.

111 Trump talked about his desire to change the pleased expression: Jeremy Diamond, "Donald Trump on Protester: 'I'd Like to Punch Him in the Face,'" CNN, February 23, 2016, http://www.cnn.com/2016/02/23/politics/donald-trump-nevada-rally-punch /index.html.

111 He then praised his supporters: Eugene Kiely, "'Temperature' at Trump Rallies," FactCheck.org, March 15, 2016, http://www.factcheck.org/2016/03/temperature -at-trump-rallies/.

111 [T]he victim said: Katie Reilly, Melissa Chan, "Donald Trump Protester Punched in the Face at North Carolina Rally," *Time*, March 10, 2016, http://time .com/4253898/donald-trump-protester-north-carolina-rally-punched/.

111 Andy Dean, a former *Apprentice* star, said: Tessa Berenson, "Meet the Members of Donald Trump's Television Army," *Time*, April 5, 2016, http://time.com/4281934 /donald-trump-tv-supporters-katrina-pierson-omarosa-jeffrey-lord/.

112 "[T]here's no violence": Tessa Berenson, "Trump Denies There Is Any Violence at His Rallies," *Time*, March 14, 2016, http://time.com/4257804/donald-trump-rally -violence-denial/.

112 "Riots aren't necessarily a bad thing": Daniel White, "Trump Supporter: 'Riots Aren't Necessarily a Bad Thing,'" *Time*, March 16, 2016, http://time.com/4262131 /trump-supporter-riots-arent-necessarily-a-bad-thing/.

112 One of the defendants wrote in a letter: Jason Riley, "Three Men Criminally Charged for Physical Harassment of a Protester at Trump Rally in Louisville," WDRB .com, July 20, 2016, http://www.wdrb.com/story/32490892/three-men-charged-with -misdemeanors-for-physical-harassment-of-donald-trump-protester.

112 As she wrote in one of her last pieces for *Breitbart News*: Michelle Fields, "Michelle Fields: In Her Own Words," *Breitbart News*, March 10, 2016, http://www.breitbart .com/big-journalism/2016/03/10/3276486/?dg.

113 The Trump campaign flatly denied that any such incident had occurred: ABC News Politics, "New: Trump Campaign Spokesperson Hope Hicks Responds to Allegations Campaign Manager Assaulted Breitbart Reporter," Twitter, March 10, 2016, https:// twitter.com/ABCPolitics/status/708003221139140608.

113 Soon enough, video and audio: Benny Johnson, "AUDIO: Listen to the Moment Trump's Campaign Manager Allegedly Assaulted Michelle Fields," *Independent Journal Review*, March 2015, http://ijr.com/2016/03/557732-audio-here-is-the-altercation -between-trumps-campaign-manager-and-michelle-fields/.

113 C-SPAN video showed Fields approaching Trump and Lewandowski: Ben Mathis-Lilley, "C-SPAN Video Shows Trump Campaign Manager Reaching Toward Reporter's Arm," *Slate*, March 11, 2016, http://www.slate.com/blogs/the_slatest/2016/03/11 /corey_lewandowski_michelle_fields_in_cspn_video.html.

114 Trump said he was the victim: Christina Wilkie, "Reporter's Pen Could Have Been 'A Little Bomb,'" *Huffington Post*, March 30, 2016, http://www.huffingtonpost.com /entry/trump-michelle-fields-pen_us_56fb3e4cc4b0daf53aedfbf4.

114 [H]er eyes were wide open: Michelle Fields, "Journalism in the Age of the Body Slam," *New York Times*, May 25, 2017, https://www.nytimes.com/2017/05/25/opinion /greg-gianforte-attack-on-media.html?_r=0.

CHAPTER 10: KAYFABE

117 [T]he Pew Research Center: Jeffrey Gottfried, Elisa Shearer, "New Use Across Social Media Platforms 2016," Pew Research Center, May 2016, http://www.journalism .org/2016/05/26/news-use-across-social-media-platforms-2016/.

118 "I was given $3,500 to protest Donald Trump's rally": Louis Jacobson, "No, Someone Wasn't Paid $3,500 to Protest Donald Trump; It's Fake News," PolitiFact, November 17, 2016, http://www.politifact.com/truth-o-meter/statements/2016/nov/17 /blog-posting/no-someone-wasnt-paid-3500-protest-donald-trump-it/.

119 He told the *Washington Post*: Caitlin Dewey, "Facebook Fake-News Writer: 'I Think Donald Trump Is in the White House Because of Me,'" *Washington Post*, November 17, 2016, https://www.washingtonpost.com/news/the-intersect/wp/2016/11/17

/facebook-fake-news-writer-i-think-donald-trump-is-in-the-white-house-because-of
-me/?utm_term=.92dc4ab25a96.

120 [A]ccording to *BuzzFeed News*: Craig Silverman, Lawrence Alexander, "How Teens in the Balkans Are Duping Trump Supporters with Fake News," *BuzzFeed News*, November 3, 2016, https://www.buzzfeed.com/craigsilverman/how-macedonia-became -a-global-hub-for-pro-trump-misinfo?utm_term=.iuw7oYa4p#.yurjxXg2B.

120 *BuzzFeed News* stated: Craig Silverman, "This Analysis Shows How Viral Fake Election News Stories Outperformed Real News on Facebook," *BuzzFeed News*, November 16, 2016, https://www.buzzfeed.com/craigsilverman/viral-fake-election-news -outperformed-real-news-on-facebook?utm_term=.eep67x9xa#.hrgG67M7W.

120 A September 2016 Rasmussen poll: "Voters Don't Trust Media Fact-Checking," Rasmussen Reports, September 30, 2016, http://www.rasmussenreports.com/public_content /politics/general_politics/september_2016/voters_don_t_trust_media_fact_checking.

121 PolitiFact demanded: W. Gardner Selby, "Ted Cruz Says Iran Annually Has Death to America Holiday," PolitiFact, March 13, 2015, http://www.politifact.com/texas/statements /2015/mar/13/ted-cruz/ted-cruz-says-iran-annually-has-death-america-holi/.

121 "A list of Iranian holidays": Ibid.

121 I could only take heart: John Nolte, "Fact Check: Ted Cruz Attack Proves PolitiFact Is Run by Gigantic Assholes," *Breitbart News*, March 14, 2015, http://www .breitbart.com/big-journalism/2015/03/14/mostly-true-ted-cruz-attack-proves-politifact-is -run-by-gigantic-assholes/.

122 Writer Caitlin Dewey said in her final column: Caitlin Dewey, "What Was Fake on the Internet This Week: Why This Is the Final Column," *Washington Post*, December 18, 2015, https://www.washingtonpost.com/news/the-intersect/wp/2015/12/18/what-was-fake-on -the-internet-this-week-why-this-is-the-final-column/?utm_term=.6f48d3605d15.

122 The Pew Research Center found: Michael Barthel, Amy Mitchell, Jesse Holcomb, "Many Americans Believe Fake News Is Sowing Confusion," Pew Research Center, December 15, 2016, http://www.journalism.org/2016/12/15/many-americans-believe -fake-news-is-sowing-confusion/.

123 Look at what happened in London: James Vincent, "Is Sharing Fake News Okay If It Feels Right?" *The Verge*, March 23, 2017, https://www.theverge.com/tldr /2017/3/23/15034018/london-terror-attack-tube-sign-fake-news.

123 Jonah Berger, a professor: Jonah Berger, Katherine Milkman, "What Makes Online Content Viral?" *Journal of Marketing Research*, 2011, https://www.ama.org/documents /online_content_viral.pdf.

123 A magazine photo of Kim Kardashian's: David Hershkovits, "How Kim Kardashian Broke the Internet with Her Butt," *Guardian*, December 17, 2014, https://www.theguardian .com/lifeandstyle/2014/dec/17/kim-kardashian-butt-break-the-internet-paper-magazine.

124 "The Paranoid Style in American Politics": Richard Hofstadter, "The Paranoid Style in American Politics," *Harper's Magazine*, November 1964, https://harpers.org /archive/1964/11/the-paranoid-style-in-american-politics/.

125 Snopes attempted to debunk the rumor: David Mikkelson, "Clinton Body Bags," Snopes, January 24, 1998, https://www.snopes.com/politics/clintons/bodycount.asp.

125 "[S]omething fishy": Jose A. DelReal, Robert Costa, "Trump Escalates Attack on Bill Clinton," *Washington Post*, May 23, 2016, https://www.washingtonpost.com /politics/trump-escalates-attack-on-bill-clinton/2016/05/23/ed109acc-2100-11e6-8690 -f14ca9de2972_story.html?utm_term=.68d0e633cb9c.

126 Here's one sample from Fox News: Malia Zimmerman, "Flight Logs Show Bill Clinton Flew on Sex Offender's Jet Much More Than Previously Known," Fox News, May 13, 2016, http://www.foxnews.com/us/2016/05/13/flight-logs-show-bill-clinton -flew-on-sex-offenders-jet-much-more-than-previously-known.html.

126 Clinton took special drugs: Jerome Corsi, "Hillary Mum on Coughing Fits, Special Eyeglasses," *WorldNetDaily*, February 19, 2016, http://www.wnd.com/2016/02 /hillary-mum-on-coughing-fits-special-eyeglasses/.

127 "Do we actually know who told Hillary": Amy Davidson Sorkin, "Yet More E-Mail Trouble for Clinton," *New Yorker*, November 7, 2016, https://www.newyorker .com/magazine/2016/11/07/yet-more-email-trouble-for-clinton.

127 According to University of Miami political scientists: Michael Shermer, "Why Do People Believe in Conspiracy Theories?" *Scientific American*, December 1, 2014, https://www .scientificamerican.com/article/why-do-people-believe-in-conspiracy-theories/.

128 Trump said: Transcript, "Donald Trump's Speech at the Republican Convention, as Prepared for Delivery," CNN, July 22, 2016, http://www.cnn.com/2016/07/22 /politics/donald-trump-rnc-speech-text/index.html.

128 Brendan Nyhan, a political science professor: Gregory Krieg, "Why People Believe Conspiracy Theories Like 'Pizza Gate,'" CNN, December 6, 2016, http://www.cnn .com/2016/12/05/politics/pizza-gate-conspiracy-theories-why-believe/index.html.

129 "Your reputation's amazing": Tina Nguyen, "Donald Trump to Prominent Conspiracy Theorist: 'Your Reputation Is Amazing,'" *Vanity Fair*, December 2, 2015, https://www .vanityfair.com/news/2015/12/donald-trump-alex-jones-interview.

129 He once described her: Media Matters Staff, "Trump Ally Alex Jones: 'I Was Told by People Around' Clinton That 'She's Demon-Possessed,'" Media Matters, October 10, 2016, https://www.mediamatters.org/video/2016/10/10/trump-ally-alex-jones-i-was -told-people-around-clinton-shes-demon-possessed/213712.

129 One of his most popular videos: The Alex Jones Channel, "Hillary Caught on Tape Birthing Alien Life Form," YouTube, September 7, 2016, https://www.youtube.com /watch?v=4fuui9qICYg.

129 Jones said: David Wright, "Obama Smells Himself, Confirms He Is Not a Demon," CNN, October 12, 2016, http://www.cnn.com/2016/10/12/politics/obama-sulfur -smell-alex-jones/index.html.

130 Obama said: Ibid.

130 "You can call me a conspiracy theorist all day long": Video, "Alex Jones Strikes

Back in Powerful Response to NYT/Obama Hit Piece," InfoWars.com, October 14, 2016, https://www.infowars.com/alex-jones-responds-to-new-york-times-hit-piece/.

130 "He's playing a character": Jonathan Tilove, "In Travis County Custody Case, Jury Will Search for Real Alex Jones," *Austin American-Statesman*, April 16, 2017, http://www.mystatesman.com/news/state--regional-govt--politics/travis-county-custody-case-jury-will-search-for-real-alex-jones/rnbWzMHnFCd5SOPgP3A34J/.

130 Sociologist Nick Rogers said: Nick Rogers, "How Wrestling Explains Alex Jones and Donald Trump," *New York Times*, April 25, 2017, https://www.nytimes.com/2017/04/25/opinion/wrestling-explains-alex-jones-and-donald-trump.html.

CHAPTER 11: THE CULT OF KEK

133 The pair described them: Anne Case, Angus Deaton, "Rising Morbidity and Mortality in Midlife Among White Non-Hispanic Americans in the 21st Century," *Proceedings of the National Academy of Sciences of the United States of America*, December 8, 2015, http://www.pnas.org/content/112/49/15078.full?tab=author-info.

134 "The recession, ever-expanding personal debt, and high-profile terrorist attacks": Daniel Sullivan, "Psychology Explains How Trump Won by Making White Men Feel Like Victims," *Quartz*, November 11, 2016, https://qz.com/834713/us-election-psychology-explains-how-donald-trump-won-by-making-white-men-feel-like-victims/.

135 "The core concept": Andrew Anglin, "A Normie's Guide to the Alt-Right," *Daily Stormer*, August 31, 2016, www.dailystormer/a-normies-guide-to-the-alt-right/.

135 His speech announcing his candidacy for presidency was a siren call: Transcript, "Full Text: Donald Trump Announces a Presidential Bid," *Washington Post*, June 16, 2015, https://www.washingtonpost.com/news/post-politics/wp/2015/06/16/full-text-donald-trump-announces-a-presidential-bid/.

135 Trump declined to denounce David Duke: Eric Bradner, "Donald Trump Stumbles on David Duke, KKK," CNN, February 29, 2016, http://www.cnn.com/2016/02/28/politics/donald-trump-white-supremacists/index.html.

135 Read carefully what Trump said: Paola Chavez, "Donald Trump Claims No One Has 'Done So Much for Equality as I Have,'" ABC News, March 1, 2016, http://abcnews.go.com/Politics/donald-trump-claims-equality/story?id=37305333.

136 "I'll use the word anchor baby": Alex Griswold, "ABC Reporter Battles over 'Anchor Baby' Term: 'It's Offensive!'" *Mediaite*, August 20, 2015, https://www.mediaite.com/tv/abc-reporter-battles-trump-over-anchor-baby-term-its-offensive/.

136 "Before Trump, our identity ideas, national ideas, they had no place to go": Jennifer Palmieri, "Our Campaign Lost the Election. But Trump's Team Must Own Up to How He Won," *Washington Post*, December 7, 2016, https://www.washingtonpost.com/opinions/our-campaign-lost-the-election-but-trumps-team-must-own-up-to-how-he-won/2016/12/07/4a6a4c24-bcbd-11e6-94ac-3d324840106c_story.html?utm_term=.a94c5edfe425.

136 "Race is real, race matters": Serge F. Kovaleski, Julie Turkewitz, Joseph Goldstein, Dan Barry, "An Alt-Right Makeover Shrouds the Swastikas," *New York Times*,

December 10, 2016, https://www.nytimes.com/2016/12/10/us/alt-right-national-socialist
-movement-white-supremacy.html.

136 Mike Cernovich said: Mike Cernovich, Twitter, October 28, 2015, https://
web.archive.org/web/20160815185116/https:/twitter.com/cernovich/status
/659472184679780352.

137 One 2015 study: Shanto Iyengar, Sean J. Westwood, "Fear and Loathing Across
Party Lines: New Evidence on Group Polarization," *American Journal of Political Science*,
2015, https://pcl.stanford.edu/research/2015/iyengar-ajps-group-polarization.pdf.

138 "[D]one in the spirit of irony and exuberance": Joshua Barajas, "Nazi Salutes 'Done
in a Spirit of Irony and Exuberance,' Alt-Right Leader Says," PBS NewsHour, November 22, 2016, https://www.pbs.org/newshour/politics/white-nationalist.

139 Neiwert wrote: David Neiwert, "What the Kek: Explaining the Alt-Right 'De-
ity' Behind Their 'Meme Magic,'" Southern Poverty Law Center, May 8, 2017, https://
www.splcenter.org/hatewatch/2017/05/08/what-kek-explaining-alt-right-deity-behind
-their-meme-magic.

139 Rush Limbaugh passed along a variation: Transcript, "Trump Was Supposed to Be
Gone by Now," *The Rush Limbaugh Show*, July 22, 2015, https://www.rushlimbaugh.com/
daily/2015/07/22/trump_was_supposed_to_be_gone_by_now/.

CHAPTER 12: HACKS

142 "[H]orrible, absolutely horrible": Donald J. Trump, "News Conference in Doral,
Florida," The American Presidency Project, July 27, 2016, http://www.presidency
.ucsb.edu/ws/index.php?pid=118047.

142 "It's so farfetched": Ibid.

143 "Russia, if you're listening": Ibid.

143 The Senate Intelligence Committee released a bipartisan report: U.S. Senate Select
Committee on Intelligence, "Assessing Russian Activities and Intentions in Recent U.S.
Elections," January 6, 2017, https://www.intelligence.senate.gov/publications/assessing
-russian-activities-and-intentions-recent-us-elections.

145 Watts testified: Clint Watts, "Clint Watts' Testimony: Russia's Info War on the
U.S. Started in 2014," *Daily Beast*, March 30, 2017, https://www.thedailybeast.com/clint
-watts-testimony-russias-info-war-on-the-us-started-in-2014.

146 Manafort asked Tapper: Transcript, *State of the Union*, CNN, August 14, 2016,
http://www.cnn.com/TRANSCRIPTS/1608/14/sotu.01.html.

CHAPTER 13: BIMBO ERUPTIONS

147 "I did not have sexual relations with that woman, Miss Lewinsky": Transcript, "President Bill Clinton," CNN, August 17, 1998, http://www.cnn.com
/ALLPOLITICS/1998/08/17/speech/transcript.html.

147 Hillary called Lewinsky a "narcissistic loony toon": Alana Goodman, "The Hillary Papers," *Washington Free Beacon*, February 9, 2014, http://freebeacon.com
/politics/the-hillary-papers/.

148 She didn't really resurface until 2014: Monica Lewinsky, "Shame and Survival," *Vanity Fair*, June 2014, http://www.vanityfair.com/style/society/2014/06/monica-lewinsky-humiliation-culture.

148 Charlie Rangel said during that time: Maureen Dowd, "Liberties; The Slander Strategy," *New York Times*, January 28, 1998, http://www.nytimes.com/1998/01/28/opinion/liberties-the-slander-strategy.html.

148 "It was a right-wing attack": Anita Kumar, Lesley Clark, "Why Do Women's Groups Treat Bill Clinton and Donald Trump Differently?" *McClatchy DC*, October 14, 2016, http://www.mcclatchydc.com/news/politics-government/election/article108304112.html.

148 Gloria Steinem did the same: Gloria Steinem, "Why Feminists Support Clinton," *New York Times*, March 22, 1998, http://www.nytimes.com/2010/09/26/opinion/eq-steinem.html.

149 Tina Brown described the president: Tina Brown, "Fax from Washington," *New Yorker*, February 16, 1998, pg. 31.

149 Nina Burleigh made her desires explicit: Howard Kurtz, "Going Weak in the Knees for Clinton," *Washington Post*, July 6, 1998, http://www.washingtonpost.com/wp-srv/politics/special/clinton/stories/medianotes070698.htm.

149 "Feminism sort of died in that period": Dylan Stableford, "Maureen Dowd: 'Feminism Died a Little Bit' Under Bill Clinton," Yahoo, October 3, 2016, https://www.yahoo.com/news/maureen-down-feminism-died-under-bill-clinton-190246356.html.

149 She wrote a barn burner of a piece: Marjorie Williams, "Lowering the Bar: Clinton and Women," *Vanity Fair*, May 1998, http://www.vanityfair.com/magazine/1998/05/williams199805.

149 Betsey Wright termed "bimbo eruptions": Gil Troy, "The Feminist Who Used Sexism to Defend Bill Clinton," *Daily Beast*, August 7, 2016, https://www.thedailybeast.com/the-feminist-who-used-sexism-to-defend-bill-clinton.

150 "His hands were all over me": Eric Lichtblau, "Willey Repeats Allegations of Clinton Groping at Trial," *Los Angeles Times*, May 5, 1999, http://articles.latimes.com/1999/may/05/news/mn-34167.

150 Hillary Clinton dismissed her: Shawn Boburg, "Enabler or Family Defender? How Hillary Clinton Responded to Husband's Accusers," *Washington Post*, September 28, 2016, https://www.washingtonpost.com/local/enabler-or-family-defender-how-hillary-clinton-responded-to-husbands-accusers/2016/09/28/58dad5d4-6fb1-11e6-8533-6b0b0ded0253_story.html?utm_term=.75b0d3ac8020.

151 [D]uring a New Hampshire event: Eric Bradner, Dan Merica, "Hillary Clinton Asked About Paula Jones," CNN, December 3, 2015, http://www.cnn.com/2015/12/03/politics/hillary-clinton-paula-jones-question/.

151 Broaddrick told *BuzzFeed News*: Katie J. M. Baker, "Juanita Broaddrick Wants to Be Believed," *BuzzFeed News*, August 14, 2016, https://www.buzzfeed.com/katiejmbaker/juanita-broaddrick-wants-to-be-believed?utm_term=.iyMgKrpoJ#.aiDkDZdNO.

151 [L]iberal feminists fell in line: Marjorie Williams, "Lowering the Bar: Clinton and Women," *Vanity Fair*, May 1998, http://www.vanityfair.com/magazine/1998/05/williams199805.

152 "[T]here's no feeling sorry for Hillary": Transcript, *Fox News Sunday*, Fox News, January 10, 2016, http://www.foxnews.com/transcript/2016/01/10/donald-trump-talks-ted-cruz-gun-control-and-clintons-denis-mcdonough-previews.html.

152 For a while, Clinton refused to fire back: Anne Gearan, "Hillary Clinton Dismisses Trump's 'Alternate Reality,'" *Washington Post*, January 4, 2016, https://www.washingtonpost.com/news/post-politics/wp/2016/01/04/hillary-clinton-dismisses-trumps-alternate-reality/?utm_term=.cd82b7597d95.

152 Trump took Bill Clinton's side: Jordyn Phelps, "Flashback: Donald Trump Called Bill Clinton's Accusers 'Terrible' and 'Unattractive' and Former President 'Terrific,'" ABC News, October 9, 2016, http://abcnews.go.com/Politics/flashback-donald-trump-called-bill-clintons-accusers-terrible/story?id=42686582.

153 Feigning he was a man of polite manners, he said: Maggie Severns, "Trump: 'I Was Going to Say Something Extremely Rough' to Clinton," *Politico*, September 26, 2016, https://www.politico.com/story/2016/09/what-was-trump-going-to-say-to-clinton-first-debate-228744.

153 Trump said he was proud: Daniella Diaz, "Trump: I Held Back on Bill Clinton's 'Indiscretions' Because of Chelsea," CNN, September 27, 2016, http://www.cnn.com/2016/09/26/politics/presidential-debate-donald-trump-debate-performance/index.html.

153 The talking points, obtained by CNN, went as follows: Jim Acosta, Theodore Schleifer, "Trump Campaign Talking Points: Bring Up Monica," CNN, September 30, 2016, http://www.cnn.com/2016/09/28/politics/donald-trump-monica-lewinsky-hillary-clinton/index.html.

CHAPTER 14: LOCK HER UP

155 On the air that night I said: Ian Schwartz, "Amanda Carpenter: Trump Is Talking About 'Sexual Assault,' No Other Way to Frame This," Real Clear Politics, October 8, 2016, https://www.realclearpolitics.com/video/2016/10/08/amanda_carpenter_trump_is_talking_about_sexual_assault_no_other_way_to_frame_this.html.

156 [S]ent out a solemn statement: Brian Flood, "Mike Pence 'Cannot Defend' Donald Trump's Remarks: 'We Pray for His Family,'" *The Wrap*, October 8, 2016, https://www.thewrap.com/mike-pence-cannot-defend-donald-trumps-remarks-we-pray-for-his-family/.

157 "Actions speak louder than words": Liam Stack, "Donald Trump Featured Paula Jones and 2 Other Women Who Accused Bill Clinton of Sexual Assault," *New York Times*, October 9, 2016, https://www.nytimes.com/2016/10/10/us/politics/bill-clinton-accusers.html?_r=0.

157 Trump said: Transcript, "Transcript of the Second Debate," *New York Times*, October 10, 2016, https://www.nytimes.com/2016/10/10/us/politics/transcript-second-debate.html.

159 "Because you'd be in jail": Ibid.

159 [A] "litmus test" of loyalty: Interview, "Steve Bannon Interview: Trump 'Access Hollywood' Tape Was a Litmus Test," CBS News, September 8, 2017, https://www.cbsnews.com/news/steve-bannon-60-minutes-interview-trump-access-hollywood-test/.

159 Pence hopped off the bench and deployed to Liberty University: Vaughn Hillyard, "Pence Gets Lukewarm Reception for Liberty University Speech," NBC News, October 12, 2016, https://www.nbcnews.com/politics/2016-election/pence-gets-lukewarm-reception-liberty-university-speech-n665316.

160 He said: Patrick Healy, Alan Rappeport, "Donald Trump Calls Allegations by Women 'False Smears,'" *New York Times*, October 13, 2016, https://www.nytimes.com/2016/10/14/us/politics/donald-trump-women.html.

160 Trump denied all allegations en masse: Jeremy Diamond, Eugene Scott, "Trump Says He'll Sue Sexual Misconduct Accusers," CNN, October 22, 2016, http://www.cnn.com/2016/10/22/politics/trump-says-hell-sue-sexual-misconduct-accusers/index.html.

160 Trump said that one of the women: Jose A. DelReal, "Trump Mocks Sexual Assault Accuser: 'She Would Not Be My First Choice,'" *Washington Post*, October 14, 2016, https://www.washingtonpost.com/news/post-politics/wp/2016/10/14/trump-mocks-sexual-assault-accuser-she-would-not-be-my-first-choice/?utm_term=.0e5d39dd855f.

161 Trump said things such as: Gabrielle Healy, "Did Trump Really Mention WikiLeaks Over 160 Times in the Last Month of the Election Cycle?" PolitiFact, April 21, 2017, http://www.politifact.com/truth-o-meter/statements/2017/apr/21/jackie-speier/did-trump-really-mention-wikileaks-over-160-times-/.

161 "The WikiLeaks revelations have exposed criminal corruption at the highest levels of our government": Donald J. Trump, "Remarks at the Phoenix Convention Center in Phoenix, Arizona," The American Presidency Project, October 29, 2016, http://www.presidency.ucsb.edu/ws/index.php?pid=119182.

162 He said in a letter to FBI employees: Sari Horwitz, "Read the Letter Comey Sent to FBI Employees Explaining His Controversial Decision on the Clinton Email Investigation," *Washington Post*, October 28, 2016, https://www.washingtonpost.com/news/post-nation/wp/2016/10/28/read-the-letter-comey-sent-to-fbi-employees-explaining-his-controversial-decision-on-the-clinton-email-investigation/?utm_term=.07fa513959e5.

CHAPTER 15: PRESIDENT TRUMP

166 "I'm going to be so presidential you will be so bored": Eun Kyung Kim, "Donald Trump Joins TODAY Show for Live Town Hall, Answers Voters' Questions," *Today*, August 21, 2016, https://www.today.com/news/donald-trump-joins-today-show-live-town-hall-answers-voters-t87551.

166 President-elect Trump tweeted: Donald J. Trump, Twitter, November 27, 2016, https://twitter.com/realdonaldtrump/status/802972944532209664?lang=en.

166 "There's no such thing, unfortunately, anymore of facts": Jack Holmes, "A Trump Surrogate Drops the Mic: 'There's No Such Thing as Facts,'" *Esquire*, December 1,

2016, http://www.esquire.com/news-politics/videos/a51152/trump-surrogate-no-such
-thing-as-facts/.

166 [G]ive a very similar assessment: "Transcript: ABC News Anchor David Muir
Interviews President Trump," ABC News, January 25, 2017, http://abcnews.go.com
/Politics/transcript-abc-news-anchor-david-muir-interviews-president/story
?id=45047602.

167 "Many mostly Democrat States": Donald J. Trump, Twitter, January 4, 2018, https://
twitter.com/realDonaldTrump/status/948872192284155904.

167 An official White House statement: Statement by the Press Secretary on the Presidential Advisory Commission on Election Integrity, January 3, 2018, https://www
.whitehouse.gov/briefings-statements/statement-press-secretary-presidential-advisory
-commission-election-integrity/.

168 "It's a lie": Remarks by President Trump and Vice President Pence at CIA Headquarters, January 21, 2017, https://www.whitehouse.gov/the-press-office/2017/01/21
/remarks-president-trump-and-vice-president-pence-cia-headquarters.

168 "[T]he largest audience to witness an inauguration": Statement by Press Secretary Sean Spicer, January 21, 2017, https://www.whitehouse.gov/the-press-of
fice/2017/01/21/statement-press-secretary-sean-spicer.

168 Spicer said that he "absolutely" regrets telling this lie: Glenn Thrush, Dave Itz-
koff, "Sean Spicer Says He Regrets Berating Reporters over Inauguration Crowds," *New
York Times*, September 18, 2017, https://www.nytimes.com/2017/09/18/arts/television
/sean-spicer-emmys.html.

168 White House senior adviser Kellyanne Conway went to work next: Transcript,
Meet the Press, NBC News, January 22, 2017, https://www.nbcnews.com/meet-the-press
/meet-press-01-22-17-n710491.

169 "Everybody acts like President Trump is the one that came up with this idea":
Transcript, *This Week*, ABC News, March 5, 2017, http://abcnews.go.com/Politics/week
-transcript-17-sarah-huckabee-sanders-josh-earnest/story?id=45911284.

169 [S]he offered some alternative facts of her own: Mike Kelly, "Kellyanne Conway
Alludes to Even Wider Surveillance of Trump Campaign," *Record*, March 15, 2017,
http://www.northjersey.com/story/news/columnists/mike-kelly/2017/03/12/mike-kelly
-conway-suggests-even-wider-surveillance-trump-campaign/99060910/.

170 Trump told: Justin Baragona, "'Wiretap Covers a Lot of Different Things': Trump
Says We'll Know More About His Claims in 'Two Weeks,'" *Mediaite*, March 15, 2017,
https://www.mediaite.com/online/wiretap-covers-a-lot-of-different-things-trump
-says-well-know-more-about-his-claims-in-two-weeks/.

170 Fox News wouldn't back up their contributor: Peter Sterne, "Fox News: 'No Evidence of Any Kind' That Obama Wiretapped Trump," *Politico*, March 17, 2017, http://
www.politico.com/blogs/on-media/2017/03/fox-news-no-evidence-trump-obama-wire
tapping-236186.

170 "All we did was quote a certain very talented legal mind": Joint Press Conference with President Trump and German Chancellor Merkel, March 17, 2017, https://

www.whitehouse.gov/the-press-office/2017/03/17/joint-press-conference-president
-trump-and-german-chancellor-merkel.

170 Trump simultaneously said: "President Trump Cites 'Made Up' Russia Story in Interview on Comey Firing," NBC News, May 11, 2017, http://www.nbcwashington.com
/news/politics/President-Trump-Lester-Holt-Russia-Made-Up-Story-422056703.html.

172 Adriana Cohen was furious: Adriana Cohen, "The Media Has Lost Its Marbles," *Boston Herald*, May 18, 2017, http://www.bostonherald.com/news/columnists/adriana
_cohen/2017/05/adriana_cohen_the_media_has_lost_its_marbles.

172 Sean Hannity went on the air: Transcript, *Hannity*, Fox News, June 20, 2017, http://www.foxnews.com/transcript/2017/06/20/levin-challenges-mueller-whats-your
-intention-gorka-us-wants-to-crush-isis-not-war-with-russia.html.

172 "Our president is under constant barrage": Joe Concha, "Dobbs: White House Communications Team 'Flatfooted and Failing' Against 'Forces of Evil,'" *The Hill*, May 17, 2017, http://thehill.com/homenews/media/333780-dobbs-white-house-communications
-team-flatfooted-and-failing-against-forces-of.

172 "Can we just cut through the crap!": Joe DePaolo, "'Can We Just Cut Through the Crap!': Former Cruz Staffer Amanda Carpenter Blasts GOP Figures Who 'Enabled' Trump," *Mediaite*, May 17, 2017, https://www.mediaite.com/online/can-we-just-cut
-through-the-crap-former-cruz-staffer-amanda-carpenter-blasts-gop-figures-who
-enabled-trump/.

CHAPTER 16: NIXON'S SHADOW

175 As Nixon wrote in one 1971 memo to H. R. Haldeman: Richard Reeves, *President Nixon: Alone in the White House*, Simon & Schuster, 2001, pg. 472.

175 "[E]nemy of the American people": David Jackson, "Trump Again Calls Media 'Enemy of the People,'" *USA Today*, February 24, 2017, https://www.usatoday.com/story
/news/politics/2017/02/24/donald-trump-cpac-media-enemy-of-the-people/98347970/.

177 Clark MacGregor said: Carl Bernstein, Bob Woodward, *All the President's Men*, Simon & Schuster, 1974, pgs. 163–64.

177 [S]ixty-nine people being charged with crimes: Bill Marsh, "When Criminal Charges Reach the White House," *New York Times*, October 30, 2005, https://query
.nytimes.com/gst/fullpage.html?res=9904E7DF1F3FF933A05753C1A9639C8B63.

178 [P]roposed far worse: G. Gordon Liddy, *Will*, St. Martin's Press, 1980, pgs. 171, 197–98, 207–10.

178 "Do you think, for Christ sakes": Richard Reeves, *President Nixon: Alone in the White House*, Simon & Schuster, 2001, pg. 339.

178 "[I]t would be an undeclared war": G. Gordon Liddy, *Will*, St. Martin's Press, 1980, pg. 182.

179 "I knew exactly what had to be done and why": Ibid., pgs. 193–94.

179 "How many of our people should we let him kill before we stop him?": Ibid., pgs. 207–10.

179 "If necessary, I'll do it": Ibid.

179 "If someone wants to shoot me": Ibid., pg. 258.

180 They called her their "secret weapon": Helen Thomas, *Front Row at the White House*, Touchstone, 1999, pg. 205.

180 Helen Thomas recalled: Ibid., pg. 201.

181 She was drugged: Winzola McLendon, *Martha*, Random House, 1979, pgs. 13–14.

181 "They threw me down on the bed": Helen Thomas, *Front Row at the White House*, Touchstone, 1999, pg. 211.

182 Haldeman said: John Dean, *The Nixon Defense*, Viking, 2014, pgs. 73–74.

182 He thought it reasonable she was heavily guarded: Winzola McLendon, "When Watergate Came, She Paid for Her Big Mouth," *Chicago Tribune*, July 29, 1979, http://archives.chicagotribune.com/1979/07/29/page/269/article/when-watergate-came-she-paid-for-her-big-mouth.

182 Ben Bradlee later recalled: Ben Bradlee, "Watergate: 25 Years Later," *Washington Post*, June 17, 1997, http://www.washingtonpost.com/wp-dyn/content/discussion/2006/10/18/DI2006101801505.html.

183 [I]n the years after his resignation he blamed *her* for Watergate!: Austin Scott, "Sought to Scrap Watergate Tapes, Nixon Discloses," *Washington Post*, September 4, 1977, https://www.washingtonpost.com/archive/politics/1977/09/04/sought-to-scrap-watergate-tapes-nixon-discloses/fe001d53-f94e-44d8-aecc-40cfbca309cd/?utm_term=.11170d15060

183 He was so enamored: David Fahrenthold, "A Little Magazine with Trump on the Cover Hangs in His Golf Clubs. It's Fake," *Washington Post*, June 27, 2017, https://www.washingtonpost.com/politics/a-time-magazine-with-trump-on-the-cover-hangs-in-his-golf-clubs-its-fake/2017/06/27/0adf96de-5850-11e7-ba90-f5875b7d1876_story.html?utm_term=.3e14a05ff40a.

184 "[N]obody's had more covers": *Time* Staff, "Read President Trump's Interview With TIME on Truth and Falsehoods," *Time*, March 23, 2017, http://time.com/4710456/donald-trump-time-interview-truth-falsehood/.

AFTERWORD: FIREPROOFING

191 [T]he political system is controlled by lizard people: Philip Bump, "12 Million Americans Believe Lizard People Run Our Country," *Atlantic*, April 2, 2013, https://www.theatlantic.com/national/archive/2013/04/12-million-americans-believe-lizard-people-run-our-country/316706/.

192 [L]ook at Marco Rubio's New Hampshire debate performance: Transcript, "Republican Candidates Debate in Manchester, New Hampshire," The American Presidency Project, February 6, 2016, http://www.presidency.ucsb.edu/ws/index.php?pid=111472.

194 Steve Bannon once complained: Joshua Green, *Devil's Bargain*, Penguin Press, 2017, pg. 188.

195 [H]is messaging on health care: Edward Pevos, "Kid Rock's Full Senate Speech from the First Little Caesars Arena Concert," MLive.com, September 12, 2017, http://www.mlive.com/music/index.ssf/2017/09/kid_rocks_entire_senate_speech.html.

196 Trump did the same in his announcement speech: *Time* Staff, "Here's Donald Trump's Presidential Announcement Speech," *Time*, June 16, 2015, http://time.com/3923128/donald-trump-announcement-speech/.

197 Jeb Bush explained his position on immigration: Transcript, "Read the Full Text of the Primetime Republican Debate," *Time*, August 11, 2015, http://time.com/3988276/republican-debate-primetime-transcript-full-text/.

197 When asked about the loss of jobs in the area: Hillary Clinton, *What Happened*, Simon & Schuster, 2017, pgs. 204–5.

APPENDIX I

203 Trump will respond, "You know, some people say": Jonathan Karl, "The Last Time Donald Trump Talked About 'Birtherism,'" ABC News, September 7, 2016, http://abcnews.go.com/Politics/time-donald-trump-talked-birtherism/story?id=41927366.

204 "I'm not going to say [THE CLAIM] because I'm not allowed to say": Jenna Johnson, "Even in Victory Trump Can't Stop Airing His Grievances," *Washington Post*, May 29, 2016, https://www.washingtonpost.com/politics/even-in-victory-donald-trump-cant-stop-airing-his-grievances/2016/05/29/a5f7a566-2526-11e6-8690-f14ca9de2972_story.html?utm_term=.f560bc23b343.

204 "I will tell you about that sometime in the very near future": Toluse Olorunnipa, "In Trump's White House, Everything's Coming in 'Two Weeks,'" Bloomberg News, June 6, 2017, https://www.bloomberg.com/news/articles/2017-06-06/in-trump-s-white-house-everything-s-coming-in-two-weeks.

204 He will vow to share the information: Remarks by President Trump at the Presidential Advisory Commission on Election Integrity Meeting, July 19, 2017, https://www.whitehouse.gov/the-press-office/2017/07/19/remarks-president-trump-and-vice-president-pence-presidential-advisory.

204 "I'll keep you in suspense": Emily Shapiro, "Trump: 'I'll Keep You in Suspense' About Accepting Election Outcome," ABC News, October 19, 2016, http://abcnews.go.com/Politics/trump-ill-suspense-accepting-election-outcome/story?id=42928015.

204 [H]e will take to Twitter to discredit them: See the *New York Times*' complete list: Jasmine C. Lee, Kevin Quealy, "The 363 People, Places, and Things Donald Trump Has Insulted on Twitter: A Complete List," *New York Times*, August 25, 2017, https://www.nytimes.com/interactive/2016/01/28/upshot/donald-trump-twitter-insults.html?mcubz=1.

205 "I can't be doing so badly": *Time* Staff, "Read President Trump's Interview with TIME on Truth and Falsehoods," *Time*, March 23, 2017, http://time.com/4710456/donald-trump-time-interview-truth-falsehood/.

205 [W]ill be dismissed as being "dishonest": Philip Rucker, John Wagner, Greg Miller, "Trump, in CIA Visit, Attacks Media for Coverage of His Inaugural Crowds,"

Washington Post, January 21, 2017, https://www.washingtonpost.com/politics/trump
-in-cia-visit-attacks-media-for-coverage-of-his-inaugural-crowds/2017/01/21/f4574dca-e019
-11e6-ad42-f3375f271c9c_story.html?utm_term=.47f4a36ce5c2.

APPENDIX II

207 Take a look at this passage: Donald J. Trump with Tony Schwartz, *Trump: The Art of the Deal*, Random House, 1987, pg. 58.

208 "I have been on their cover": Remarks by President Trump and Vice President Pence at CIA Headquarters, January 21, 2017, https://www.whitehouse.gov/the-press-office/2017/01/21/remarks-president-trump-and-vice-president-pence-cia-headquarters.

208 "I got a standing ovation": "Transcript: ABC News Anchor David Muir Interviews President Trump," ABC News, January 25, 2017, http://abcnews.go.com/Politics/transcript-abc-news-anchor-david-muir-interviews-president/story?id=45047602.

208 "I have been given as President": Greg Miller, Julie Vitkovskaya, Reuben Fischer-Baum, "'This Deal Will Make Me Look Terrible': Full Transcripts of Trump's Calls with Mexico and Australia," *Washington Post*, August 3, 2017, https://www.washingtonpost.com/graphics/2017/politics/australia-mexico-transcripts/?utm_term=.f4e565deb5b2.

208 "It is a disgrace": Donald J. Trump, Twitter, February 7, 2017, https://twitter.com/realdonaldtrump/status/829133645055135750.

208 "I guess it was the biggest Electoral College win": Remarks by President Trump in Press Conference, February 16, 2017, https://www.whitehouse.gov/the-press-office/2017/02/16/remarks-president-trump-press-conference.

209 "'You will go down as one of the great presidents'": *New York Times* Staff, "Partial Transcript: Trump's Interview with the Times," *New York Times*, April 5, 2017, https://www.nytimes.com/2017/04/05/us/politics/donald-trump-interview-new-york-times-transcript.html.

209 "No administration has accomplished more": Remarks by President Trump on Buy American, Hire American Executive Order, April 18, 2017, https://www.whitehouse.gov/the-press-office/2017/04/18/remarks-president-trump-buy-american-hire-american-executive-order.

209 "I don't think anybody has ever done this much": Interview, "President Trump Reflects on His First 100 Days," Fox News, April 28, 2017, http://www.foxnews.com/transcript/2017/04/28/president-trump-reflects-on-his-first-100-days.html.

209 "The Fake News media is officially out of control": Donald J. Trump, Twitter, May 4, 2017, https://twitter.com/realdonaldtrump/status/860087334519414784.

209 "I came up with it a couple of days ago": Interview, "Transcript: Interview with Donald Trump," *Economist*, May 11, 2017, http://www.economist.com/Trumptranscript.

209 "No politician in history": Dan Merica, "Trump to Graduates: 'No Politician in History . . . Has Been Treated Worse,'" CNN, May 18, 2017, http://www.cnn.com/2017/05/17/politics/trump-coast-guard-speech/index.html.

209 "[T]here's never been anything like it": Transcript, *Wolf*, CNN, June 7, 2017, http:// transcripts.cnn.com/TRANSCRIPTS/1706/07/wolf.01.html.

210 "The Fake News Media has never been so wrong or so dirty": Donald J. Trump, Twitter, June 13, 2017, https://twitter.com/realdonaldtrump/status/874576057579565056.

210 "You are witnessing the single greatest WITCH HUNT": Donald J. Trump, Twitter, June 15, 2017, https://twitter.com/realdonaldtrump/status/875321478849363968.

210 "This is the greatest Witch Hunt in political history": Donald J. Trump, Twitter, July 12, 2017, https://twitter.com/realdonaldtrump/status/885081181980590084?lang=en.

210 "We have done more in five months": Reuters Staff, "Highlights of Reuters Interview with President Trump," Reuters, July 12, 2017, http://www .reuters.com/article/us-usa-trump-interview-highlights/highlights-of-reuters-interview -with-trump-idUSKBN19X34X.

210 "We've signed more bills": Michael D. Shear, Karen Yourish, "Trump Says He Has Signed More Bills Than Any President, Ever. He Hasn't," *New York Times*, July 17, 2017, https://www.nytimes.com/2017/07/17/us/politics/trump-laws-bills.html?_r=0.

210 "You're going to be saying, Merry Christmas again": Remarks by President Trump at 2017 National Boy Scout Jamboree, July 24, 2017, https://www.whitehouse.gov /the-press-office/2017/07/24/remarks-president-trump-2017-national-scout-jamboree.

210 "That was a standing ovation": Josh Dawsey, Hadas Gold, "Full Transcript: Trump's Wall Street Journal Interview," *Politico*, August 1, 2017, http://www.politico .com/story/2017/08/01/trump-wall-street-journal-interview-full-transcript-241214.

210 "Just think of the amazing moments in history": Remarks by President Trump to the American Legion Boys Nation and the American Legion Auxiliary Girls Nation, July 26, 2017, https://www.whitehouse.gov/the-press-office/2017/07/26/remarks-president -trump-american-legion-boys-nation-and-american-legion.

211 "I can be more presidential": Chris Cillizza, "Donald Trump Ranked Himself 2nd on a List of Most 'Presidential' Presidents," CNN, July 26, 2017, http://www.cnn .com/2017/07/26/politics/donald-trump-abe-lincoln/index.html.

211 "Business spirit is the highest it's ever been": Remarks by President Trump After Swearing In General John Kelly as White House Chief of Staff, July 31, 2017, https:// www.whitehouse.gov/the-press-office/2017/07/31/remarks-president-trump-after -swearing-general-john-kelly-white-house.

211 "Nobody has greater respect for intelligence": Aaron Blake, "Trump's Tough-on-North Korea, Toned-Down-on-Russia Q&A Session, Annotated," *Washington Post*, August 11, 2017, https://www.washingtonpost.com/news/the-fix/wp/2017/08/11/president -trumps-contrarian-qa-session-with-reporters-annotated/?utm_term=.21e7a7d934ab.

211 "The Obstructionist Democrats have given us": Donald J. Trump, Twitter, August 14, 2017, https://twitter.com/realdonaldtrump/status/897048688639574016.

211 "We have the highest employment numbers": Remarks by President Trump on Infrastructure, August 15, 2017, https://www.whitehouse.gov/the-press-office/2017/08/15 /remarks-president-trump-infrastructure.

211 "Few, if any, Administrations have done more": Donald J. Trump, Twitter, August 25, 2017, https://twitter.com/realdonaldtrump/status/901032475111116800?lang=en.

212 "Nobody could have": Donald J. Trump, Twitter, October 8, 2017, https://twitter.com/realdonaldtrump/status/917172144710103040?lang=en.

212 "I would say we are substantially ahead of schedule": Remarks by President Trump at the 2017 Values Voter Summit, October 13, 2017, https://www.whitehouse.gov/the-press-office/2017/10/13/remarks-president-trump-2017-values-voter-summit.

212 "I'm not going to blame myself": Remarks by President Trump in Cabinet Meeting, October 17, 2017, https://www.whitehouse.gov/the-press-office/2017/10/16/remarks-president-trump-cabinet-meeting.

APPENDIX III

213 "[W]e're keeping a list": Joe Perticone, "Omarosa: Republicans Who Vote Against Trump Will Be Put on 'A List,'" *Independent Journal Review*, November 8, 2017, http://ijr.com/2016/11/732006-omarosa-republicans-who-vote-against-donald-trump-will-be-put-on-a-list/.

213 "I've never met anyone more dedicated": Remarks by President Trump and Vice President Pence at CIA Headquarters, January 21, 2017, https://www.whitehouse.gov/the-press-office/2017/01/21/remarks-president-trump-and-vice-president-pence-cia-headquarters.

214 "[U]nited the civilized world": Sean Spicer, White House Press Briefing, May 30, 2017, https://www.whitehouse.gov/the-press-office/2017/05/30/daily-press-briefing-press-secretary-sean-spicer-51.

215 "This is a war, dammit": Matthew Balan, "'This Is a War, Dammit': Lou Dobbs Rips 'Flatfooted' Trump Staff," *Mediaite*, May 16, 2017, https://www.mediaite.com/tv/this-is-a-war-dammit-lou-dobbs-rips-flatfooted-trump-staff/.

215 "President Trump has a magnetic personality": Callum Borchers, "This White House Statement on Trump's 'Positive Energy' Reads Like a Parody," *Washington Post*, May 30, 2017, https://www.washingtonpost.com/news/the-fix/wp/2017/05/30/this-white-house-statement-on-trumps-positive-energy-reads-like-a-parody/?utm_term=.55de8f3e75a3.

215 "I would take a bullet for him": Rebecca Berg, "Trump Loyalists Fume as WH Sway Diminishes," Real Clear Politics, September 6, 2017, https://www.realclearpolitics.com/articles/2017/09/06/trump_loyalists_fume_as_outsiders_gain_sway_at_wh_134921.html.

215 "Somebody has to be the president's pit bull": Interview, "Dr. Gorka: I'm Ready to Be the President's Pit Bull," Fox News, July 14, 2017, http://www.foxnews.com/transcript/2017/07/14/dr-gorka-im-ready-to-be-presidents-pit-bull.html.

215 "If the president asks you, you don't say no": Katelyn Polantz, "Trump Lawyer Cobb Describes Role, Says He Took Job with 'Rocks in My Head and Steel Balls,'" *National Law Journal*, July 21, 2017, http://www.nationallawjournal.com/id=1202793656625/Trump-Lawyer-Cobb-Describes-Role-Says-He-Took-Job-With-Rocks-in-My-Head-and-Steel-Balls?slreturn=20170818144946.

215 "I think there has been": Anthony Scaramucci, White House Press Briefing, July 21, 2017, https://www.whitehouse.gov/the-press-office/2017/07/21/press-briefing-white-house-principal-deputy-press-secretary-sarah.

216 "'I don't know why people don't like you'": White House Press Briefing by Press Secretary Sarah Sanders, July 26, 2017, https://www.whitehouse.gov/the-press-office/2017/07/26/press-briefing-press-secretary-sarah-sanders-7262017-1.

216 "Hey, everybody. I'm Kayleigh McEnany": Aaron Blake, "Trump TV's 'Real News' Sounds More Like Real Propaganda," *Washington Post*, August 7, 2017, https://www.washingtonpost.com/news/the-fix/wp/2017/08/07/trump-tvs-real-news-sounds-more-like-real-propaganda/?utm_term=.bb9a1969a685.

217 "Anybody who thinks they are gonna change the President": Joe Bilello, "Corey Lewandowski: Trump Is 'Greatest Communicator We Have Ever Seen,'" *Mediaite*, August 1, 2017, https://www.mediaite.com/tv/corey-lewandowski-trump-is-greatest-communicator-we-have-ever-seen/.

217 "President Trump is the most gifted politician of our time": Tom Boggioni, "Watch: Stephen Miller Stuns by Claiming President Trump Is the 'Best Orator' to Hold That Office in Generations," *Raw Story*, August 8, 2017, https://www.rawstory.com/2017/08/watch-stephen-miller-stuns-by-claiming-president-trump-is-the-best-orator-to-hold-that-office-in-generations/.

217 "I stand before you today": Remarks by Vice President Pence at Official Governor's Portrait Unveiling, August 11, 2017, https://www.whitehouse.gov/the-press-office/2017/08/11/remarks-vice-president-pence-official-governors-portrait-unveiling.

218 "The president is about two months into being covertly drugged": Jack Holmes, "Alex Jones Thinks President Trump's Soda Is Being Drugged Each Day," *Esquire*, September 11, 2017, http://www.esquire.com/news-politics/a12222847/alex-jones-trump-drug-diet-coke.

218 "[T]he president can use whatever language he wants to use": Transcript, *This Week*, ABC News, September 24, 2017, http://abcnews.go.com/Politics/week-transcript-24-17-treasury-secretary-steven-mnuchin/story?id=50046004.

219 "I think Donald Trump has the potential to be the greatest President since Abraham Lincoln": Josh Feldman, "Jerry Falwell Jr.: Trump 'Has the Potential to be the Greatest President Since Abraham Lincoln,'" *Mediaite*, October 15, 2017, https://www.mediaite.com/tv/jerry-falwell-jr-trump-has-the-potential-to-be-the-greatest-president-since-abraham-lincoln/.

219 "What are President Trump's flaws?": Erik Wemple, "White House's Sanders: Trump's Flaw Is Having to 'Deal with You Guys on a Daily Basis,'" *Washington Post*, November 1, 2017, https://www.washingtonpost.com/blogs/erik-wemple/wp/2017/11/01/white-houses-sanders-trumps-flaw-is-having-to-deal-with-you-guys-on-a-daily-basis/?utm_term=.59f6f9f4c6da.

INDEX

ABOUT THE AUTHOR

AMANDA CARPENTER is a CNN political commentator, writer, and former senior staffer to Senators Jim DeMint and Ted Cruz. She has written for the *Washington Post, Politico, Refinery29*, Cosmo.com, the *Washington Times*, and *Human Events*.